HANDBOOKS

TAMPA & ST. PETERSBURG

LAURA REILEY

Contents

Discover Tampa & St. Petersburg

Except for Alaska, Florida has the longest coastline of any state – 1,350 miles. The majority of that length is on the Gulf side, the west coast of Florida – a maze of barrier islands, intracoastal waterways, and deep bays. And so much of life here centers on all that sustaining water. In fact, the greater Tampa Bay area, the largest metro area in the state, is really a region made up of many distinct communities built around the bay, the Gulf of Mexico, and waterways like the Hillsborough River, all laced together with bridges and causeways.

Still, Tampa in Hillsborough County and St. Petersburg in Pinellas County have distinct relationships with all that water. Tampa fronts Tampa Bay, not the Gulf of Mexico. With a huge working port, it doesn't have any beaches to speak of. From the distinct Latin roots of Tampa's historic Ybor City to the high-rise downtown, from the thrills of Busch Gardens to the many spectator sporting opportunities, Tampa is nonetheless a slick vacation destination.

Across the bay, St. Petersburg and Pinellas County share Tampa's geography and climate, but both offer a more low-rise and historic spin on sun and sand. On the bay side, St. Petersburg is a draw for museum buffs, while those nearly in the buff come to sunbathe on the west side of the peninsula in St. Pete Beach, Clearwater Beach, and all the Gulf-side communities in between.

The beachy beauty of west-central Florida offers the kind of rough-edged, front-row view into the natural world that is hard to come by these days. Add to that posh and culturally rich neighborhoods, enduring historical sites, as well as family-friendly attractions to rival Disney, and it's certainly among the Sunshine State's most delectable destinations.

Planning Your Trip

▶ WHERE TO GO

Downtown Tampa and Channelside

Like a number of American cities, Tampa's downtown is waking up. It's been the city's financial and cultural center for decades, but only in the new millennium have people begun moving into downtown condo high-rises. To go along with that, the city's downtown infrastructure of restaurants, shops, and other amenities has had to keep pace. Finally, the convention center and surrounding hotels are not marooned at night in a sea of locked office buildings.

Located dockside at the Port of Tampa where all the cruise ships come in, the shopping/dining/entertainment complex called Channelside has a big movie theater with IMAX, a fun upscale bowling alley, little boutiques, and about a dozen restaurants. The St. Pete Times Forum is also located here, home to Tampa's professional hockey team, the Tampa Bay Lightning.

South Tampa and Hyde Park

The city's first residential suburb, Hyde Park was, and still is, the residential area of choice for prominent citizens. Many of the 19th-century bungalows and Princess Anne–style cottages are still occupied today, and the Old Hyde Park Village collection of boutiques and restaurants is one of the city's biggest draws (also because historically Tampa's downtown hasn't had a retail center).

Davis Islands

Two little islands off downtown Tampa, where the Hillsborough River empties into Hillsborough Bay, became booming real estate developments at the turn of the 19th century. Today, the islands are home to an airport, Tampa General Hospital, a yacht club, and more than 100 of the original homes. It also has a cute street-that-time-forgot business district.

the Tampa skyline

Ybor City

Party central in Tampa, the century-old cigar-rolling center of town exhibits little of its Cuban heritage these days. Seventh Avenue is the main drag, closed off to cars on weekend evenings so that the throngs of moderately impaired revelers are less likely to be roadkill on their way to see the next band or get the next tattoo. During the week, the area is more sedate—a better time to try out one or more of the many restaurants that range all over the gastronomic map.

Busch Gardens and North Tampa

Busch Gardens is located 20 minutes north of downtown in an area that for a long time was not much more than cow pastures and the slowly spreading campus of the University of South Florida. The university has blossomed in recent years, shucking its reputation as a commuter school, and the area to its north has become among the most desirable residential communities in the Bay area. It's all new construction—a home that dates back to 1990 is considered old.

Greater Tampa

A testament to the abundance of wealthy international air travelers, this area to the southwest of downtown is chock-full of business-friendly hotels and fine shopping. With anchor stores Neiman Marcus and Nordstrom, International Plaza, opened in 2001, gets the nod for fanciest shopping. Really, it's the poshest assembly of stores in any shopping center on the Gulf Coast, served by an open-air village of restaurants called Bay Street. About a minute away, Westshore Plaza features more than 100 similarly fancy specialty shops and four major department stores, including a lovely Saks Fifth Avenue.

Downtown St. Petersburg

Today, St. Petersburg is Florida's fourth-

the Beach Theatre in St. Pete Beach

largest city, the anchor of Pinellas County. It's had another boom period in recent years, an influx of high-tech businesses drawing younger families and driving down the median age (the area until the 1990s was more of a retirement community). The city's downtown—on the bayside, mind you, not the Gulf side—has seen lots of new growth, from pricey condos to the $40 million BayWalk shopping complex. It has more history, more of a sense of place and sophistication than the beach towns along the Gulf side. There are romantic bed-and-breakfasts, fine restaurants, and cultural attractions.

St. Pete Beach

St. Pete Beach is not just the shortened name for St. Petersburg Beach. St. Petersburg is the big city adjacent to Old Tampa Bay, which looks out across at the big city of Tampa. St. Pete Beach, on the other hand, is an autonomous barrier-island town to the south and west of St. Petersburg. It's a classic Florida beach town, with late-night waterside clubs, deep-water fishing, and low-slung motels with views of the beach.

Gulfport

Gulfport is known as the Gateway to the Gulf as it is the point of departure for the Gulf of Mexico. It faces Boca Ciega Bay, which leads to the Gulf. It has a sleepy, old-timey charm that lures many snowbirds into staying year-round.

Clearwater and Clearwater Beach

Clearwater Beach offers a wide, inviting shore, serious beach volleyball, and loads of nightlife and casual seafood restaurants. Clearwater has perhaps the densest concentration of beachside accommodations—often tall resort hotels and condos right on the beach.

Dunedin

One of the oldest towns on the West Coast of Florida, Dunedin has a wooded and subtropical setting with four miles of picturesque waterfront. The closest the Gulf Coast comes to hippie culture, Dunedin boasts a relaxed boat-centric lifestyle, with comfy bars and flip-flop wearing denizens. Just off the coast of Dunedin are two of the area's most wonderful beaches: Honeymoon and Caladesi Islands. Oldsmar is the adjacent, mostly residential community that skews a little more toward retirees.

▶ WHEN TO GO

This part of Florida is a year-round destination. A huge family draw, partly because of its big airport and proximity to Orlando and Walt Disney World, the area is at its busiest during school vacations. Thanksgiving to Easter are peak visitor times, but numbers also spike during summer vacation— still, I won't lie to you, summer weather is like hot breath on your neck all the time, no remittance, and gloomy, stormy skies many afternoons. This area is also a huge draw for Grapefruit League spring training devotees, so the month of March sees many high-energy, Copenhagen-chewing ball fans cheering on their beloved teams.

Snowbirds also bump up the local population in the winter months (especially on the Pinellas County side). Their timing isn't arbitrary—February, March, and April along much of Florida's Gulf Coast are magical. Temperatures in the high 70s, a little breeze, low humidity, little rain, and Gulf water just warm enough for swimming.

That said, if you visit just after the snowbirds fly home and before summer sets in you'll find plenty of accommodations, unoccupied tables

Springtime is magical along the Gulf Coast.

in restaurants, and room to roam unhindered on the beaches. You may also find that it's a little cheaper after Easter. The same can be said of the fall, before the huge winter influx of visitors. September and October are lovely in the Tampa Bay area, but it's also hurricane season, something not to be taken lightly.

▶ BEFORE YOU GO

Getting There and Around

Tampa's airport is the largest on the Gulf Coast, clean, organized, and easy to navigate. Rental cars can be reserved in advance from the airport. Cabs, buses, and shuttles will also ferry you from airport to hotel, but the Tampa/St. Petersburg area is very difficult to navigate if you don't have your own wheels. For instance, if you're staying at a big downtown Tampa hotel but would like to spend a day at one of Pinellas's world-class beaches, you need a car. Or, say you're staying in a charming bed-and-breakfast in old St. Petersburg but would like to take in a Buccaneers game at Raymond James Stadium. Auto required.

Busch Gardens, fishing charters, sporting events, and museum admissions can all be arranged upon your arrival (bearing in mind that March and April are especially congested with exuberant vacationers).

What to Take

Because of climate and general temperament, this part of Florida is casual, with all the good and bad that that entails. There are very few women on the Gulf Coast who could spot a knock-off Hermès Birkin bag at 20 paces. That's not all bad. In the absence of high fashion, what to pack is largely a function of comfort.

Very few places require a jacket and tie, but for nicer restaurants you may feel more comfortable in something festive. The preponderance of outdoor activities also necessitates a change of shoes: something for dinner, sneakers for hiking or athletics, and swim shoes or flip-flops.

Even if you're visiting in the summer, bring a sweater. Everything is over-air-conditioned. In the winter, a long-sleeved pullover with light slacks is usually fine.

If you aim to take full advantage of the area's outdoor allures, bring sunscreen, binoculars, polarized sunglasses (for seeing depth when you fish), a bird book, snorkel, swim flippers, a juicy novel, more bathing suits than you can use, bug spray, and flip-flops.

Once you're there, you can rent bikes, scooters, skates, strollers, beach chairs, boogie or surf boards, fishing equipment, motorboats, Jet Skis, kayaks, canoes, and sailboats.

fisherman at sunset

Explore Tampa & St. Petersburg

▶ THREE-DAY BEST OF TAMPA & ST. PETERSBURG

DAY 1

Begin your visit with a trip to Tampa's Busch Gardens, the only thing in these parts to rival the wild rides nearby in Orlando. This is a full day of being outdoors in the sun, capped off with a visit to one of Hyde Park's many restaurants along South Howard Avenue (alternately, if you're just starving after all those roller coasters, adjacent to the park is one of Tampa's most venerable quickies, Mel's Hot Dogs).

DAY 2

Drive over the Howard Frankland bridge to downtown St. Petersburg. Wander the galleries of the Museum of Fine Arts, have a little lunch in its MFA Cafe, then stroll Beach and Central Avenues, doing a little window shopping or credit-card calisthenics. If American Stage has a show on, stop in for Japanese at Pacific Wave next door before settling into the theater.

DAY 3

Sift sand between your toes on one of Pinellas's world-class beaches (Caladesi, Honeymoon, and Clearwater Beach all have their distinct allures), hire a single-day fishing charter out of Hubbards Marina in St. John's Pass, or head out into the Gulf of Mexico for a dolphin-watching cruise. Finish up by watching the sun set from the outdoor patio at The Hurricane while getting your hands around a fat grouper sandwich (one of the local delicacies).

Museum of Fine Arts in St. Petersburg

FOUL-WEATHER FUN

bench outside the Salvador Dalí Museum

Remember the beginning of *The Cat in the Hat*? "The sun did not shine. It was too wet to play. So we sat in the house all that cold, cold wet day." Except for the "cold, cold" part, it sounds a little like Tampa Bay in the storm season, every afternoon given over to an impressive deluge or, at the very least, some ominous gloom. But you don't need that rascally Cat, or even Thing One or Thing Two, to help you while away a wet afternoon. Here are just a handful of ways to keep away those rainy-day blues.

OK, maybe that's overambitious, but you can at least hang out and look studious. First stop: University of Tampa. Regal yet totally out of place with its minarets, keyhole arches, and ornate Moorish revival architecture, the university's **Henry B. Plant Museum's** opulent restored rooms with original furnishings provide a window on America's Gilded Age, Tampa's history, and the life and work of Henry Plant.

Now head north to University of South Florida. An enormous institution that casts its imposing shadow over the cultural scene of Tampa, it nonetheless is seldom visited by locals who aren't lugging backpacks and books. A visit to the **University of South Florida Contemporary Art Museum** is a good excuse to explore the university campus before parking at the small gallery containing a permanent collection of sculpture multiples by artists such as Roy Lichtenstein, Robert Rauschenberg, and James Rosenquist.

Or spend some time in rented shoes. **Splitsville** is Tampa's finest bowling alley-cum-restaurant. Good food, a whimsical environment, and the coolest bowling shoes ever.

But what's more appropriate in moist conditions than swimming with the fishes (also, homage to the long-suffering goldfish in *The Cat in the Hat*)? The **Clearwater Marine Aquarium** is a working research facility and home to rescued and recuperating marine mammals and the **Konger Tarpon Springs Aquarium** has a 120,000-gallon main tank aquarium swarming with more than 30 species of fish.

But speaking of dripping, to see some of the world's most famous molten clocks, head to St. Petersburg's **Salvador Dalí Museum**, the most comprehensive collection of permanent works by the famous Spanish master who himself is the most recognized artist in history (the waxed mustache, arched eyebrows, and psychotic expression don't hurt).

▶ KIDS' STUFF

An obvious choice for family travel, Florida's 800-pound rodent resides an hour to the east of Tampa in Orlando. Still, this part of the state has ample allures for kids even if you eschew all things Disney.

Day 1

The first stop is a day at Tampa's Busch Gardens for a ride on the Montu, the ShieKra, the Kumba, the Scorpion, and the tooth-rattling Gwazi, in descending order of priority. It's a full-day park for all ages, with a mix of big, scary coasters and sweet animal attractions.

Day 2

Right across the street from Busch Gardens is Tampa's Museum of Science & Industry (MOSI), probably the best science museum on the Gulf Coast. It's nearly impossible to combine this in a day with Busch Gardens, so visit MOSI on your second day, with the

Busch Gardens

other half of the day spent wandering either at the The Florida Aquarium (with a stop for lunch across the street at the portside dining/entertainment complex of Channelside) or the Lowry Park Zoo. Both of these attractions are midsize, thus very walkable and requiring under four hours to fully explore. Before you get out of Tampa, take one of the aquarium's Dolphin Quest Eco-Tours out into the bay to get an eagle-eye view of dolphins, manatees, and migratory birds.

Day 3

Spend the next day lolling on the sand at one of Pinellas's top beaches—Clearwater Beach or St. Pete Beach if you want easy access to refreshments and amenities; Honeymoon Island or Caladesi Island if you prize natural beauty and getting away from the hoards.

Day 4

If you find yourself with the luxury of another day, head an hour north on Highway 19 so the kids can experience something entirely memorable. You may need to stay overnight in Homosassa or Crystal River to get a jump on the day. You're going to commune with the West Indian manatee, still listed as an endangered species. From October 15 to March 31, you'll find hundreds of these gentle giants swimming in the warm waters of Kings Bay in Crystal River and the Blue Waters area of the Homosassa River. They are huge herbivores, and playful. Manatee Tour & Dive or Birds Underwater will take whole families out for snorkel trips with the manatees. You're not supposed to touch, but sometimes they like you to rub their bellies.

▶ THE BEST OF THE BEACHES

You see your first castle in Europe. "Fabulous, awe-inspiring." You see 10 such castles and it's a case of "seen one, you seen 'em all." You get castle callous; it's unavoidable. So it is with beaches—blue water lapping, the horizon a long line in the distance, gulls wheeling. The first day it's paradise; the fifth day it's sandy. Pinellas County's beaches are the answer, as

they provide a diverse array of natural settings and an equally wide range of waterside activity.

Start with a fairly urban city beach, Clearwater Beach, a long, wide stretch offering showers, restrooms, concessions, cabanas, umbrella rentals, volleyball, and metered parking. Pier 60, where the beach

WHERE THE HEART IS

TAMPA BAY REVEALS ITS MOST ROMANTIC SPOTS

Now, there's been a lot of talk about some crafty chemical in chocolate simulating the feeling of being in love. I don't know if I buy that, but chocolate is indubitably a good way to begin an amorous foray. Even more so if it's Chocolate-Chocolate-Chocolate. That's actually the name of the demure chocolate-shellacked cylinder packing chocolate cheesecake, chocolate mousse and chocolate pie into one deadly package served with aplomb at **Harry Waugh Dessert Room** at Bern's Steak House. And if the romance leaves you cold, the sheer quantity of sugar, high-octane coffee, and gorgeous after-dinner drinks are bound to give you a little thrill.

On the other hand, nothing gets the heart pumping like a brush with danger. **Big Cat Rescue** the world's largest accredited sanctuary for big cats, lets you and your sweetie stay overnight with the jaguars, snow leopards, etc. Just hope you're not breakfast in bed. On the third hand (now that's extremely handy), **Skydive City** in Zephyrhills (in Pasco County, to the north of Tampa) is one of the world's most famous "drop zones." Why here? According to owner T.K. Hayes, "It's in the middle of nowhere, with not a single picturesque thing about it. It's really about the people—Zephyrhills is the largest skydiving place in the world." Tandem jumping (where a rookie jumps physically harnessed to an instructor) has opened skydiving up to people who might never have otherwise taken the plunge.

Renaissance Vinoy Resort & Golf Club

Then again, you could take to the sea. Ahoy, mates and would-be mates. Climb aboard **Yacht StarShip** Tampa's premier dining yacht, while the sunset casts its sherbet hues across the Bay. It's the *Love Boat*, only not as interminable and without all the crew in white knee socks.

So far, this is mostly stunt-romance. For Old School champagne-and-caviar, culminating in good bed linens and discreet room service, head to the **Renaissance Vinoy Resort & Golf Club**, St. Petersburg's exquisitely restored Mediterranean Revival resort that exudes the kind of rarefied glamour that helps put life's quotidian woes behind you.

Caledesi Island State Park

meets the causeway, has a regular sunset celebration with entertainers and live music. But this is the warm-up, just to get your feet wet, so to speak. The area's other best beaches require more of a commitment and are more of a full-day adventure.

If you have some time on your hands, head to Caladesi Island State Park in Dunedin or Fort De Soto State Park in St. Petersburg, both of which make it on the lists of top beaches in the world. The former is only accessible by ferry from Honeymoon Island State Recreation Area off Alternate Highway 19 in Dunedin. The island is three and a half miles long with a marina and swim beach right near where the ferry lets you off, but the rest of the island remains undeveloped. The bay side of the island is worth exploring, with a mangrove shoreline and seagrass flats (rent canoes and paddle the 3.5-mile canoe trail that meanders through the bay side).

Or take Highway 19 south 14 miles, merge onto I-275 south for seven miles, and take Pinellas Bayway (Rte. 679 south) 6.5 miles

to Fort De Soto State Park, a beach and history lesson in one. The fort was built in 1898 to protect Tampa Bay during the Spanish-American War. Explore the old fort and its history museum before you head on to one of the two swim beaches, the better of which is the North Beach Swim Center (they have concessions). Fort De Soto State Park also has some of the most coveted beachside camping spots along the Gulf Coast.

Fort De Soto State Park

SIGHTS

From Busch Gardens to Ybor City, to the lovely beaches on the Gulf Coast, the Tampa and St. Petersburg area has much to offer. In terms of sightseeing, the region has more of a recreational spin—but don't let that be misleading. A walk along Bayshore Boulevard allows one to soak up the riches of Tampa, from the stately homes in Hyde Park to a stunning view of the downtown skyline. Busch Gardens is a family dream come true—but if culture is what you seek, Ybor City's Cuban influence still holds strong not far from downtown. Ybor City is where to experience the legacy of the Cuban cigar industry, and not without plenty of opportunity for sampling the goods. Animals more your thing? The Lowry Park Zoo is the perfect place to spend an afternoon watching white tiger cubs and learning about manatee rehabilitation. If you've got kids in tow, don't miss the Museum of Science and Industry—guaranteed to entertain even the most finicky of children with a plethora of hands-on exhibits.

At first glance, St. Petersburg and surroundings may seem to be all about the beaches, but Pinellas County is a treasure trove of riches including St. Petersburg's charming, tourist-friendly downtown area. Add to that the liveliness of the Pier—the heart of the area, where you can depart on a sightseeing charter—and a myriad of museums and aquariums, you won't lack for things to do and see.

HIGHLIGHTS

LOOK FOR  TO FIND
RECOMMENDED SIGHTS.

 **Best Place to Go Eye to Eye with a Goliath Grouper:** The **Florida Aquarium** is a marvelous Tampa attraction, a 152,000-square-foot center that focuses on Florida's relationship to the Gulf, estuaries, rivers, and other waterways, with a strong environmental message (page 16).

 **Best Way to Puff a Local Smoke:** **7th Avenue** in Ybor City was once known as the Cigar Capital of the World, with nearly 12,000 cigar makers employed in 200 factories that produced 700 million cigars a year. Tampa's Latin Quarter is one of only three National Historic Landmark Districts in Florida. Today it has something of a Jekyll and Hyde personality that offers visitors historic shops by day and the city's most vital nightlife and dining when the sun goes down (page 19).

 **Best Loop-the-Loops:** Thrill seekers won't need to be reminded to visit **Busch Gardens.** The park's inverted steel roller coaster called the Montu won ninth place in *Amusement Today Magazine's* survey of top roller coasters worldwide. The park's Kumba took the 19th spot. The park is an unusual mix of thrill rides, animal attractions (it was the first in the U.S. to create an open-range animal habitat), and entertainment. It's a something-for-everyone approach that really works (page 20).

 **Where to Catch a Big One:** The bright yellow **Sunshine Skyway Bridge,** the world's longest cable-stayed bridge, is a Pinellas County icon. But the repurposed remnants of the old bridge have become the **Sunshine Skyway Fishing Piers** – the world's longest fishing pier, with a tremendous concentration of sportfish lurking in the deep waters below. You can rent fishing gear on the pier (page 26).

The Florida Aquarium was essentially designed "from the inside out."

Downtown Tampa and Channelside   Map 1

AMERICAN VICTORY MARINER'S MEMORIAL & MUSEUM SHIP

705 Channelside Dr., 813/228-8766

HOURS: Tues.-Sat. 10 A.M.-4 P.M., Sun. noon-4 P.M.

COST: $8 adults, $4 children, children under three free

Liberty ships were sitting ducks. Or slow-moving ducks. They traveled a maximum speed of 11 knots, easy targets for WWII submarines. Thus was the Victory ship born. These newcomers zipped along at 17 knots thanks to cross-compound steam turbine engines that delivered 6,000 or 8,500 horsepower. They were 455 feet long and 62 feet wide. They had reinforced hull plates and included one 5-inch stern gun, one 3-inch bow antiaircraft gun and eight 20-mm machine guns at various locations onboard.

To explore one of these feats of engineering, visit the SS *American Victory,* a 61-year old merchant ship which served during World War II, and the Korean and Vietnam Wars as a military cargo carrier. It sits off of Channelside, offering self-guided tours of the ship and guided tours that illuminate the restoration process.

BAYSHORE BOULEVARD

Skirting Hillsborough Bay from Swann to Interbay Blvd.

HOURS: Always open

COST: Free

Bayshore Boulevard may or may not be the world's longest continuous sidewalk, but it borders Tampa Bay for nearly five miles without a break in the gorgeousness. Joggers, walkers, skaters, and bikers dot its length, which goes from downtown through Hyde Park. Home to the fanciest homes in Tampa, the boulevard was named one of AAA's "Top Roads" for its panoramic views. Even if you don't feel like walking it, it's Tampa's most signature drive. (Also, Tampa Preservation has an excellent driving tour of Hyde Park and a walking tour of part of the neighborhood geared for younger readers; for copies call 813/248-5437.)

CHANNELSIDE

615 Channelside Dr.

HOURS: daily 11 A.M.-11 P.M.

COST: Free

Channelside is a bit like what an entrepreneurial Martian would produce after seeing satellite photos of Baltimore's Inner Harbor. It's *almost* right, *nearly* a big tourist draw, and *kinda* fun. Located dockside at the Port of Tampa where all the cruise ships come in, the shopping/dining/entertainment complex has a big movie theater with IMAX, a fun upscale bowling alley, little boutiques, and about a dozen restaurants and cafés. Adjacent to the complex you'll find the aquarium, a sports and concert venue, and an ambitious yet mostly empty condo complex.

COURTESY OF VISIT FLORIDA

Claimed as the world's longest continuous sidewalk, Bayshore Boulevard borders Tampa Bay for 4.5 miles without a break.

The Florida Aquarium offers a dramatic look at all that swims, floats, and lurks in Florida waters.

◖ FLORIDA AQUARIUM

701 Channelside Dr., 813/273-4000,
www.flaquarium.org

HOURS: Daily 9:30 A.M.–5 P.M.

COST: $17.95 adults, $14.95 seniors, $12.95 children under 12

They've tried to gussy up this aquarium in the past few years with outdoor water play areas and such, but the Florida Aquarium doesn't want for anything, in my opinion. Opened in 1995, the 152,000-square-foot aquarium is smart, focusing on the waters of Florida. It doesn't contain an exhaustive catalog of the world's aquatic creatures, but it tells a very compelling story about Florida's relationship to the Gulf, estuaries, rivers, and other waterways. There are some exotic exhibits (the otherworldly sea dragons, like sea horses mated with philodendrons), but the best parts are the open freshwater tanks of otters, spoonbills, gators, Florida softshell turtles, and snakes. The aquarium manages to convey a very strong environmental message in its natives-versus-exotics exhibits, but it's all fun, never seeming pious or heavy-handed. There's also a wonderful, big shark tank, a colorful coral grotto, and a sea urchin touch tank. It's a small enough aquarium that three hours is plenty of time, and not so crowded that kids can't do a little wandering on their own. Regularly scheduled shows involve native Florida birds and small mammals, as well as shark feeding (in fact, the aquarium offers "swim with the fishes" wetsuit dives into the shark tank for the stalwart). A new cell phone audio tour may be the coolest thing yet.

After perusing the marinelife within the eye-catching shell-shaped building, you can take your newfound knowledge out on the bay with one of the aquarium-run **Dolphin Quest Eco-Tours** ($19.95 adults, $18.95 seniors, $14.95 children under 12). Tampa Bay is home to more than 400 bottlenose dolphins. Tickets are available at the aquarium box office the day of the tour only, when you'll head out in a 64-foot, 49-passenger

TALL TALE

Anyone who's spent time in the Tampa Bay area has idly wondered about the big white tower off I-275. What does it do? How did it get there? And most people never get to the bottom of the 231-foot-tall mystery at the corner of Florida Avenue and Bird Street. Until now.

The Sulphur Springs Water Tower was a north Tampa landmark almost instantly upon its completion in 1927. Like a lot of construction around that time, it was aimed at the state's new vacationing hordes. The introduction of Henry Ford's affordable $400 Model-T just after the turn of that century triggered the phenomenon of road tripping, folks hopping in the car in search of sun, sand, and a little fun. And Josiah Richardson aimed to be ready for them.

He built a hotel and tourist cottages along the Hillsborough River. He built a mammoth waterslide with a spring-fed swimming hole, a bathhouse, a shopping arcade, and an alligator farm. Just one problem: Richardson needed a reliable water source for the complex, which he called Sulphur Springs Hotel and Arcade.

So he mortgaged the whole kit and caboodle and hired Grover Pool to build a water tower for him. They excavated 45 feet down into the rock, with eight-inch-thick poured concrete walls reinforced with railroad rails. When it was finished, it stored 125,000 gallons of water from nearby artesian springs.

The pressure was great, the water clear, the supply dependable. If only everything were so steadfast: In 1933 the Tampa Electric Company dam collapsed and the complex was flooded. Coupled with the Great Depression, the disaster brought the Sulphur Springs complex to its knees. Richardson lost everything.

But the water tower did last. Through the 1960s it provided water to some of the neighborhood that bears its name. In the 1970s, dry at last, it became the architectural icon of the Tower Drive-In theater, graffiti slowly adding a lacy filigree across the tower's white surface. A sheen of fresh, graffiti-proof paint in 1979 failed to change the tower's plight — drugs and crime in the area ensured that it remained overlooked until Walgreens put in a bid to buy the 13-acre spot in 2002.

The hue and cry of Tampa residents made it clear that this tall drink of water was locally beloved. A grassroots group called Save Our Tower sprung up overnight, cajoling and nudging city officials. The City of Tampa bought the site the next year, and renamed the surrounding area River Tower Park. Current plans are ambitious — a boardwalk, a botanical garden, a jogging trail, picnic tables, and a small pier are in the works. But no matter what becomes of the lush bit of green space in Sulphur Springs, it will be presided over by the stalwart water tower of Josiah Richardson's abandoned dream.

Caribbean catamaran, watching all the while for dolphins, manatees, and a huge number of migratory birds.

THE PORT OF TAMPA

Seaport Street Terminal, 651 Channelside Dr., Terminal #2, 813/272-0558

HOURS: Port offices, 7:30 A.M.–5 P.M.

COST: Free

The Port of Tampa is said to be the fastest-growing cruise port in North America, with a passenger count going from 200,000 in 1998 to more than a million in the past couple of years. Cruise lines evidently beget cruise lines,

with newer and larger vessels steaming into the downtown Channelside port all the time. It started with Carnival and Holland America cruise lines back in 1994, but these days a number of lines head out of Tampa on 4-, 5-, 7-, 10-, 11-, and 14-day itineraries.

Tampa now homeports four vessels from three cruise lines: Carnival Cruise Lines, Holland America, and Royal Caribbean, offering the variety of 4-, 5-, 7-, and 14-day cruise itineraries. Carnival Legend has seven-day cruises to the Western Caribbean.

Grandeur of the Seas, a luxury cruise liner operated by Royal Caribbean International and home ported at Tampa, offers four- and five-day cruises to Mexico and Central America.

Holland America Lines's *Veendam* offers passengers 7- and 14-day itineraries of the western and southern Caribbean and Mexico.

The Port's cruise terminals include customer-friendly information areas, superior security, full passenger amenities, and on-terminal parking, at $12 per day (no reservations are needed). Valet services are also available. The port is in close proximity to the interstate highway system.

South Tampa and Hyde Park   Map 2

OLD HYDE PARK VILLAGE

West Swann Ave., South Dakota Ave., and Snow Ave., 813/251-3500

HOURS: Hours vary

COST: Prices vary

Tampa's downtown doesn't really have a retail center. For that, you need to visit Hyde Park. It's not vast, but the outdoor shopping/dining area is the most appealing shopping destination in town, especially when the weather's nice. There's a large covered parking lot, free to shoppers, and a lovely landscaped plaza at the center. Pottery Barn and Williams-Sonoma are among the bigger stores, with Ann Taylor, Brooks Brothers, Anthropologie, Talbots, and Tommy Bahama. Top restaurants include the Cal-Ital Wine Exchange, the indoor-outdoor Sinatra-addled Timpano Italian Chophouse, and a slick pan-Asian bistro called Restaurant BT. In the summer, Old Hyde Park Village hosts a free evening movie series, the classic films projected outside on a huge screen. The area has seen a great deal of flux in the past couple of years—stores playing musical chairs,

Stores come and go in Old Hyde Park Village, but it's still always a notable collection of chic boutiques.

buildings torn down, condos going up—let's hope it's all in the name of progress. In 2007, the Tampa City Council approved the rezoning required for the Village's proposed $100 million redevelopment, which will add 37,000 square feet of retail space and 163 luxury condos.

Davis Islands   Map 2

DAVIS ISLAND YACHT CLUB
1315 Severn Ave., 813/251-1158
HOURS: Thurs. 7 P.M., Sun. 2 P.M.
COST: Free to watch

What a spectator sport. Drive over the causeway to Davis Islands, then across the length of the island to the unassuming, squatty yacht club. It's free to watch racing, even free to crew for the evening if you have experience and a skipper will take you on. In the winter, the races take place at 2 P.M. on Sundays, but in the warm weather you can watch different classes of sailboats heading out into the bay on Thursday nights at 7 P.M. with the backdrop of Tampa's downtown bathed in a rosy sunset glow. It's beautiful, especially when all the colorful, billowing spinnakers head out.

Ybor City   Map 3

CENTRO YBOR
1600 E. 8th Ave., 813/242-4660
HOURS: Sun.-Thurs. 11 A.M.-11 P.M., until 2 A.M. weekends
COST: No entrance fee

Given up for ages as a slightly seedy adult playground at night, Ybor City has become more family friendly with the addition of Centro Ybor, which opened at the beginning of the millennium in the former Centro Español social club. It's a shopping, dining, and entertainment complex right at the pulsing heart of the neighborhood. None of the restaurants here will stir you to poetic excess, but the complex is anchored by the Muvico Centro 20 Ybor Theater, with a GameWorks location, The Improv for nighttime adult comedy, Urban Outfitters, and a number of familiar shops. The complex has its own parking structure, and is on the TECO streetcar line.

◖ 7TH AVENUE
7th Ave. from 13th to 23rd Sts.
HOURS: Vary by business
COST: Free

During the day visitors can still see cigars being hand-rolled and munch a Cuban sandwich, while at night Ybor is the city's nightlife district, drawing 40,000 visitors on weekends to dine at sidewalk cafés and drink and dance at nightclubs. Whether you explore during the day or at night, park your car in one of the many parking lots or garages (metered parking is strictly enforced 24 hours), and walk around or take the Ybor City trolley. You can still see little cigar shops and Latin social clubs mixed in with tattoo parlors and restaurants along La Setima (7th Ave.).

You get the most three-dimensional look at Ybor just by walking around: Walk by La Union Marti-Maceo mural (226 Seventh Ave.), pick up a copy of *La Gaceta* (the neighborhood's Spanish-language weekly for the past 75 years), and walk by the restored former cigar workers' casitas on your way to buy a cigar at **Metropolitan Cigars** (2014 East 7th Ave., 813/248-3304), a 1,700-square-foot walk-in humidor, or to get a Cubano sandwich. A Cubano is a long loaf, 36 inches long, with thin flaky crust and soft, pillowy interior. This gets piled high with roast pork and Genoa salami (a strictly Tampa twist), Swiss cheese (some say Emanthaler), sour pickles, and spicy mustard—the whole thing warmed and flattened in a special hot-press. Outside crisp, inside warm and a little gooey. It's perfection.

Shopping along Seventh yields some interesting finds. It's a little gritty, with a few vintage clothing shops, a fair amount of racy lingerie, GBX Fashion Shoes, and a funky Urban Outfitters. Seventh is also the locale of some of the city's biggest parties: Gasparilla Sant'Yago Night Parade in February, Guavaween in October, the Rough Rider's St. Patrick's Night Parade, and the Tampa Cigar Heritage Festival mid-November.

Busch Gardens and North Tampa   Map 4

ADVENTURE ISLAND
Adjacent to Busch Gardens, 4500 Bougainvillea Ave., 813/987-5660, www.adventureisland.com
HOURS: March–Oct., hours and days vary
COST: $36.95 adult, $34.95 children 3-9, free for children 2 and under

This park will wet your whistle, and pretty much everything else. It's a 30-acre water park, with slides, corkscrews, waterfalls, a monstrous 17,000-square-foot wave pool, and a children's play area. There are 50 lifeguards on duty, but it's still only appropriate for the truly water-safe. There's also a championship white-sand volleyball complex. If you buy a ticket to Busch Gardens, you can combine it with a ticket here for a discount.

◼ BUSCH GARDENS
Corner of Busch Blvd. and 40th St., eight miles northeast of downtown Tampa, 888/800-5447, www.buschgardens.com
HOURS: In winter daily 9:30 A.M.–6 P.M.; in summer daily 9 A.M.–10 P.M.
COST: $64.95 adults, $54.95 children 3-9, free for children 2 and under; parking an additional $9, with a free shuttle from the parking lot to the park's entrance

Busch Gardens is expensive. Is it worth it? Definitely. It is a wonderful full-day extravaganza for people of any age (if you don't like rides, go to Beer School, where you listen to some guy talk for a while about hops before you get free samples). Busch Gardens can entertain you for a full two days, but if you do just one day everyone will be clamoring for more. A 14-day 5 Park Orlando FlexTicket ($234.95 adults, $199.95 kids) is a fairly good deal if you have the stamina to hit SeaWorld Orlando, Universal Studios Florida, Islands of Adventure, and Wet 'n' Wild along with Busch Gardens.

Rides for Little Kids: Some people swear by the Myers-Briggs Type Indicator. Psychologists use the 16 personality factors to determine personality type. I think it all comes down to this: There are two personality types—those who ride the rides, and those who stay on the ground and hold the cotton candy for those who ride the rides. Using Skinnerian methods, I am trying to ensure that my child is the first type.

Busch Gardens is right there with me. The amusement park has a huge section of the park geared to children 2–7 years old (in a Dragon-centric part of the park to the far left when you're looking at the map, near **Stanleyville**, as well as in sections near the **Congo** and in **Timbuktu**). This is one of the biggest parks I've seen where there are those vexing height limitations that preclude you from riding if you're *taller* than the marker.

And therein lies a slight conceptual flaw. Hyping it fiendishly for days, parents bring their toddlers for their first taste of the intoxicating chills and thrills of the midway—mini tilt-a-whirls, little roller coasters, real training-wheels rides. The children are strapped in by the flat-lining teens who work Busch Gardens, and then the terror sets in. Some scream, others go dead white with their lips flattened in a grim look of determination. Parents stand on the ground, waving furiously and shouting encouragements while the children persevere, around and around. Is it torture? You be the judge.

COURTESY OF VISIT FLORIDA

Kumba was Busch Gardens' first multi-loop coaster.

I have advice. Drawing on the microscopic amount I know about developmental psychology, I say use modeling, to show *your* enthusiasm for the rides in order to sway them. Show them how to squeal on the vertical-lift rides, how to make catcalls to the folks down below you on the boring rides, and let them in on the unbridled joy of screaming really loudly while waving your arms in the air. They can hold the cotton candy while they watch you ride the big kid rides.

Rides for Big Kids: Major coasters are the biggest draw for those over 48 inches tall (for Montu, Kumba, and SheiKra it's 54 inches) and with no serious health problems. The rides at Busch Gardens are either little-kiddie or pee-your-pants huge. The roller coasters, in descending order of excellence: The **Montu** at the far right of the park is one of the tallest and longest inverted roller coasters in the world. You are strapped in from above, so your feet dangle while you travel at 60 mph through 60-foot vertical loops and stuff. The **SheiKra** opened in 2005 as The Next Big Thing at

Busch Gardens. It's got an incredible 90-degrees-straight-down thrill at the beginning, an underground tunnel, speeds of 70 mph, and water features late in the ride, but overall the ride is too short. It went "floorless" in 2007 to add another level of thrill, but it still doesn't make top billing in my book. **Kumba** is third best, with a full three seconds of weightlessness, an initial 135-foot drop, some cool 360-degree spirals. Good speed, long ride, one of the world's largest vertical loops. The **Python** has a double spiraling corkscrew and gut-lurching 70-foot plunge, but it's too short a ride, over in seconds. And the **Gwazi** is for purists—an old double wooden coaster, it's got that tooth-rattling charm as it barrels over the boards in 7,000 feet of track.

Beyond the coasters, the **Tidal Wave, Stanley Falls,** and **Congo River Rapids** boat ride are guaranteed to fully saturate you with water—so time them for the hottest part of the day and not right before you go see the modestly amusing 3-D movie called *Pirates 4-D.*

Animal Attractions: Busch Gardens contains

something like 2,700 animals. Colorful lorikeets will land on your shoulder or flirt shamelessly with you in the **Lory Landing** aviary, there's a **Birds of Prey** show, but the best animal attraction is the **Serengeti Plain,** which really takes up the whole right half of the park—you see it all by getting on the Serengeti Express Railway (or the Skyride or a Serengeti Safari). Ostriches may race the train; there are big cats and huffing rhinos. It's thrilling *and* a wonderful opportunity to sit down a spell and regroup. (The lamest attraction at the park, though, is Rhino Rally. Don't bother.)

In spring 2008, the park opened Jungala, what it's calling its most ambitious park enhancement project to date. Set in the Congo area, the four-acre attraction has guests mingling with exotic creatures, exploring a village hidden deep in the jungle, and connecting with the inhabitants of the lush landscape through up-close animal interactions, multistory family play areas, rides, and live entertainment.

If you visit in the summer, count on heavy rains in the afternoon. Bathrooms are plentiful and clean, there are scads of strollers to rent, the food is much better than it needs to be (Zambia Smokehouse serves good ribs and chicken), and they even have a dog kennel to watch your pet while you enjoy the park.

LOWRY PARK ZOO
1101 W. Sligh Ave., 813/932-0245,
www.lowryparkzoo.com
HOURS: Daily 9:30 A.M.–5 P.M.
COST: $18.95 adults, $17.95 seniors, $14.95 children 3–11
This zoo has recently made the overt decision to take it to the Big Time, going mano a mano with San Diego and the other big zoo kahunas. To this end, they imported four African elephants (for a stunning account of all this, read the *St. Petersburg Times's* nine-part series on the subject that should have been bound for Pulitzerhood, www.sptimes.com/2007/web specials07/special_reports/zoo) and created a huge habitat for them. (Their previous elephant program was curtailed years ago when a trainer was killed by a panicked pachyderm.)

For years this zoo languished at the bottom of the heap with old-school cages and dubious animal husbandry. All that has changed—recently, *Child* magazine ranked it the No. 1 zoo for families. I agree. Generally I prefer midsize zoos like this. The San Diego and San Francisco zoos are fine, with their wide-open spaces and generously configured habitats. But sometimes going to them is like going to a Rolling Stones concert: That speck in the distance may be a hamadryas baboon or it may be Mick Jagger, there's no telling. Little kids don't know from habitats, they just want to see the animals up close and personal. With lots of space at their disposal at zoos like that, the big cats can pull a no-show with other animals coyly revealing only a tail or an ear in the deep grass.

At the Lowry Park Zoo, habitats are naturalistic and nicely landscaped, but they are still designed for maximum viewing. All told there are around 2,000 native and exotic animals (white tiger cubs are a big draw), organized into sensible housing developments (Wallaroo Station, Safari Africa). Lots of shade provided by big lush tropicals seems to keep all species fat and sassy, even in the fairly substantial summer heat. One of the zoo's highlights is its Manatee and Aquatic Center, one of only three hospitals and rehabilitation facilities in the state of Florida for lugubrious, sick sea cows (also, Tampa's Lowry Park Zoo and Sunline Cruises have come together to present the first-ever River Odyssey Ecotour on the Hillsborough River; $14 adults, $10 children).

MOSI
4801 E. Fowler Ave., 813/987-6300, www.mosi.org
HOURS: Mon.-Fri. 9 A.M.–5 P.M., Sat. and Sun.
9 A.M.–6 P.M.
COST: $20.95 adults, $18.95 seniors,
$16.95 children 2–12
Tampa's Museum of Science & Industry is a wonderful resource for local schools, family vacationers, or local parents when they're just out of bullets (not literally). It's a sprawling modern structure that contains 450 hands-on activities grouped into learning areas. There's some goofy stuff (the Gulf Coast Hurricane Chamber, which really just blows a bunch of

loud air), but ignore that and head to the High Wire Bicycle, the longest high-wire bike in a museum, which allows visitors to pedal while balanced on a one-inch steel cable suspended 30 feet above ground. The exhibit The Amazing You teaches all about the human body. The museum has an IMAX theater and hosts traveling exhibits as well. Part of an all-new, sleek squadron of indoor Virtual Reality fighter-jet rides, the two-seater FS2000 Jet Fighter Simulator allows "pilots" to control the sharp banks, sky loops and screaming dives of pulse-pounding aerial combat. The museum has an IMAX dome and hosts traveling exhibits as well. If you time your visit to allow some cooler temperatures, the free-flying butterfly garden is a treat, with microscope viewing, magnifying glasses, and chemistry stations.

TAMPA GREYHOUND TRACK

8300 N. Nebraska Ave., 813/932-4313,
www.tampadogs.com
HOURS: Daily noon-midnight
COST: $2-4

Tampa lost its dogs in 2007. Half the year, greyhounds used to thunder around the track after that elusive little bunny. These days its a slightly seedy place to see simulcasting and do a little wagering on thoroughbreds, trotters,

jai-alai, and lots of stuff that capitalizes on the country's new mania for Texas Hold 'Em and other poker games.

USF

4202 E. Fowler Ave., 813/974-2011

The University of South Florida is one of the nation's top 63 public research universities, awarded more than $300 million in research contracts and grants in 2007 and with a $1.6 billion annual budget. The University offers 219 degree programs at the undergraduate, graduate, specialist, and doctoral levels, including the doctor of medicine. It serves more than 45,000 students on campuses in Tampa, St. Petersburg, Sarasota-Manatee, and Lakeland.

All that said, it's not the most gorgeous campus you've ever strolled. It was originally a commuter school, with parking lots spread across a wide, 1,700-acre campus for all those cars. There's no real central quad, the place where you think "this is the center of all academic shenanigans," no ivy-draped buildings or older men in tired tweed smoking pipes. Still, it's a member of the Big East Athletic Conference and thus a wealth of spectator sporting options. It also hosts lecture series, concerts at the Sun Dome, and exhibits in the Contemporary Art Museum.

Greater Tampa   Map 5

BIG CAT RESCUE

12802 Easy St., across from Citrus Park Town Center down a dirt road next to McDonald's, 813/920-4130, www.BigCatRescue.org
HOURS: Regular tours Mon.-Fri. 9 A.M. and 3 P.M., Sat. 9:30 A.M., 11:30 A.M., and 1:30 P.M.; children's tour 9 A.M. Sat.; feeding tours 4:30 P.M. Fri. and Sat., Big Cat Adventure 2-4 P.M. Sat. and last Fri. of the month
COST: Regular tour $20 (for ages 10 and over), children's tour $10, feeding tour $50, Big Cat Adventure $100

The world's largest accredited sanctuary for big cats, Big Cat Rescue provides a permanent retirement home to over 200 animals. For the

visitor, the center offers tours, outreach presentations, animal interaction, and the opportunity to spend an evening in the heart of the sanctuary. On the last Friday of each month, register for the Wild Eyes at Night tour, in which guests roam the grounds equipped with flashlights that illuminate the hundreds of shining eyes in the cat enclosures. Or be a zookeeper for a day with the all-day Big Cat Adventure. You'll get an education in animal husbandry, care, and feeding, and if you plan it for the last Friday of the month you can combine it with the exciting nighttime tour. (If an evening tour doesn't sound spooky enough,

BALLOONING

Up, up, and away in a beautiful hot-air balloon, and all you have to bring is a camera and your loved ones. Meet before dawn at a restaurant on the commerce strip of Dale Mabry, whereupon you are whisked into the **Big Red Balloon Sightseeing Adventures** (8710 W. Hillsborough Ave.; meeting place Mimi's Café, 11702 N. Dale Mabry, 813/969-1518, www.bigredballoon.com, 6-10 A.M. daily, year-round by reservation only, weather permitting, $185 adults, $160 children) van and taken to your agreed-upon launch site (there are more than 30 in the greater Tampa area from which to choose). Once inflated, the solid red balloon, the largest in the southeastern U.S., is 8.5 stories tall and contains 210,000 cubic feet of air. The balloon, which comfortably accommodates eight passengers, takes a one-hour sunrise flight at up to 1,000 feet, drifting over New Tampa, southeast Pasco County, Lutz, and Land O' Lakes. A champagne toast followed by a hearty breakfast back at Mimi's is included in the price.

During the champagne toast in the landing field, the pilot recites a traditional balloonist prayer, "The winds have welcomed you with softness, the sun has left you with warm hands, you have flown so high, and so well, that God has joined you in your laughter, and set you gently back again into the loving arms of Mother Earth." Feel free to join in.

listen to this: The woman who founded the sanctuary had a first husband who died under mysterious circumstances. His body was never found. Shudder.)

MACDILL AIRFORCE BASE
Public Affairs Office, 813/828-2215
HOURS: Tour times by appointment only
COST: Free

Tampa is fairly urban to the south, where it runs into MacDill Air Force Base, which takes up the entire southern third of the Tampa peninsula and is home to the United States Central Command (coordinating all U.S. military operations in Africa and the Middle East). Used as a staging area as far back as the Spanish-American War, it wasn't formally given to the War Department until 1939, dedicated in 1941. The base trained aircrews for overseas deployments in World War II and was crucial during the Cuban Missile Crisis and the Cold War.

Base tours are conducted on an extremely limited basis due to security measures in place since 9-11. In general, MacDill Public Affairs only schedules base tours once a week, typically on Thursdays. Tours last approximately four hours and are scheduled on a first-come, first-serve basis. The tour schedule fills up quickly, so contact MacDill Public Affairs early. Tour group size is 15–40 people (enough for one commercial bus). Priority scheduling is given to Junior ROTC students and other youth groups serving high-school-age students. Military reunions, civic and business organizations, or senior citizen groups are also welcome.

RAYMOND JAMES STADIUM
4201 N. Dale Mabry Hwy., 813/287-8844, www.ticketmaster.com
HOURS: Hours vary
COST: Prices vary

Locals are gearing up for Super Bowl XLIII in 2009. Even if your tickets are not for that game, Raymond James Stadium is a wonderful venue in which to see Tampa's beloved Buccaneers or the USF Bulls football teams. Raymond James Stadium, completed in 1998, holds more than 66,000 fans—52,000 in general seating—with a cool 103-foot-long, 43-ton pirate ship that blasts its cannons (confetti and foam footballs) every time the Bucs score.

Downtown St. Petersburg
Map 6

DOWNTOWN AREA

Along Bayshore Dr. and Beach Dr. and
First St. and Second St.

St. Petersburg has a charming, waterfront
downtown area, tourist friendly and rich in
architecture, historic buildings, attractions,
and water vistas. Most of the museums, The
Pier, and several public parks (most notably
Vinoy Park) are there. The city owns miles of
bay front, which allows for pleasant strolling,
biking, rollerblading, whatever. Parking and
traffic are usually not a problem, and decent
restaurants abound. On Central Avenue, between Second and Seventh Streets, there are
assorted galleries, shops, and restaurants.

The Looper is a super way to get around
downtown. Hop aboard the light blue motor-
ized trolleys, and enjoy a half-hour tour of St.
Petersburg's top attractions, museums, and hotels. There are 13 stops along the way.

THE PIER

800 Second Ave. NE, 727/821-6443,
www.stpetepier.com
HOURS: Shop hours vary
COST: $3 for parking; $2 admission for aquarium on
2nd floor

The Pier is really the heart and soul of visitor activity in St. Petersburg, looking like
a five-story inverted pyramid, or the good
guys' home base in a sci-fi movie. You can
rent bikes; grab a rental rod and reel and fish
off the end; depart from the Pier on a sightseeing boat charter (or on the *Dolphin Queen,*
a 44-foot catamaran that sails several times
daily; $20 adults); rent an electric boat at The
Electric Marina for half an hour, one hour,
or all day (boats seat up to 10 people and you
drive it yourself; 727/898-2628); see a flick
at the 20-screen movie theater; visit the little
aquarium; dine in the family-friendly food

COURTESY OF ST. PETERSBURG/CLEARWATER AREA CVB

The landmark Pier in the heart of St. Petersburg is a unique piece of Florida architecture
that offers visitors a chance to experience the waterfront along Tampa Bay.

court; or browse the complex's many shops. It's not high-end stuff, more touristy—there's a pet accouterment store, an entertainment-celebrity collectibles shop, candle store, T-shirt stores, that kind of thing. It is often the winter home of *The Bounty,* which offers tours when in port. Even if it sounds hokey and touristy, the views of the bay and the waterfront are delightful, with pelicans and dolphins cavorting nearby.

Clearwater and Clearwater Beach   Map 8

CLEARWATER MARINE AQUARIUM
249 Windward Passage, 727/441-1790
HOURS: Mon.-Sat. 9 A.M.-5 P.M., Sun. 10 A.M.-5 P.M.
COST: $11 adults, $9 seniors, $7.50 children 3-12

Just over the bay in Tampa, the Florida Aquarium usually gets the bulk of the kudos. And many people happen into The Pier Aquarium downtown in St. Petersburg. Clearwater Marine Aquarium is a less touristy, more modest facility with, in some ways, loftier aims. Reopened in 2008 after some major renovations, it's a working research facility and home to rescued and recuperating marine mammals (dolphins, whales, otters, etc.). For the visitor, the thrust is on education, with hourly animal care and training presentations and exhibits on animal rescue, rehabilitation, and release—and how the public can help to protect and conserve endangered marinelife. It's like the ACLU for fish. The aquarium offers on-site feeding and care programs for interested guests and operates a daily two-hour-long **Sea Life Safari** (25 Causeway Blvd., Slip #58, Clearwater Beach, 727/462-2628) that takes visitors around the Clearwater estuary and Intracoastal Waterway, with commentary by a marine biologist.

Greater Pinellas County   Map 9

◖ SUNSHINE SKYWAY BRIDGE AND FISHING PIERS
I-275 South toward Bradenton
HOURS: Always open
COST: $1

This cable-stay bridge, the largest in the world, at the southern end of St. Petersburg connects the city with Manatee County. It is a serious 29,000 feet long. The design allows stunning, unobstructed views of the water. However, this bright-yellow beauty, freshly repainted in 2007, is not for those with a fear of heights, since drivers ascend to 190 feet above the water. Bridge workers are sometimes called to bring down white-knuckled drivers frozen from height anxiety.

The ends of the old Sunshine Skyway, which was demolished some years back, are now the 0.75-mile-long North Pier and a 1.5-mile-long South Pier—together said to be the world's longest fishing pier. You can drive your car onto the pier and park it right next to your fishing spot, parallel parking on the left lane, with room for cars to drive and walkways on either side of the span. There are restrooms on both piers, and bait shops sell live and frozen bait, tackle, drinks, and snacks. They also rent rods. The North Pier has a large picnic area next to the bait shop.

RESTAURANTS

The Tampa Bay area is the home base of numerous national and regional chains: Hooters, Durango Steakhouse, Beef O' Brady's, Checkers, Shells' Seafood Restaurant, Carrabba's, Outback Steakhouse, and that's just the tip of the iceberg. Maybe it's residents' deep streak of loyalty, maybe their plodding constancy, but marketing geniuses have determined that Tampa Bay is the perfect test market for new chain restaurant concepts. They are trotted out here, and if they fly, launched upon the rest of the country.

Still, the past number of years has seen the arrival of a raft of new unique, discrete, and more-or-less independently owned restaurants. Chefs on both sides of Hillsborough Bay are beginning to question where their product comes from, to espouse the virtues of local, sustainable, organic, and naturally raised foods. Trends and culinary fads from elsewhere in the country require a bit longer to take root here, and there's not that frenetic Cult of the New that one sees in many big metro areas. Meaning, reservations aren't impossible at the temple of the latest macaroni maestro, the newest sushi shaman.

In terms of cuisine, Tampa Bay is something of a generalist. St. Louis boasts the legendary toasted ravioli. In Philly, it's all about the cheesesteak. Let other cities each have their personal gastronomic monomania, here it's a little bit of everything, impacted by the availability of fresh Gulf of Mexico seafood.

COURTESY OF TAMPA BAY CVB

RESTAURANTS

HIGHLIGHTS

LOOK FOR (TO FIND
RECOMMENDED RESTAURANTS.

(**Best Place to Indulge Your Urge to Graze:** Downtown Tampa's **Fly Bar and Restaurant** can get airstrip-loud with hipsters enthusing about the kobe sliders or baby beets with a mantle of Humboldt Fog goat cheese (page 29).

(**Best Place to Dabble in Veganism:** **Grass Root's** "live spaghetti with treatballs" brings lush spirals of zucchini "noodles" paired with mushroom-dense meatballs and two gorgeous sauces (page 32).

(**Best Place to See Two Cuisines Coexist:** When B.T. Nguyen's **Restaurant B.T.** is described as "fusion," she's likely to be a little irked. "The word fusion has been misused. What I do is classic Vietnamese and classic French, with a few dishes that cross over. I'm determined to maintain this concept and stay true to what worked in history – a lot of dishes came out of French colonial rule. And I like the attitude and passion of French cuisine" (page 33).

(**Best Steak with Side Order of Kitsch: Bern's Steak House** has been a Tampa institution for more than 50 years, making national Best Steak lists the whole time. It's a bordello-like warren of rooms, think flocked wallpaper and ornate gilt mirrors, with an over-the-top romantic dessert room upstairs. Take the tour of the kitchen and wine cellar (the largest restaurant wine cellar in the country) for added entertainment (page 36).

(**Best Hot Date and Handroll Locale:** An old favorite in St. Petersburg, **Pacific Wave** changed hands early in 2007, not upsetting the apple cart in the slightest. New owner Dan Smith has gussied up the space a bit and devoted himself to acquiring top-notch Hawaiian fish for his sushi and Japanese-inflected entrées (page 47).

COURTESY OF GRASS ROOT

Grass Root is Tampa's only raw, vegan, vegetarian, and certified green restaurant.

(**Best Place to Practice Saying "Bruschetta":** A local watering hole and slick sidewalk-table Italian, downtown St. Petersburg's **Bella Brava** does a fabulous fritto misto calamari, lengths of fennel, and thin wheels of fried lemon, as well as addictive thin-crust pizzas (page 48).

(**Where to Eat Amongst the Art:** Brand new in 2008 along with the new Hazel Hough Wing at St. Petersburg's Museum of Fine Art, the **MFA Café** is one of the most stylish lunches around (smoked tomato soup, a to-die-for burger), smack dab in the museum's soaring atrium (page 49).

(**Where to Find the Area's Most Red Haute Fare:** Chris Ponte may be the closest thing Tampa Bay has to a celebrity chef. Aside from a formidable culinary pedigree, his calling card at **Cafe Ponte** is Cal-Ital, sometimes with hints of Mediterranean, but always super luxurious and New York-sophisticated. The Clearwater dining room is lovely as well (page 58).

Downtown Tampa and Channelside   Map 1

AMERICAN
THE BUNGALOW BISTRO $$

5137 N. Florida Ave., Seminole Heights, 813/237-2000

HOURS: Tues.-Sat. 11 A.M.-10 P.M., Sun. 10 A.M.-3 P.M.

Located just north of downtown in the neighborhood of Seminole Heights, Bungalow Bistro is Elizabeth and Michael Graham's labor of love. It was a building saved from demolition in 2000 when Hillsborough Avenue was widened. They moved two buildings, turning the main house into Forever Beautiful Salon and Day Spa and the garage house into Bungalow Bistro. It's just like going to dinner at a friend's house, one who is a good cook and who feels the need to charge you a fair-minded price. Top honors: a drippy gorgonzola burger. Next best: espresso chocolate cookies that will rock your world and almond marzipan cookies that will give it a little jiggle. The rest of the menu is mid-priced, homey American food. No liquor license, so BYOB.

ECLECTIC
🎬 FLY BAR AND RESTAURANT $$

1202 Franklin St., 813/275-5000, www.flybarandrestaurant.com/tampa

HOURS: Mon.-Fri. 11:30 A.M.-3 P.M., Mon.-Thurs. 5:30 P.M.-midnight, Fri. and Sat. until 1 A.M.

The Fly is two years old, and its buzz is still deafening. The brainchild of Tampa native Leslie Shirah, this bastion of hip has since gained a devoted following among Tampa foodies and revelers. Shirah honed the concept during a 15-year stint in San Francisco, where she still owns three restaurants. The concept is this: an all-day menu until late-late; a share-it-with-friends approach to international small plates; suave cocktails; a little live music; and a minimalist-hip decor. New chef Rene Caceres has raised the bar further: Tiny golden and red beets are roasted, herbed, and given a molten blanket of tangy Humboldt Fog goat cheese. A delicious contrast of flavors, it's rivaled by a bowl of caramelized brussels sprouts, their earthiness accented with a sharp grain mustard vinaigrette. He has added fish tacos with fruity tomatillo salsa, an heirloom tomato salad,

PRICE KEY

$ Most entrées less than $10

$$ Most entrées between $10-25

$$$ Most entrées more than $25

and tucked onions and cheddar cheese in the center of the lush kobe sliders.

FRENCH
L'EDEN $$

500 Tampa St., 813/221-4795

HOURS: Mon.-Sat. 10 A.M.-3 P.M., Fri. and Sat. 5-11 P.M.

A new addition to downtown Tampa's paucity of restaurants is always welcome, and indeed this tiny French bistro has charm. It seems most thronged for weekday lunch, when soups, crepes, and salads fuel downtown workers. At night, service can be very mixed and the small-plate approach contains some oddities ("India curry chicken" ends up being tiny croissants containing chicken salad with curry-flavored mayonnaise—not what you'd expect, but tasty). Dessert crepes, a nice meal ender, come with several choices of fillings.

ITALIAN
AVANZARE $$$

Hyatt Regency Tampa, 211 N. Tampa St., 813/225-1234

HOURS: Daily 6-10 A.M., 11:30 A.M.-2 P.M., and 5-11 P.M.

Situated blocks from Tampa Bay Performing Arts Center, the Hyatt's restaurant is dreamy for dinner and a show. A waterfall cascades in the five-story atrium, but the restaurant maintains a relaxed intimacy common to fine Italian trattorias. At breakfast and lunch it's straight-ahead American with fillips of Mediterranean, but in the evening Avanzare goes upscale and sinfully Italian. The kitchen meanders across the geography of Italy, sending out inspired regional dishes to folks celebrating special

TAMPA'S "RISING STARS"

Many people argue that cooking is craft, while baking is science. It's about chemical reactions that some might say are magical, the results transporting. Don't even get Marcel Proust started about his beloved madeleine. Tampa has a growing array of bakeries that manage to break new ground, cooking up fresh temptations for local diners.

Chances are you've eaten their crisp, golden Cuban bread if you've dined anywhere in Ybor City. But why not go to the source? Rumor has it **La Segunda Central Bakery** (2512 N. 15th St., 813/248-1531) churns out 6,000 Cuban loaves daily. You only need one, in the form of the archetypal Cubano sandwich. They're about 36 inches long, with a zipperlike seam down the top. What's that charred leaf on the top of your bread? It's the remnants of a palmetto leaf, used during baking to hold the top of the bread together and create the signature crack along the top. It means you've got yourself an authentic loaf of Cuban bread, comprende?

Sami's Pita Bakery (4920 E. Busch Blvd., 877/989-2722) specializes in breads and baked goods for the health-conscious or those with allergies. For breads, this means flat breads, sliced breads, and rolls that are made from milled flours other than wheat — from millet and flax spinach lavash to pizza crusts and low-carb seven-grain fiber bread. Even sweets get virtuous, from sweet Middle Eastern walnut baklava to low-carb/high-protein cheesecake.

What's that smell wafting through Soho? It's the stunning whole-grain breads of **Great Harvest Bread Co.** (500 S. Howard Ave., 813/259-3700). Part of a small franchise chain of bakeries, it has a free, piping-hot bread-tasting bar that puts those little spoons at Baskin Robbins to shame. Slather a little butter on that warm cheddar garlic bread and get a preview of Keri Eisenbeis and Michael Matthews' addic-tive goods. The mostly-bread bakery, opened in August 2003, is hip, lively, and fun — an easy place to blow (and eat) a lot of dough. Employees, old and young, have the kind of earnest, evangelical zeal of the recently converted. And it's easy to see why.

For a rustic boule, an elegant batard, or a slab of heavenly, herb-flecked focaccia, aficionados have long known they need to get in the car and drive down MacDill to **Pane Rustica** (3225 S. Macdill Ave., 813/902-8828). Its name says it all: dense loaves dotted with black olive, a hearty seven-grain that makes any sandwich a party, even thin, bubbled pizza crusts that rival the best in New York. Their current location has been the stage for some of Tampa's best lunching. You walk in and pick your sandwich, salad, pizza, or other baked good from the short blackboard menu or from the mouthwatering display along the long glassed counter.

And **Alessi Bakery** (2909 W. Cypress St., 813/871-2286) is Tampa's original Old World family-owned Sicilian bakery, known especially for its flaky-pastried chocolate cream-filled cannoli — "leave the guns, and take the cannoli," indeed. Their chocolate biscotti are worthy of your richest cup of joe, and their princess cake has been a local legend since the bakery's opening in 1912. Pastries run the gamut from Cuban to Italian to all-American, with 16 tortes offered for a dose of instant dessert heroism.

On the other hand, baker Michael Baugh is often called the Michelangelo of chocolate. You can test the assertion at **Let Them Eat Cake** (3805 S. Westshore Blvd., 813/837-6888). Baugh has a local TV show called *Chocolate Is My Crayon*, teaches cake baking and chocolate sculpting, and makes over-the-top decadent wedding cakes, birthday cakes, or even just who-needs-a-reason-to-eat-cake cakes.

occasions or those sophisticates who just choose to indulge like this for no particular reason.

STEAKHOUSE
GALLAGHER'S ❸❸❸
615 Channelside Dr., Ste. 203, 813/229-8000,
www.gallagherstampa.com
HOURS: Sun.-Thurs. 5-10 P.M., Fri. and Sat. until 11 P.M.

Opened in 2007, Gallagher's Steak House in Channelside is the fifth franchise that plays tribute to the historic New York flagship steak emporium of the same name. The space was inherited from the short-lived Signature Room (itself an homage to the original, at the top of Chicago's Hancock Building), a pleasant bewindowed corner spot with a spare, masculine aesthetic. Construction issues delayed the opening by a few weeks, which left extra time for staff training—it shows. Servers are expertly versed in the menu, steeped in the arcana that surround aged prime and Angus beef. Plates contain precious few superfluous knickknacks and doodads; the meat and nothing but the meat. Not surprisingly, the wine list is weighted to big cabs to accommodate the steaks, and a heap of pinot noirs to appeal to current tastes. And after the booze and the rare meat? Then comes the chocolate.

MALIO'S PRIME ❸❸❸
400 N. Ashley Drive, 813/223-7746,
www.maliosprime.com
HOURS: Mon.-Thurs. 11 A.M.-11 P.M., Fri. until midnight, Sat. 4 P.M.-midnight

He knew everyone, made people feel good, kissed the ladies. Malio Iavarone was the consummate restaurateur and showman, his restaurant an iconic dining destination. It opened in 1969 and closed in 2005, a long run in restaurant years. And now it's back, kind of. Malio's son, Derek, and a buddy launched Malio's Prime in downtown Tampa's 31-story Rivergate Tower (the one that looks like a beer can). It's an anchor of sorts for the whole Riverwalk initiative, a vote of confidence that Mayor Pam Iorio's vision of a riverfront renaissance will become reality. It's a gorgeous space, with a familiar menu of steaks and chops, but

YACHT STARSHIP

Ahoy, mates and would-be mates. Climb aboard **Yacht StarShip** (departs from 603 Channelside Dr., 813/223-7999, www.yachtstarship.com, dinner cruise $80, but there are sometimes discounts; the boat boards at 6:30 P.M., departs at 7 P.M., and returns at 9:30 P.M.), Tampa's premier dining yacht, while the sunset casts its sherbet hues across the Bay. It's the *Love Boat*, only not as interminable and without all the crew in white knee socks. Imagine yourself plowing into hand-carved beef tenderloin with garlic mashed potatoes napped with wild mushroom demiglace, or maybe grilled swordfish nestled under a tomato-caper beurre blanc and served with sautéed spinach. Now add in a little gentle rocking, the salty sea air, and a tangerine sunset illuminating the downtown Tampa skyline. In 2.5 hours, you can have the cruise of a lifetime aboard this three-story, 180-foot yacht, which has recently undergone a capacity expansion. Arrive a half-hour before departure to sign in and board. The boat does not wait for latecomers!

as an evening progresses in the 8,000-square-foot restaurant, the noise level swells, making lingering somewhat unattractive.

TAPAS
TINATAPA'S ❸❸
615 Channelside Dr., Ste. 120, 813/514-8462
HOURS: Mon.-Thurs. 4-11 P.M., Fri. 11 A.M.-2 A.M., Sat. noon-2 A.M., Sun. noon-10 P.M.

The restaurant is named in homage—just a tongue-twister away—to the famous Tipatina's in New Orleans, so if you know your Big Easy, you'll know Tinatapa's is going to be a fun, loud, raucous place to end an evening. Barcelona mosaics and logs for rafters give the spare, round room a decidedly European feel. There isn't total verisimilitude with some of the Spanish small plates—baked goat cheese with tomato sauce and salmon with a horseradish

Baby spinach, sunflower sprouts, crisp apple, maple glazed walnuts, and an herbed apple vinaigrette – just one of the dishes that await you at Grass Root.

glaze might flummox the average barfly in Madrid. Still, flavors are bright and assertive, prices are low, and sharing makes it an adventure (but for those who have trouble sharing, house specialties come in full entrée sizes, paired with black beans and Spanish rice).

VEGETARIAN
GRASS ROOT $$
2702 N. Florida Ave., 813/221-7668,
www.thegrassrootlife.com
HOURS: Tues.-Sat. 11 A.M.-9 P.M.

Not just vegetarian, but 100 percent vegan. Not just vegan, but much of the menu upholds the tenets of raw foodism, nothing taken above 110 degrees to kill off all those good enzymes. Still, this funky outpost in a slightly sketchy neighborhood is not at all about asceticism. At Grass Root, diners can dive into platters of "live spaghetti with treatballs,"

raw sushi, exotic wraps, and lush miso "sipp" with sliced coconut noodles. Hardly the food of deprivation and hippie delirium, dishes are colorful, flavorful, and satisfying, even for the unreconstructed carnivore. Spencer Sterling's list of fresh-made juices are lovely and sustaining.

VIETNAMESE
BAMBOOZLE $
516 N. Tampa St., 813/223-7320
HOURS: Mon.-Fri. 11 A.M.-2 P.M.

New on the scene, Bamboozle is packing them in downtown. Quick and healthy Vietnamese fusion has charmed office workers at lunch (breakfast and dinner are possibly on the horizon), with classic pho and traditional noodle salads, followed up by the oh-so-sweet Vietnamese coffee lush with sweetened condensed milk. Very vegetarian friendly.

South Tampa and Hyde Park   Map 2

AMERICAN

MISE EN PLACE $$$

442 W. Kennedy Blvd., 813/254-5373

HOURS: Tues.-Fri. 11:30 A.M.-2:30 P.M., Tues.-Thurs.
5:30-10 P.M., Fri. until 11 P.M., Sat. only 5-11 P.M.

Mise en Place has been at the cutting edge of Tampa dining for years; Marty Blitz is a local culinary legend. Look out at the minarets of the University of Tampa as you scroll through the oversized one-page menu. It's hard to characterize the sensibility in the kitchen when the weekly-changing menu ranges from pizza with chorizo, roast corn, chilies, and manchego to mole spice–rubbed seared tuna with purple potatoes, vanilla bean pineapple salad, and a prickly pear habanero vinaigrette. They also take great care to accommodate folks with special diets and it's one of the only places in town with a sophisticated cheese program: maybe a firm, smoky, aged sheep's milk cheese, a Grafton Cloth Bound cheddar, and one most excellent runny-stinky selection from the Cote d'Or.

SQUARE ONE $$

3701 Henderson Blvd., 813/414-0101,
www.square1burgers.com

HOURS: Sun.-Thurs. 11:30 A.M.-10 P.M., Fri. and Sat.
until midnight

Bill Shumate opened his first burger joint in 1964 in Norman, Oklahoma. Many restaurants and concepts later (like Bella's on S. Howard), he and his partner Joanie Corneil have returned to these roots, back to square one with, um, Square One. It's burgers and lots of them, with nine basic types (Meyer Angus beef, kobe, sashimi tuna, portobello) with a whole passel of toppers (teriyaki ginger sauce, roasted black bean and corn salsa) and three types of buns. The menu shows admirable focus, but these are fancy burgers: Think Angus beef topped with caramelized onion, sun-dried tomatoes, and brie. Nearly the best burger in Tampa (despite the fact that the fries need another minute in the fryer), often a mob scene of young families.

THE WINE EXCHANGE $$

1609 Snow Ave., 813/254-9463

HOURS: Sun.-Thurs. 11:30 A.M.-10 P.M., Fri. and Sat.
until 11 P.M.

Despite a recent move, it's been around for a long time as a top dog in the Old Hyde Park Village area, beloved by Hyde Park shop-and-lunchers for its Mediterranean-inflected salads and sandwiches. At dinner, the dusk-cooled outdoor patio beckons from beneath the limbs of a craggy old live oak, while the little interior dining room is a stage set for convivial conversation. Still, the greatest come-hither allure is the wine list. The Wine Exchange has one of the most intriguing, well-priced, and downright spunky lists around. At any given time they boast an array of 50 world-beat wines by the glass (tempranillos next to mourvedres jostling up against delicate riesling kabinetts) and a changing palette of tasting flights (a trio of perfumy viogniers, that kind of thing). Alas, food is just so-so.

ASIAN

RESTAURANT B.T. $$$

1633 W. Snow Ave., 813/258-1916

HOURS: Daily 11:30 A.M.-2:30 P.M., Mon.-Thurs.
5:30-9:30 P.M., Fri. and Sat. until 10:30 P.M.

After 15 years of being at the forefront of Tampa's gastronomic scene, B.T. Nguyen may have reached her pinnacle in Restaurant B.T., located dead center in Old Hyde Park Village. Classic Vietnamese and French dishes (Vietnam was under French colonial rule 1858–1954, thus French and Vietnamese cuisines had ample time for fraternizing, swapping tips and techniques, and generally commingling) appear in a swirl of lemongrass and hot chiles, always innovatively presented in stylish, architectural flights of fancy that echo the sophistication of this indoor/outdoor dining room. Trained as a sommelier, Nguyen's wine list is also laudable, as is her short list of exotic cocktails, which explains the locale's popularity as an evening gathering place for the city's beautiful people.

TC CHOY ASIAN BISTRO $$

301 S. Howard Ave., 813/251-1191

HOURS: Mon.-Thurs. 11:30 A.M.-2:30 P.M. and
5:30-10 P.M., Fri. until 11 P.M., Sat. and Sun. 11 A.M.-3 P.M.
and 5:30-11 P.M.

Remember when salsa supplanted ketchup as
America's favorite condiment? Wasabi has to
be nipping at salsa's heels. Sushi turns up everywhere, from the ball game to convenience
stores to—and here's the strange part—a
whole bunch of different kinds of Asian restaurants. You don't have to go to a Japanese
restaurant to dig into a California roll—you'll
find them at area Chinese restaurants, Thai
restaurants, even Vietnamese restaurants. It's
part of a recent trend to purvey a greatest-hits
list of pan-Asian dishes under the same roof,
an enticing mélange of pad Thai, tekka maki,
and kung pao chicken sure to please everyone.
TC Choy's Asian Bistro in Hyde Park is a textbook example of the species. Anchoring a long
row of restaurants along South Howard, TC
Choy's traffics in carefully constructed dishes
from Thailand, Singapore, China, Japan, and
Malaysia, all served in an oversized, stylish
dining room. Best offerings: noonday dim sum
with big tables perfect for large parties.

WATER $$

1015 1/2 S. Howard Ave., 813/251-8406,
www.ciccioandtonys.com

HOURS: Daily 6-10 P.M.

Dead center on Restaurant Row, Water is a
savvy Japanese-inspired seafood joint and a
late-night hangout for the neighborhood's
beautiful people. Water specializes in rice-pa-
per rolled sushi (no nori) paired with punchy
sauces and dynamic side dishes. A minimalist
design aesthetic and a no-reservations policy
cannot douse the enthusiasm for vibrant combos like unagi, banana, and avocado.

BARBECUE
SMOKE BARBECUE & GRILL $$

901 Platt St., 813/254-7070

HOURS: Mon.-Fri. 11:30 A.M.-2:30 P.M.,
Mon.-Sat. 5-10 P.M.

Opened in May 2008, this barbecue joint is

another project from local über-restaurateur
Gordon Davis (of Ceviche and others). This
is in a "New World barbecue" idiom, with traditional dry-rubbed pork shoulder, brisket,
spareribs, and beef ribs; a Hawaiian rotisserie
chicken; skewers of shrimp and scallops; and
other skewers of veggies. Whole meal prices
will hover between $15 and $21, with side
dishes that include sweet potato fries, Asian-
inflected cole slaw, and sautéed greens. A liquor
license is still pending, but the aim is just beer
and wine in this old converted auto body shop
with gas lamps and rustic brick.

ECLECTIC
SEVEN 17 SOUTH $$$

717 S. Howard Ave., 813/250-1661

HOURS: Mon.-Fri. 11:30 A.M.-2:30 P.M.,
Mon.-Sat. 5-10 P.M.

Two fully realized culinary strategies are adopted simultaneously—each separate but
equal. One side of the menu deals in kicky
pan-Asian dishes as the other offers up sturdy
Italian classics (lasagna, veal scaloppini). It's
something for everyone, but not all on the
same schizophrenic plate. Its success isn't just
about the food: A sleek, clubby interior (visit
just for a peek at the stunning art deco canvasses set against deep lapis lazuli walls) draws
a hip, fashion-forward crowd. Service is warm
and attentive, with glamorous hostesses bustling around as each evening amps up. The
bartenders' mixology skills don't hurt, either,
to lure a robust bar business most nights. Not
every dish is a slam-dunk, but most diners' de-
sires can be satisfied somewhere in the pages
of the long menu.

SIDEBERN'S $$$

2208 W. Morrison Ave., 813/258-2233

HOURS: Mon.-Thurs. 5-10 P.M., Fri. and Sat. until 11 P.M.

If the steakhouse Bern's doesn't sound like
your cup of tea, try the more contemporary
approach at the affiliated SideBern's. They
lost their chef/partner Jeannie Pierola at the
end of 2007, but the kitchen is still turning
out gorgeous dim sum and world-beat small
plates. The daily-changing selection of breads

CUPCAKE NATION

Babycakes was taken. So was Cupcake Café, The Cupcakery, Casa Cupcake, even Hello, Cupcake. All trademarked already. So when Nicole Rogers applied for a business name, she settled on **The Cupcake Spot** (2401 S. Dale Mabry Hwy., Tampa, 813/258-3111, Tues.-Fri. 11 A.M.-6:30 P.M., Sat. 10 A.M.-5 P.M.) for the little storefront she opened at the end of 2007.

A perfectly lovely name, paired with a plucky, cherry-topped, anthropomorphized cupcake logo, Tampa's C-Spot is our first entry in the national cupcake craze. New York City's Magnolia Bakery is credited with starting the frenzy in the mid-1990s, its buttercreamy allures immortalized in an episode of *Sex and the City* (and later in a *Saturday Night Live* skit).

Then Oprah brought Los Angeles's Sprinkles Cupcakes to our collective consciousness (a gift from Barbra Streisand, they were Oprah's absolute faves). Not to be outdone, Ellen DeGeneres went on to enumerate the 10 best cupcakes in America.

There are more than a dozen craven cupcaker blogs, including one launched in 2004 by Rachel Kramer Bussel, a former sex columnist for *The Village Voice*. One blog, the appropriately named www.cupcakefetish.com, puts the number of cupcake shops at 475, spread through 13 countries.

And now Tampa has its own. But what has taken cupcakes from the homeroom mom's sticky chore to adult obsession?

"Part of it is a nostalgic feeling about childhood," says Rogers. "It doesn't matter if you're 1 or 101, it plays to our ego. You get your very own cake and you're not sharing. They're portable, they're cute. and they're portion controlled so you don't overindulge."

Yeah, right. The Cupcake Spot has a 1950s diner motif, lots of chrome and hot pink. There are funky armchairs and bold black-and-white tile floors. But where X marks the Spot is the glass case of sweet stuff. They make about 14 varieties each day, so while each is a single-serving cake, there's no law that you may have just one. Top honors go to the Chocolate Elvis (banana cupcake, peanut butter buttercream and a dollop of chocolate ganache), the Berry Squared (strawberry cake topped with strawberry-raspberry cream cheese icing) and the Va-Va-Vanilla (a regular vanilla cake/icing combo elevated by black dots of vanilla bean). Prices run $2.75 per cupcake, $15.50 per half dozen, and $30 per dozen.

is absolutely knockout (curry sesame flatbread, kalamata and fig loaf). Veggies are first rate: a first course salad of sliced roasted red beets, goat cheese and spring mix in a lovely Dijon vinaigrette; a heavenly cipollini onion soup with white truffle foam. Cocktails are pricey but worth a splurge.

ETHIOPIAN
QUEEN OF SHEBA $

3636 Henderson Blvd., 813/872-6000
HOURS: Daily 11 A.M.-10 P.M.

The space is one of those Bermuda Triangle sites that has seen the demise of a number of restaurant ventures. Queen of Sheba will stick, though, on the basis of its huge family-style platter of spiced legume or meat stews called wats, its chicken drumsticks, and the hard-boiled eggs. The platters are lined with injera, a staple Ethiopian bread made of tef flour (gluten-free, a boon to wheat allergies or celiac disease sufferers). Spongy and elastic, more injera doubles as utensil, tiny pieces used to scoop dabs of stew.

ITALIAN
CAFFE PARADISO $$

4205 S. MacDill Ave., 813/835-6622
HOURS: Mon.-Sat. 5:30-10 P.M.

"Are you ready to hear the evening's specials?" Sure, why not, how ready do we have to be, we thought. After about the 10th dish, we started panicking. What was that first one again, with the fish? Did he say something about manicotti? Not to worry, the waiter was patient with us, repeating as necessary. Giving advice, cajoling gently to ensure we'd ordered well. It's that kind of place: friendly, casual, with comforting Italian cuisine served up by guys who, if they aren't Italian, have the warmth and tendency to gesticulate that makes them seem so. It's the kind of place that's familiar and reminiscent of home—regardless of your heritage. It's nothing too snazzy from the outside, just a little storefront in the St. Croix Plaza on South MacDill Avenue. Inside, it's comfy and dark, with crisp linens and lots of regulars.

PANE RUSTICA $$

3225 S. MacDill Ave., 813/902-8828,
www.panerusticabakery.com
HOURS: Tues. 8 A.M.–6 P.M., Wed.-Sat. 8 A.M.-10 P.M.,
Sun. 8 A.M.-3 P.M.

A thin-crust pizza hotshot by day, from Wednesday to Saturday Pane Rustica hosts some of the most sophisticated Cal-Ital dinners around, with full table service and an elegant short wine list. You can still opt for one of those luscious thin-crust pizzas (maybe one with a mantle of gorgonzola hiding sweet lengths of caramelized shallot? or perhaps ricotta salata enlivened with olive tapenade and sun-dried tomatoes?) or even a laid-back burger gussied up with brie and roasted red peppers. But the breadth of alluring choices might sway you toward something a bit more refined. Don't miss Kevin and Karyn Kruszewski's stupendous cookies, cakes, and other housemade confections for dessert.

SPANISH/TAPAS

CEVICHE TAPAS BAR & RESTAURANT $$

1502 S. Howard Ave., 813/250-0203
HOURS: Tues.-Thurs. 5-11 P.M., Fri. and Sat. until 3 A.M.

Despite a recent move to the site of another longtime Hyde Park favorite (the defunct St. Bart's Island House), Ceviche hasn't skipped a beat, serving its namesake citrus-cured fish, sea scallops with manchego, and an array of little dishes with addictive olives and almonds, all in a sleek nightclub atmosphere. Its new location has a special flamenco room for live music and dance, a suave late-night hangout for Hyde Park's hipsters, purple-teethed from pitchers of delicious sangria.

CHEAP $

309 S. Howard Ave., 813/258-5878
HOURS: Tues.-Sat. 5 P.M.-2 A.M.

Cheap has most of the elements of an exciting new small-plate restaurant, but it needs to tinker with its menu. An industrial-chic, low-light, loud-music place with good buzz, a high funk-factor is provided by wonderful found-object murals and the use of minivan banquettes in the booths, complete with seatbelts. Cheap boasts colorful mix-and-match china, gorgeous sangria pitchers, and lovely swirled stemware. Half the menu is "crudos," cold raw seafood dishes like tartares, ceviches, and sashimis. The other half is "epulae" (a Latin word that means loosely "feast"). On either side, most dishes lack textural contrast of something crunchy, and the vegetarian hasn't much from which to choose.

STEAKHOUSE

BERN'S STEAK HOUSE $$$

1208 S. Howard Ave., 813/251-2421
HOURS: Daily 5-11 P.M.

It's the biggest gorilla of them all on the Tampa dining scene, the restaurant known around the world. It's on what is now a slightly seedy stretch of South Howard, but fans are undeterred. It's a more than 50-year-old landmark, with a wine list that could break a toe and a menu that reaches new levels of hyperbole. Waiters go through a grueling years-long apprenticeship, resulting in a staff that could, and does, quote verbatim from the offerings. Steaks are so lovingly described that it wouldn't be surprising to hear the eye color, hat size, or hobbies of the cows in question. It's prime beef, aged and nurtured in Bern's own meat lockers, and you, the customer, dictate the size, cut, cooking temperature, and way too many other details. Just bring me a nice steak. Still, you gotta go to Bern's, if only to revel in the bordello-like decor of gilded plaster columns, red wallpaper, Tiffany lamps, and murals of French vineyards. After dinner take the tour of the kitchen and wine cellar.

Then head upstairs to **The Harry Waugh Dessert Room at Bern's Steak House.**

Nothing prepares you for it. Not even the rococo excess of Bern's downstairs. People tell you, "You dine in individual hollowed-out wine casks." Someone says, "There are individual wall-mounted radio thingies to set the mood at your table." You hear a rumor about an accordionist, maybe something about flambéing waiters. The romantic date-night possibilities

of this dessert-only upstairs of Bern's (named after a wine-writing crony of Bern himself) get the heart racing. If that's not enough, there's Chocolate-Chocolate-Chocolate. That's actually the name of the demure chocolate-shellacked cylinder packing chocolate cheese pie, chocolate mousse, and chocolate cheesecake into one deadly package.

Davis Islands   Map 2

AMERICAN
220 EAST $$
220 E. Davis Blvd., 813/259-1220
HOURS: Mon.-Thurs. 11:30 A.M.-3 P.M. and 5-10 P.M., Fri. 11 A.M.-3 P.M. and 4-11 P.M., Sat. 11 A.M.-11 P.M.

Nestled in the cute street-that-time-forgot business district of Davis Island, this longtimer beckons with a cheery turquoise-and-grape awning. Opinions are divided about the best tables—out front at one of the handful on the patio, or inside at one of the deep green booths. Either way, most tables are full of islanders and pilgrims from elsewhere in the Bay Area eager for a friendly face and a fairly priced, unfussy meal that ranges affably through American, Asian, or even Cajun dishes.

ASIAN FUSION
JACKSON'S BISTRO-BAR-SUSHI $$$
Wyndham Harbour Island Hotel, 601 S. Harbour Island Blvd., 813/277-0112, www.jacksonsbistro.com
HOURS: Mon.-Thurs. 11:30 A.M.-2:30 P.M. and 5-10 P.M., Fri. and Sat. 11:30 A.M.-2:30 P.M. and 5-11 P.M., Sun. 10:30 A.M.-2:30 P.M. and 5-10 P.M.

Really on Harbour Island, an adjacent tiny island within a stone's throw of Davis Islands, Jackson's opened in 1997 and has waited for everything, and everyone, around it to arrive at its sophistication level. Judging from the hip, bustling crowd—they've arrived. And the sleek restaurant embraces the throngs with a laudably broad wine list and a something-for-everyone culinary approach that includes pistachio-crusted red snapper, lush prime rib eye steaks, and a smart array of familiar *nigiri* and *makimono* sushi rolls.

Backjack's is the restaurant's locale for weekend entertainment. It's a vast, clubby, mahogany-lined room containing a lengthy three-sided bar and some of the city's most diehard revelers. Despite its island locale, it's one block from the Tampa Convention Center, Marriott Waterside, and the Hartline Trolley.

FRENCH
CHEZ BRYCE $$$
238 E. Davis Blvd., 813/258-8100
HOURS: Tues.-Sat. 11:30 A.M.-3 P.M. and 6-10P.M., Sun 10:30A.M.-3P.M. and 6-10P.M.

Tampa native Bryce Whittlesey opened his own restaurant in 2007 in a big and quirky space with a fountained courtyard that is the height of romance in sweet weather. You might aim for the utterly fabulous house-smoked salmon salad—fragrant at five paces with the scents of Meyer lemon and fresh tarragon, a perfect vinaigrette napping endive and watercress, and plush swaths of salmon. Iced stone crab claws beckon from the raw bar, and individual Puckish (Wolfgang, not Shakespeare) pizzas come gussied with thoughtful toppings (fennel, goat cheese, and more of that smoked salmon). The single certainty is dessert, as in must have it. Whittlesey goes classic French, with vacherins, tartes Tatin, and pots de crème.

MEXICAN
ESTELA'S $
209 E. Davis Blvd., 813/251-0558
HOURS: Weekdays 11 A.M.-10 P.M., weekends until 11 P.M.

Across the street from 220 East and equally

COURTESY OF VISIT FLORIDA

Fresh seafood is a perk of visiting waterfront locales.

beloved, Estela's is known for exemplary carne asada (a rib eye with lots of thinly sliced onions and a limey piquancy, served with a cheese enchilada and refried beans) and chocolate tacos. Margaritas are big and quenching; there's mariachi on the weekend. Unsurprisingly, Estela's has spawned additional locations in New Port Richey, St. Petersburg, and Brandon.

Ybor City   Map 3

AMERICAN

TAMPA BAY BREWING COMPANY $$

Centro Ybor, 1600 E. 8th Ave., plaza level under Muvico, 813/247-1422, www.tbbco.com

HOURS: Mon.-Tues. 11 A.M.-11 P.M., Wed.-Sat. 11 A.M.-2 A.M., Sun. 1 P.M.-midnight

One of Tampa's beloved brewpubs, it recently moved from elsewhere in Ybor City to anchor the Centro Ybor, a welcome addition. There's good live music, excellent proprietary brews (watch the Redeye Ale, it's a humdinger), and an ambitious American bistro menu.

GREEK

ACROPOLIS GREEK TAVERN $$

1833 E. 7th Ave., 813/242-4545, www.acropolistaverna.com

HOURS: Mon.-Thurs. 11 A.M.-midnight, Fri. 11 A.M.-3 A.M., Sat. noon-3 A.M., Sun. noon-midnight

Belly dancers Fridays, Saturdays, and Sundays; a frenetic bouzouki band; or the stirring Greek song stylings of Babi Lavidas. Then add to that people leaping up to gyrate through a quick *ze-bekiko* or *sousta,* punctuated by the occasional sound of plates breaking, and you have yourself a Hellenic hootenanny. Tables outside are nice, but you might miss out on the action in the becolumned dining room. Owners Sam and Costa Waez have taken a traditional Greek taverna set-up and infused it with Ybor fun. The menu is all that the blue-and-white color scheme promises, with gyros, spanakopita, moussaka, and such. But vegetarians will be especially pleased at their range of options: tahini-lush hummus and baba ganoush; a roasted veggie sandwich anchored by nutty eggplant; falafel offered as a wrap or app, drizzled with more tangy tahini sauce.

JAPANESE
SAMURAI BLUE SUSHI AND SAKE BAR 💲💲
Centro Ybor, 1600 E 8th Ave # C208, 813/242-6688, www.samuraiblue.com
HOURS: 11:30 A.M.-midnight Mon.-Fri., 5 P.M.-1 A.M. Sat., 5-11 P.M. Sun.

A longtimer in the ever-changing lineup of Centro Ybor restaurants, Samurai is a big, frenetic joint serving sake bombers, "spontaneous combustion rolls," and other kooky spins on Japanese bar staples. You've had better chilled soba noodles and tekka maki, but it doesn't matter much once you've relaxed with something from the suave saketini menu.

ITALIAN
BERNINI OF YBOR 💲💲💲
1702 E. 7th Ave., 813/248-0099, www.berniniofybor.com
HOURS: Weekdays 11:30 A.M.-10 P.M., weekends until midnight, Sun. 4-10 P.M.

People watching is a robust pastime in Ybor City, with occasional catcalling and trash-talking adding a fillip of drama. For the best sidewalk seat in town, pull up a chair at Bernini. It's set in the historic Bank of Ybor City building and serves sophisticated Cal-Ital cuisine—salmon carpaccio, lemon-scented calamari, and filet mignon sparked with a wild mushroom risotto and topped with heady truffle butter. It attracts a more mature crowd than the bars and clubs all around it, partly because of the thoughtful wine list and partly because the mixologists know their way around the bar. Given Bernini's namesake painter, Bernini's

Italian chocolate kiss martini is suitably over-the-top, go-for-Baroque, pairing Ketel One vodka, Godiva white and dark liqueurs, and a hint of Frangelico, all sealed with a kiss. Certainly easier on the breath than the punchy puttanesca pizza (olives, anchovy, capers, etc.), but it all depends on your priorities.

MEXICAN
ADOBE GILA'S 💲
Centro Ybor, 1600 E. 8th Ave., 813/241-8588, www.adobegilas.com
HOURS: Daily 11 A.M.-3 A.M.

Named for a cantankerous (and poisonous) Gila monster, Adobe Gilas is more a drinking establishment, a fun place in which to pick your poison and let it rip. Think you can handle a 64-ounce margarita? Feel free to attempt it amongst these consummate 'rita professionals. Food runs to dips and chips (burgers and "tortilla pizza" are strictly serviceable), so the draw is the rustic second-story indoor-outdoor space and abounding good cheer. After all this revelry, regroup at the Centro Ybor movie theater across the plaza.

MEMA'S ALASKAN TACOS 💲
1724 E. 8th Ave., 813/242-8226
HOURS: Tues. 11 A.M.-1 A.M., Wed.-Sat. 11 A.M.-3 A.M.

Alright, Mexican may be stretching the category a bit. It's tacos, namely $3 fish tacos, largely consumed in the waning hours of a night of debauchery. A post-clubbing pit stop, Mema's attracts even those who are all dressed up to have one last Corona with a tamale or black beans. No one's saying it's art, but if the time is right, it sure tastes good.

SPANISH
COLUMBIA RESTAURANT 💲💲💲
2117 E. 7th Ave., 813/248-4961
HOURS: Mon.-Thurs. 11 A.M.-10 P.M., Fri. and Sat. until 11 P.M., Sun. noon-9 P.M.

The Columbia bears the distinction of being the oldest restaurant in Florida (started in 1905) and the nation's largest Spanish/Cuban restaurant (13 rooms extending one city block). Frankly, the food's not spectacular these days,

COURTESY OF TAMPA BAY & CO.

The Columbia Restaurant in Ybor City offers an evening flamenco show.

but the experience is worth picking through ho-hum paella or sipping pedestrian sangria. Some of these waiters have been here a lifetime, the many rooms manage to stay packed, and there are stirring flamenco shows Monday–Saturday nights.

Busch Gardens and North Tampa   Map 4

AMERICAN
SKIPPER'S SMOKEHOUSE $$
910 Skipper Rd., 813/971-0666
HOURS: Tues.-Fri. 11 A.M.-10 P.M., Sat. noon-11 P.M., Sun. 1-10 P.M.

New Tampa (the residential area northeast of downtown), as the name indicates, is all new. The upside is that things are clean, pristine, hygienic; the downside is that there's no sense of history, no gritty, time-worn ambience. If you are jonesing for something that seems older than a decade or so, Skipper's Smokehouse has the ambience of a place 10 times its age. It's Tampa's best live music venue (blues, alt rock, Tuvan throat singers, the gamut), with concerts held outdoors under the canopy of a huge, moss-festooned live oak. It has a lively 30s-and-up bar scene (a mighty fine mojito), and a ramshackle restaurant serves a wonderful blackened grouper sandwich, gator nuggets, and black beans.

CALIFORNIA
CICCIO & TONY'S $$
16019 Tampa Palms Blvd., 813/975-1222
HOURS: Mon.-Thurs. 11:30 A.M.-2:30 P.M. and 5-9:30 P.M., Fri. 11:30 A.M.-2:30 P.M. and 5-10:30 P.M., Sat. noon-3 P.M. and 5-10:30 P.M., Sun. 5-9:30 P.M.

Everyone's favorite neighborhood restaurant in New Tampa is Ciccio & Tony's. Most nights it teems with families devoted to this health-conscious neighborhood favorite. C&T hits everything right: Thin, crunchy New York–style pizzas come topped with caramelized eggplant and goat cheese, while a turkey club chop chop pairs turkey breast with high-protein soy bacon bits, ripe tomato, crisp lettuce, and savory yellow rice.

CHINESE
HO HO CHOY $

1441 E. Fletcher Ave., 813/962-2159
HOURS: Sun.-Thurs. 11 A.M.-10 P.M., Fri. and Sat. until 11 P.M.

Relocating from a spot on Dale Mabry, Ho Ho Choy is a purveyor of appealing and straightforward Chinese dishes as well as an array of less familiar dim sum. The fried and steamed dumplings are served all day (whereas in China the small dishes are served primarily for lunch), offered in small, individual portions. Ho Ho Choy's fried sesame ball is prototypical, featuring a crunchy, sesame seed-coated exterior giving way to a smooth red bean paste center. An order of pork buns brings airy, soft white bread cradling a sweet, electric-pink barbecued pork filling. The pan-fried dumplings are the best, with their crisp fried exteriors contrasting the rest of the slithery dumpling, and a savory, gingery ground pork filling.

GREEK
ACROPOLIS BAR & GRILL $$

14947 Bruce B. Downs Blvd., 813/971-1787
HOURS: Mon.-Thurs. 11 A.M.-midnight, Fri. and Sat. until 3 A.M., Sun. noon-midnight

The staff is young, attractive, and prone to launching into a fit of grapevine dancing at the slightest provocation. They yell "Opa" and break plates, a belly dancer undulates on the weekends, a DJ spins world music late night. The same menu at lunch and dinner means it's a little splurgy at lunch, consummately affordable at dinner. The owners have stayed focused in the kitchen, ditching things that may not be accessible to timid palates (fishy taramasalata) and keeping the Greek crowd pleasers (flaming cheese, watch the eyebrows). Generally,

portions are big and entrées come with a choice of soup or salad—hard to choose, because the soup is often a delicious lemony avgolemono (like eggdrop soup, Greek-style) and the salad is a generous Greek topped with a wedge of perfect feta.

MEXICAN
THE LIME $

16023 Tampa Palms Blvd., 813/979-LIME
HOURS: Mon.-Fri. 11:30 A.M.-2:30 P.M. and 5-9:30 P.M., weekends 11:30A.M.-midnight

The same crew that owns Ciccio & Tony's opened an outpost of its hip Tex-Mex nightspot in New Tampa in 2007. Lime green ostrich banquettes and pretty people don't mask the fact that this is essentially a sports bar with decent tacos and such. On any given night you'll find gussied-up USF students on their way in to mingle as the soccer moms and their progeny are finishing up a burrito and basket of chips.

VIETNAMESE
PHO QUYEN $

2740 E. Fowler Ave., 813/632-3444
HOURS: Sun.-Thurs. 10:30 A.M.-9 P.M., Fri. and Sat. until 10 P.M.

Pho (pronounced FUH—say foot without the *t*) is the Vietnamese national breakfast. Pho Quyen provides a glorious introduction to the species. In the little shopping center near USF shared by Staples and JoAnne's Fabrics, this Southeast Asian restaurant, at the site of a former Chinese eatery, has filled a void—bringing the clean, vibrant flavors of Vietnam to New Tampa, all at very affordable prices. Food fiends claim that pho, like Japanese miso or Jewish chicken soup, functions as an analeptic, stimulating the central nervous system when you're sick, sad, or hungover. I don't know if I buy that, but there's just about nothing else more wholesome. Pho Quyen's interior is simple and utilitarian, with green vinyl booths, a few huge silk orchids, and jolly green plaid tablecloths that gussy up the spare dining room of peach and green walls.

RESTAURANTS

Greater Tampa Map 5

AMERICAN
GRILLE ONE SIXTEEN ⓢⓢⓢ
15405 N. Dale Mabry, 813/265-0116
HOURS: Sun.-Thurs. 11 A.M.-9 P.M., Fri. and Sat. until 10 P.M.

New in Carrollwood in 2007, Grille One Sixteen has made waves with its hip-like-Miami design. House music pulses; waiters scoot around in modish all-black; an elegant long bar is packed with the glamorous or at least fashion-intrepid. Chef James Maita has a strong New American palette with a world-beat sense of play. Not every time at bat yields a home run, but he usually gets on base. That exhausts my baseball metaphors.

MICHAEL'S GRILL ⓢⓢ
11720 N. Dale Mabry, 813/964-8334
HOURS: Mon.-Thurs. 11 A.M.-9 P.M., Fri. and Sat. until 10 P.M.

In the sophisticated neighborhood of Carrollwood, Andrea and Michael Reilly's little restaurant has become an institution, as much for the warm greeting and neighborly service as it is for the convivial patio and spare, brasserie-style dining room. You can eat your French onion soup or penne Bolognese at the bar and take in all the drama of the bustling open kitchen, but through the French doors and out onto the leafy patio the well-heeled crowd always seems to be having more fun. Borders Books next door makes a nice after-dinner browse.

BRAZILIAN
BOIZAO STEAKHOUSE ⓢⓢⓢ
4606 W. Boy Scout Blvd., 813/286-7100
HOURS: Mon.-Fri. 11 A.M.-2:30 P.M., Sun.-Thurs. 5-10 P.M., Fri. and Sat. until 11 P.M.

Eating at a classic Brazilian *churrascaria* is a little like fielding a series of telemarketing calls during dinner. Every minute or two you have to stop what you're doing—eating, talking, whatever. Only in this case, it's because someone is repeatedly offering you meat on a long skewer: Oh, yes, please. No, none of that, thanks. Each diner gets a tabletop card: Green side means go, red side means stop. Pronounced boy-ZOUN, this newcomer seems to draw the expense-account businessfolk who stay in nearby Tampa International Airport/Westshore hotels. It's a vast, slick space with a festive, all-you-can-eat party vibe. The waft of rotisseried meats greets you at the door; a huge salad bar buffet anchors the airy room; the lavish glassed-in wine cellar holds enticing heavy-hitters and oversized bottles.

CHINESE
CHINA YUAN SEAFOOD RESTAURANT ⓢ
8502 N. Armenia Ave., # 1A, 813/936-7388
HOURS: Mon.-Thurs. 11 A.M.-10 P.M., Fri. and Sat. 10:30 A.M.-11 P.M., Sun. 10:30 A.M.-10 P.M.

China Yuan was always good, its burnished-skinned ducks practically flying out of their glass case and onto plates of the eager and the lucky. But the dining room was punitively bright, bare-bones, a little cold, and a lot cramped. All that changed at the end of 2007 when the doors reopened after an expansion and major remodeling. The new space is airy, fronted by a bank of windows and populated by generous round tables suitable for big parties. An array of dim sum, not cart service, brings delicate shrimp har gow and cup-shaped meat siu mai, roast pork buns (like meat-filled doughnuts, what's not to like?), and flaky fried chive dumplings. A major carb-load best mitigated with an order of spicy eggplant with garlic or sautéed pea sprouts.

YUMMY HOUSE ⓢ
2202 W. Waters Ave., Ste. 1, 813/915-2828
HOURS: Daily 5-9:30 P.M.

This newish strip-mall restaurant, on an unlovely stretch of Waters Avenue, purveys just about the best Chinese food I've had in years. The kitchen traffics in bright sautéed greens, still-crisp veggies, burnished-skin ducks, and

IN THE CUPS

Java, mud, joe – call it what you will, but Tampa Bay has gone gaga for coffee. Yup, cappuccino is officially as American as apple pie. In fact, the frothy coffee drink goes right nicely with a slice of pie. In the past 15 years, coffee mania has swept the nation: even the average Joe can hold forth on Central American versus Indonesian beans and the relative merits of Braun or Krups coffee makers, with or without the gold filter. Everyone's gotten a bit like J. Alfred Prufrock, measuring out their lives with coffee spoons, or at least those little wooden stirring sticks.

The Tampa Bay area has been bitten by the bean bug right along with the rest of the country. While clear dominance has been exerted handily by super-roaster Starbuck's, other coffee roasters, shops and cafes dot the landscape with such density that the deep, pungent aroma of roasted beans is not uncommon wafting through the urban landscape.

In New Tampa, **The Coffee Beanery** (17032 Palm Pointe Dr., 813/977-7400) gets its share of java junkies. Closer to USF, **Sacred Grounds** (4819 E Busch Blvd., 813/983-0837) is the place to chill and sip your soy latte in the evening; **Joffrey's Coffee Company** (615 Channelside Dr # 101, 813/275-0721) is the local brew in Channelside; also a locally based company, **Indigo Coffee** has several locations in Tampa (my favorite is 3908 N. Marguerite St., 813/224-0315).

In Pinellas County, **Daily Grind** (111 2nd Ave NE # 100, St. Petersburg, 727/824-0866) serves downtown business people in need of a caffeine fix; **Mazzaro's** (2909 22nd Avenue N, St. Petersburg, 727/321-2400) is the long-standing favorite for real Italian deli, pastries, and the kind of intense espresso, topped with textbook crema, that puts hair on your chest. And then there's **Globe Coffee Lounge** in St. Petersburg, where owner JoEllen Schilke and staff craft latte art (you know, where the steamed milk gets swirled into self-expressive submission by a pierced and soulful barista).

RESTAURANTS

cracked crabs redolent of ginger and scallion, served to a mostly Chinese clientele. Already, the place has a huge and devoted fan base, people who recognize that there's real Hong Kong know-how at work in the kitchen. It's packed on most nights, the simple square dining room loud with the raised voices of big families and gastronomic enthusiasm. Just slightly understaffed, the few waiters seem always at a near-jog, brusque but efficient in their task of bringing and taking away. There's no liquor; beverages are limited to a soda case and pots of strong black tea.

INDIAN
UDIPI CAFÉ $

14422 N. Dale Mabry Hwy., 813/962-7300
HOURS: Tues.-Sun. 11:30 A.M.–9:30 P.M.

Forget lamb vindaloo—south Indian vegetarian will blow your taste buds sky-high with spicy eggplant curry. A bare-bones setting for an exotic cuisine, but don't expect a gastronomic tour guide. Go for the masala dosa, a huge, thin rice-and-lentil pancake rolled into tube so it looks like a sleeping bag on a platter, served with curry-spiked potato and onion paste, coconut chutney, and sambar. Or head for one of the *uthapam,* a soft white pancake in which things like tomato, peas, cilantro, and onion are embedded. Easiest eaten in triangular wedges dotted with sauce, it's like an Indian spin on pizza. No alcohol.

ITALIAN
ARMANI'S $$$

6200 Courtney Campbell Causeway, 813/207-6800
HOURS: Mon.-Thurs. 6-10 P.M., Fri. and Sat. until 11 P.M.

When you want to get a sense of Tampa's scale, distance, and scope, you have to dig deep into your wallet and head to Armani's atop the Hyatt Regency Westshore. It's the undisputed top special-occasion and god-I-need-to-clinch-this-deal restaurant in town, partly for the view, partly for the solicitous service, and partly for the scaloppine Armani (thin-pounded veal sautéed with wild mushrooms and cognac in a creamy truffle sauce) or the grilled duck breast stuffed with liver pâté and dried cherries in a subtle vanilla sauce. The wine list shows depth and breadth, with an emphasis on important California/French wines.

MEXICAN
McKENITA MEXICAN GRILL $
17623 N. Dale Mabry, Lutz, 813/264-1212
HOURS: Mon.-Sat. 11 A.M.-9 P.M.

Rand Packer, Roy's celebrated former chef, went out on his own in 2007, opening Mariposa, with a second location opened in 2008 in the Trinity Town Center. It's an order-at-the-counter, funky and affordable outpost of regional Mexican cuisine—cooking from Oaxaca, the land of seven moles. Best dishes are the *sopes* and the smoked pork tacos.

PACIFIC RIM
ROY'S $$$
4342 W. Boy Scout Blvd., 813/873-7697,
www.roysrestaurant.com
HOURS: Sun.-Thurs. 5:30-10 P.M., Fri. and Sat.
until 10:30 P.M.

The Tampa dining cognoscenti has embraced the lively and über-stylish Hawaiian-fusion cuisine of celebrity chef Roy Yamaguchi. Even on a Monday night, Roy's has got the kind of buzz that could cover a whole bunch of power tools in action. Not that the sleek interior needs any touch-ups. Expanses of richly buffed wood and sea grass are punctuated by blown-glass sconces and Asian-inspired wrought-iron fixtures. About the prettiest dining room in Tampa, it seems only fitting that the clientele is a mix of the beautiful, the affluent, and the preternaturally suave. The nightly-changing menu always features some of the "Roy's classics," such as the justifiably famous miso-charred butterfish with its zingy kimchee-lime infusion. Don't miss the macadamia tart or the oozy chocolate soufflé.

STEAKHOUSE
CHARLEY'S STEAKHOUSE $$$
4444 W. Cypress St., 813/353-9706
HOURS: Sun.-Thurs. 5-10 P.M., Fri. and Sat. until 11 P.M.

Part of a small, family-owned, Florida-based chain of steakhouses of the same name, this is all about fat, grilled steaks and sturdy California cabs, served in a warren of formal, but a little tired looking, rooms. It started in 1974 and is one of Tampa's original men's clubs for 1,100-degree seared steaks (3-inch-thick filet mignon, 32-ounce porterhouse, 18-ounce boneless New York strip). The signature dish is the ultimate surf and turf: a 50-ounce filet mignon paired with a 2-pound Australian lobster tail. 'Nuff said.

COUNCIL OAK $$$
5223 North Orient Rd., 813/627-7628
HOURS: Sun.-Thurs. 5-10 P.M., Fri. and Sat.
until midnight

Owned by the Seminole tribe (as is the restaurant of the same name in Hollywood), Council Oaks is a new contender in the great American steakhouse wars. Morton's, Sullivan's Steakhouse, Don Shula's, Fleming's, The Palm, Ruth's Chris—they all have a similar masculine vibe and an à la carte approach to steaks and chops. It opened with much fanfare as part of the Seminole Hard Rock Hotel & Casino, Tampa's big expansion at the end of 2007. Smack in the center of the gaming pandemonium, it's an elegant bastion of luxe seafood followed by big red meat, all capably prepared for the most part and presided over by a remarkably knowledgeable waitstaff.

THE PALM $$$
205 Westshore Plaza, 813/849-7256
HOURS: Mon.-Fri. 11:30 A.M.-11 P.M., Sat. 5-11 P.M.,
Sun. 5-10 P.M.

One of 25 in the chain, The Palm features prime Angus steaks and caricatures of Bay Area politicos and luminaries on the wall. All the usual steakhouse bells and whistles are offered à la carte.

SHULA'S $$$
InterContinental Tampa, 4860 W. Kennedy Blvd.,
813/286-4366
HOURS: Mon.-Fri. 11:30 A.M.-2 P.M., Mon.-Thurs.
5:30-10 P.M., Fri. and Sat. until 10:30 P.M., Sun.
until 9:30 P.M.

Not surprisingly given coach Don Shula's hand in it, Shula's features decor that is all in tribute to

FAST FOOD FAVORITES

Fast food may be increasingly un-PC, but that doesn't mean you don't occasionally need something quick and cheap. The Virginia-based **Five Guys Famous Burgers and Fries** (2702 E. Fowler Ave., Tampa, 813/977-4400; 7054 U.S. 19 N., Pinellas Park, 727/526-7800; 13149 N. Dale Mabry Hwy.; 3841 W. Kennedy Blvd., Tampa, and at Westfield Brandon Mall) is gaining market share locally due to its free in-the-shell peanuts, spectacular fries, and burgers lavishly accessorized then packaged in no-frills, no-logos, brown-paper bags like the olden days.

Despite its McDonalds parentage, **Chipotle** (2662 Gulf to Bay Blvd., Clearwater, 727/724-1768; 3700 Park Blvd., Pinellas Park, 727/525-2484; 780 4th St. N., St. Petersburg, 727/895-6050; 309 N. Westshore Blvd., Tampa, 813/289-9820; 533 S. Howard Ave., Tampa, 813/254-6450; 2576 E. Fowler Ave.,

Tampa, 813/971-4360; 12827 N. Dale Mabry, Tampa, 813/961-1444) is a new fastie that's doing some things right, emphasizing spice and health in their burrito bowls.

The same could be said of Miami-based newcomer **Pollo Tropicale** (3900 Park Blvd., Pinellas Park, 727/362-9600; 6276 W. Waters Ave., Tampa, 813/319-6360; 3285 W. Hillsborough Ave., Tampa, 813/319-1850), trafficking in Caribbean-style, citrus-marinated grilled chicken served in a clean, bright, fast-food environment. By most accounts it's still working out the kinks, but PF Chang's fast concept, **Pei Wei Asian Diner** (12927 N. Dale Mabry Hwy., Tampa, 813/960-2031; 1402 66th St., St. Petersburg, 727/347-1351) stays focused on healthful choices with its Mandarin-wokked Thai, Vietnamese, Japanese, and Chinese noodle and rice dishes.

RESTAURANTS

© WWW.123RF.COM/BARBARA HELGASON

Tampa has its share of laudable grab-n-go fasties.

the Miami Dolphins. It's the kind of steakhouse where they parade the meat in front of you before you select your slab (48-ounce porterhouse?!).

AT INTERNATIONAL PLAZA
American
BAR LOUIE $

International Plaza, 2223 N. Westshore Blvd., 813/874-1919
HOURS: Sun.-Thurs. 11 A.M.-2 A.M., Fri. and Sat. until 3 A.M.
Tuesday nights it's $1 burgers, very competent. Also, there are tater tots. Napoleon Dynamite would approve. The '80s soundtrack is a guilty pleasure, especially delicious when taken concurrently with a couple of the 40 beers on tap. With funky artwork and an echoey urban-industrial interior, it's more bar than restaurant.

BLUE MARTINI $$

International Plaza, 2223 N. Westshore Blvd., 813/873-2583
HOURS: Mon.-Fri. 4 P.M.-3 A.M., Sat. and Sun. 1 P.M.-3 A.M.
This may be the most fun on Bay Street. The menu leans to attractive and contemporary small plates (seared tuna, hummus and pita chips). Essentially a bar for full-fledged adults, there's an elevated stage behind the bar on which to see live rock.

NORDSTROM CAFÉ BISTRO $$

International Plaza, 2223 N. Westshore Blvd., 813/875-4400
HOURS: Mon.-Sat. 10 A.M.-9 P.M., Sun. noon-6 P.M.
When Nordstrom has an especially good shoe sale you don't want to get too far from the action. Sophisticated salads and brick-oven pizzas emanate from a lively demonstration kitchen. Ladies who lunch and fatigued shopping casualties enjoy the respite on Nordstrom's upper level.

Deli
TOOJAY'S ORIGINAL GOURMET DELI $

International Plaza, 2223 N. Westshore Blvd., 813/348-4101
HOURS: Sun.-Thurs. 8 A.M.-9 P.M., Fri. and Sat. until 10 P.M.
These are fat, old-school New York–style deli sammies, no froufrou chutneys, but very solid (go for corned beef or the Italiano). There are 24 locations, only in Florida, very family-friendly. The chicken noodle soup and blintzes will cure the shopping-trip blues and not set you back much.

Italian
PELAGIA TRATTORIA $$$

International Plaza, 2223 N. Westshore Blvd., 813/313-3235
HOURS: Daily 6:30 A.M.-10:30 A.M., 11:30 A.M.-3 P.M., and 5:30-10 P.M.
Opened in August 2004, this swanky hotel eatery has turned a lot of heads. The bold Mediterranean palate in the dining room is echoed in Chef Fabrizio Schenardi's lush cuisine. At breakfast, this means waffles with cappuccino mousse and walnuts; at lunch, crunchy fried olives stuffed with three meats or mussels braised with merguez; and for dinner, the stylish crowd enthuses about the rack of lamb with fig-port sauce. It's the prettiest hotel restaurant in all of Tampa, located on the main level in the Renaissance Tampa Hotel, Bay Street. A new "express lunch" menu gets people in and out lickety-split.

Wine Bar
THE GRAPE $$

International Plaza, 2223 N. Westshore Blvd., 813/354-9463
HOURS: Mon.-Sat. 11 A.M.-10 P.M., Sun. noon-10 P.M.
Cool purple club chairs invite lengthy investigation of the more than 120 wines available by the bottle, glass, or half glass, divided into categories by relative weight or body of the wines. Goofy descriptions and lack of vintage years make the list a little frustrating for the serious oenophile, but a menu of cheeses, pâtés, and spreads marries nicely with the quaffs. Some evenings it's lively girls' night out as ladies heft glasses of pinot noir amongst a sea of shopping bags. Menu high notes include a tasty spinach salad and a worth-the-extra-dry cleaning chocolate fondue.

Downtown St. Petersburg   Map 6

ASIAN
❸ PACIFIC WAVE $$$
211 2nd St. S., 727/822-5235,
www.pacificwaverestaurant.com
HOURS: Mon.-Thurs. 5-10 P.M., Fri. and Sat. until 11 P.M.

Downtown's Pacific Wave is proof positive that a restaurant that's been around a while has had time to mature, to settle—really to grow up. The restaurant's interior exudes casual elegance. It's not too loud, too frenetic, or too dark. It's got date night written all over it, but seems equally amenable to office parties and boisterous groups. The strengths of the menu are sophisticated but traditional sushi and sashimi, but also Japanese- and Pacific Rim–inspired cooked dishes (special emphasis on Pacific fish from Hawaii) and an appealing short wine list and alluring cocktail list. A real treat is the polished and seasoned servers; they pace a meal appropriately and show a deep knowledge of the menu's ingredients and flavors.

BRITISH PUB
MOON UNDER WATER $$
332 Beach Dr. NE, 727/896-6160
HOURS: Sun.-Thurs. 11:30 A.M.-11 P.M., Fri. and Sat. until midnight

Since 1996, the comfy British pub's calling card has been a loose, ethnically diverse array of pub grub, all able accompaniments to a delicious, foam-capped black and tan. The signature dish, chicken curry is something of a party, arriving with a hot metal bowl of saffron-yellow basmati, another of dusky curry, a crisp, peppery pappadam, an oblong of warm naan, and little bowls of mango chutney, onion pickle, and cuke-spiked yogurt. Perhaps reflecting Britain's other colonial interests, the menu features quite a number of Middle Eastern dishes, but you'll also find laudable fish and chips.

COFFEEHOUSE
GLOBE COFFEE LOUNGE $
532 1st Ave. N., 727/898-5282,
www.globecoffeelounge.com
HOURS: Mon.-Thurs. 11 A.M.-1 A.M., Fri. and Sat. until 2 A.M.

Owner JoEllen Schilke is a DJ on local public radio station WMNF 88.5 FM, hosting a weekly arts interview and review show Fridays 1–2 P.M. She's a warm, bohemian spirit, whose personality permeates Globe. Sandwiches and vegetarian-friendly comfort foods make up the menu, and the top-notch coffee comes complete with seasonal latte art. Frequent live music.

ECLECTIC
THE TABLE $$$
535 Central Ave., 727/823-3700
HOURS: Mon.-Fri. 11:30 A.M.-2 A.M., Sat. 5:30 P.M.-2 A.M.

Opened near the beginning of 2008, The Table follows in the footsteps of its big brother to the south in Sarasota. The concept is Atlantic-rim cuisine, which traipses through South America, the Caribbean, eastern America, and a hint of Spain. It's extremely stylish in a glammy-Miami way, but the food seems so literally all over the map that things start tasting muddy. Peruvian potatoes, herbs from elsewhere in South America—when you start to think of the carbon footprint of all this food trekked in, it seems irresponsible unless it's all fabulous. Sadly, it's not. But the mojito list is spectacular.

FRENCH
L'OLIVIER $$
111 Second Ave. NE, 727/821-3846
HOURS: Daily 11 A.M.-10 P.M.

L'Olivier is the dream of Olivier Cuevas, realized beautifully in the courtyard of the Tower Plaza adjacent to BayWalk. The intimate café has one of the most romantic, candlelit patios around, the menu an equally romantic greatest-hits list of classic bistro fare: coq au

RESTAURANTS

TOP DOGS

I like them dragged through the garden. That's what you call it when a Chicago-style hot dog is packed to capacity with traditional fixings: yellow mustard, alarmingly neon green relish, a dill pickle spear, tomato slices that never seem to quite fit, chopped onion, "sport peppers" (hot little babies packed in vinegar), and a couple shakes of celery salt. A Chicago bun is flecked with poppy seeds, the dog itself is all-beef and pretty darned salty.

For a Coney Island dog with its full complement of bells and whistles, you want it "all the way." Except, confusingly, there are two kinds of Coney Island dogs, the New York beef franks made famous by Nathan's, et al., but also a style of dog in Michigan that is topped with all-meat chili, yellow mustard, and diced yellow onion.

Tampa dog aficionados have been crowding into **Mel's Hot Dogs** (4136 E. Busch Blvd., Tampa, 813/985-8000) since 1973. It's a fine dog, the house special packed with sauerkraut, onion, mustard, relish and pickle. Still, the Polish sausage is a fat, juicy choice, accessorized with brown mustard and grilled onions. On the Pinellas side, the alpha dog is clearly **Coney Island** (250 Dr. Martin Luther King Jr. St. N., St. Petersburg, 727/822-4493), which goes all the way back to 1926. The coin of the realm is the Michigan-style chili dog (a mere $1.72; the topping is technically called Coney sauce), eaten swiftly atop a stool at the counter, washed down with an impossibly thick chocolate shake. Sexagenarian **Dairy Inn** (1201 Dr. Martin Luther King St. N., St. Petersburg, 727/822-6971) also serves up a dandy dog, but it is sometimes eclipsed by the Coney Island chili or the housemade root beer.

Chi-Town Dogs (4115 66th St. N., St. Petersburg, 727/343-9003) is plugging along, doing a fine job with regular and Polish dogs along with major Chicago staples: Italian beef ladled with gravy, Chicago beef tamales (they look like hotdogs), Jays potato chips, and Salerno butter cookies; while **Yummy's** (2914 Beach Blvd. S., Gulfport, 727/321-9869) opened mid-2008 in an adorable house on the main drag in Gulfport. The Yummy dog is textbook, the snappy tube steak hunkered under the sweet relish, sport peppers, etc. The place itself has a high funk factor (yard sale tchotchkes function as decor and impulse buys), and the owners could not be more friendly.

---

vin, beef bourguignon, quiche lorraine—but the stars of the show are the crepes. Dinner crepes, made of one-quarter tangy buckwheat flour, are filled with things like slow-cooked ratatouille, brie, spinach, walnut, and honey or ham, emmental, mushroom, and diced tomato, all of which are served with a scoop of luxurious potato gratin. One crepe is plenty, especially if your aim is to finish with a classic suzette (flambéed with Grand Marnier) or a homey banana and Nutella crepe and a good coffee or glass of champagne.

ITALIAN
🄲 BELLA BRAVA $$$

515 Central Ave., 727/895-5515, www.bellabrava.net
HOURS: Mon.-Fri. 11:30 A.M.-2:30 P.M., Sun.-Thurs.
5-10 P.M., Fri. and Sat. until 11 P.M.

What makes a place Italian? The presence of pasta? A marked propensity for checked tablecloths and candles in Chianti bottles? Maybe molten mantles of mozzarella cheese oozing over some unsuspecting eggplant or chicken? Na, it's more nebulous than that, a kind of vibe thing. Take Bella Brava: concrete floors, liberal use of stainless steel, exposed ducting and high-tech circular Italian track lighting are all warmed through a bold color palette of caramel and pale pea. A floating mezzanine level and streetside balcony bump up the seating to nearly 200. Somehow all of the decor functions as shorthand for "expect slick northern Italian food." And Bella Brava delivers. There are the bruschetta, risotti, and antipasti that new generations of Tampa Bay area residents are being weaned on, all served at fairly reasonable prices.

MEDITERRANEAN
CAFE ALMA 🟢🟢

260 1st Ave. S., 727/502-5002, www.cafealma.com
HOURS: Mon.-Fri. 11 A.M.-3 P.M., Mon.-Wed. 5-10 P.M., Thurs.-Sat. until midnight, Sun. 10:30 A.M.-3 P.M.

Downtown St. Petersburg owes a bit of its recent hipness (so much so that celebrity chef Robert Irvine was set to open two restaurants here in 2008 before he was defrocked as a fraud) to trendy downtown gathering spots like Café Alma, one of its originals. Open from lunch to late night, the atmosphere sets the mood for the stimulating yet charmingly straightforward Mediterranean-inspired dishes. Entrées include Spanish-inflected paella alongside traditional French bouillabaisse and peppercorn-crusted Hudson Valley duck breast served atop a sweet corn pancake. While lunchtime brings business diners, at night the vibe is decidedly more festive. New ownership in 2008 has thus far not signaled much change at this local favorite.

MARCHAND'S GRILL 🟢🟢🟢

Renaissance Vinoy Resort, 501 5th Ave. NE, 727/894-1000
HOURS: Daily 11:30 A.M.-2:30 P.M. and 5:30-10 P.M.

In keeping with the glamour of the historic Vinoy, its restaurant, Marchand's sparkles with opulent appointments and an equally opulent clientele. The restaurant has undergone some major changes recently. Its entrance now shows off the central Vinoy Bar; heavy new armchairs in sumptuous velvet have been added; and a small wine cellar room provides an enviably intimate dining space for four. But perhaps the biggest change is the chef and the dining concept: One side used to be Marchand's, with a Mediterranean menu; the other the Terrace Room, seafood-heavy American. Now it's all called Marchand's. The kitchen has wisely kept the seafood focus, but dishes reflect a more stylish and still loosely Mediterranean sensibility with saucing and garniture.

NEW AMERICAN
🟢 MFA CAFÉ 🟢🟢

255 Beach Dr. NE, 727/822-1032
HOURS: Mon.-Sat. 11 A.M.-3 P.M., occasional Sunday brunch

Unveiled along with the lovely new Hazel Hough Wing, the MFA Café may prove to be one of the museum's most appreciated works of art. Chef James Canter did stints at a number of stylish San Francisco restaurants before settling in along Straub Park and Tampa Bay. The café is really a cordoned-off section of the soaring atrium at the museum's center, light streaming in from floor-to-ceiling windows. It's a prime locale for special parties and glamorous soirees, but during the day it's given over to some of the most sophisticated lunches around: soups (a stunning creamy smoked tomato), salads (think smoked duck paired with citrus-dressed frisée, crisp apple, and toasted walnut), and a burger that alone justifies paying the $12 museum admission price.

PARKSHORE GRILL 🟢🟢🟢

300 Beach Dr. NE, 727/896-9463, www.parkshoregrill.com
HOURS: Sun.-Thurs. 11 A.M.-10 P.M., Fri. and Sat. until 11 P.M.

With its outside patio within eyesight of the Museum of Fine Arts, Parkshore is a place to linger. The bar is lively but elegant, and the menu leans to very smart spins on contemporary American cuisine (pan-seared scallops, lobster pasta, great martinis).

SPANISH
CEVICHE 🟢🟢

10 Beach Dr., 727/209-2302
HOURS: Sun. and Mon. 5-10 P.M., Tues.-Thurs. 5 P.M.-midnight, Fri. and Sat. 5 P.M.-1 A.M.

Ceviche serves its namesake citrus-cured fish, sea scallops with manchego, and an array of little dishes with addictive olives and almonds, all in a sleek nightclub atmosphere. Special plaudits for its *albondigas*—that's Spanish for delicious little veal, chorizo, and pork meatballs bobbing in an addictively rich tomato sauce. Sister restaurant **Pincho y Pincho**, next door, seems plucked right off the streets of Barcelona, an any-time-of-the-day hangout

FROZEN DELIGHTS

The rousing success of new fro-yo places like Pinkberry in Los Angeles may have led to a Tampa Bay area frozen-confection renaissance. **CaliYogurt** (2303 W. Morrison Ave., Tampa, 813/254-2362) is getting high marks for its green tea and plain (exactly the flavors Pinkberry sells). Very tangy, it's not too sweet, offered with lots of fun toppings. Same again with **Berryism** (701 S. Dale Mabry Hwy., Tampa, 813/873-2377) and **SunniBunni** (1413 S. Howard Ave., Tampa, 813/251-8383). Expect to pay around $4 for a small serving with one topping.

That's all in Tampa. Pinellas County has been slower to jump on that particular bandwagon, preferring their cones filled with more traditional old-school delights. **Ritter's Frozen Custard** (2655 East Lake Rd., Palm Harbor, 727/784-0220) is wowing customers with their glaciers, shakes, malts, sundaes, and good old-fashioned frozen custard. The peanut butter mountain sundae and the turtle sundae are big sellers, as is the turtle custard made on Tuesdays and Saturdays.

Downtown St. Petersburg is home to **Paciugo** (that's pa-CHU-go; 300 Beach Dr. NE, Suite 120, St. Petersburg, 727/209-0298), a quick study in the glories of gelato, which is denser, softer, creamier than American ice cream. Gelato often incorporates purees of fruits or nuts, and it is kept at a warmer temperature, making it more amenable to cups than cones. The rationale for the warmer temperature is that your palate isn't coated with icy cold, so you perceive greater richness and intensity of flavor.

With a changing array of 32-34 flavors each day, it's hard to choose. Aim for the stracciatella (chocolate chip) or the panna cotta (shades of wedding cake) for sheer lusciousness. In a small cup (about $3.50-5) you can mix three flavors together. Think long and hard about pairing the intense chocolate fondante with a bit of lush hazelnut, the most popular flavor in Italy, and then tie them together with a third selection of gianduja (that's chocolate and hazelnut together, like Nutella). If you are a fruit lover, all of the pureed fruit flavors are intensely tangy – lemon and a sophisticated strawberry/balsamic are at the top of the heap.

where you can linger over a big bowl of milky coffee or wrestle with an open-face ham and manchego sandwich while watching pedestrians amble by.

TAPAS AND SUSHI
THE VENUE 🟡🟡
2675 Ulmerton Road, 727/571-2222,
www.thevenueclub.com
HOURS: Takara daily 4 P.M.–1:30 A.M.; Viaggio Sun.-Wed. 4-10 P.M., Thurs.-Sat. until 11 P.M.

More than 27,000 square feet of bars and restaurants are tucked, warrenlike, into the Feather Sound space that used to be Storman's Palace. Ultra lounge, martini bar, deck bar, champagne lounge, private wine room, cabana deck, VIP rooms, sushi bar, tapas restaurant—this playground is aimed at making four hours heady with options and high expectations. On one side the tapas bar Viaggio brings plates that are architectural and carefully sauced, with a focus on name-brand meats (Harris Ranch beef, Maple Leaf duck) and as much organic and local produce as is available. On the other side, sushi chef Tada "Yoshi" Kohazama presides over Takara, with hand rolls, *nigiri, maki,* and luxurious combo rolls.

St. Pete Beach   Map 7

CONTINENTAL
MARITANA GRILLE AT THE DON CESAR $$$
3400 Gulf Blvd., 727/360-1881, www.doncesar.com
HOURS: Sun.-Thurs. 5:30-10 P.M., Fri. and Sat. until 11 P.M.

Located in St. Pete Beach's iconic pink hotel, this has special occasion written all over it. There's a great chef's table for groups up to eight, at which executive chef Eric Neri is put through his Floribbean-cuisine paces, from marmalade-roasted Gulf red snapper served with pea vines or grilled filet mignon with truffled mashed potatoes and candied shallots. The restaurant's interior is lovely, patrons surrounded by 1,500 gallons of saltwater aquariums and indigenous Florida fish.

SEAFOOD
DOCKSIDE DAVE'S
7141 Gulf Blvd., 727/360-4200, www.docksidedavesgrill.com
HOURS: Mon.-Sat. 11 A.M.-10 P.M., Sun. noon-10 P.M.

It's no longer in its original, divey location in Madiera Beach (condos forced it out). Still, it's beloved as one of the local fish sandwich superstars, onion rings on the side. The decor isn't much, but it's a good place to try one of the local specialties, smoked amberjack spread. Perhaps an acquired taste.

MAD FISH $$$
5200 Gulf Blvd., 727/360-9200, www.madfishonline.com
HOURS: Sun.-Thurs. 4-10 P.M., Fri. and Sat. until 11 P.M.

A newcomer in 2007, Mad Fish was opened by chef Dan Casey. Set in a blue neon and gleaming chrome diner, the inside has been wrapped in lustrous African mahogany. Reminiscent of the dining cars on vintage trains, it's elegant, with an extensive wine bar and an emphasis on fresh fish. According to Casey, Mad Fish services nearby convention and hotel business. Look for the signature shrimp Guanajuato, a tomato-based shrimp cocktail enlivened by Mexican orange soda, and a dessert caddy of still-warm cookies served with glasses of banana milk shake.

Gulfport   Map 7

AMERICAN
ELEMENTS GLOBAL CUISINE $$
3121 Beach Blvd., 727/343-9894
HOURS: Mon.-Sat. 11:30 A.M.-3:30 P.M. and 5-9:30 P.M.

Gulfport has exploded on the dining scene in the past few years, with worthwhile restaurants lining several blocks. At Elements, owners Jose Luis and Catherine Pawelek offer a short globe-trotting menu that includes dishes like Kona-braised short ribs with a coffee rub for a little bitterness, a Kahlua glaze for a little sweetness, all nestled in a wide pool of soft Gorgonzola polenta. Jose Luis's Argentine heritage is apparent in the hearty, flavorful grilled flank steak entrée, rosy slices elevated by a zippy citrus-based chimichurri with garlic and parsley. Its balance of spicy/salty/sweet is echoed in other well-executed dishes like Indonesian-Thai inspired chicken and veggie stir fry or portobello ravioli with a smoldering Madras coconut milk curry.

BRAZILIAN *CHURRASCARIA*
LA FOGATA $$$
2832-2838 Beach Blvd. S., 727/327-4200
HOURS: Tues.-Sun. 5:30-10 P.M.

New in 2007, La Fogata is clubby and dark, with a wine wall of riveted, distressed copper sheeting and an architectural arrangement of bottles; booths are gorgeous faux ostrich. Bellini, its sister property, attached at the back,

RESTAURANTS

RIPE FOR THE PICKING

Most of us are so far removed from where our food comes from that it's hard to even envision its provenance. If we concentrate, we may conjure long, symmetrical rows of green leaves fringing the tops of loamy soil hillocks, farmhands parting the thicket to extract jewel-tone strawberries or giving a little yank to unearth a young carrot.

That's part of the picture, but taking a field trip to local pick-your-own farms reveals 21st century farms that look nothing like this. New technology is changing the way farmers coax their crop into being. Many of these farms are hydroponic, the advantages for the consumer being that the hydrostacker pots rotate, much like a spinning sunglass display in a drugstore, making it easier for pickers to find what's ripe and obviating the need for any kneeling or squatting.

While prices fluctuate, they still are invariably lower than that at the grocery store, making picking your own a natural for the thrifty shopper.

Interested shoppers can visit the following local farms:

Hydro Harvest Farms, 1101 Shell Point Rd. E., Ruskin, 941/915-7208; hydroponic vegetables and strawberries, year-round Mon.-Sat. 10 A.M.-5 P.M., Sun. 10 A.M.-4 P.M.

Parke Hydro Farms, 3715 Tanner Rd., Dover, 813/927-4049; hydroponic vegetables and strawberries, year-round Tues.-Sat. 9 A.M.-5 P.M.

Wheeler Farms, 14801 Balm Rd., Balm (southern Hillsborough County), 813/634-1868; beans and peas, May and June

Lee Vineyards, 10251 McIntosh Rd., Dover, 813/335-1865; tropical and exotic fruits, grapes, during the summer

Favorite Farms, 10070 McIntosh Rd., Dover, 813/986-3949; strawberries, only open for pick-your-own after the commercial season, the last weeks of March and the beginning of April

Glover's Blueberry Farm, 5615 W.O. Griffin Rd., Plant City, 813/245-6818; blueberries, only open for pick-your-own after the commercial season, mid-May through June 1

Hunsader Farms, 5500 County Road 675, Bradenton, 941/331-1212; strawberries, rhubarb, cauliflower, broccoli, onions and other vegetables, year-round Mon.-Sat. 8 A.M.-4 P.M.

hand-picked strawberries

is a New York City–cool lounge with its own short tapas menu. You pay one price, either for the full *churrascaria* meat service or just the salad buffet, the offerings nuanced and carefully thought out, from seared tuna with wasabi and a tangle of seaweed salad to lovely Thai shrimp salad with cilantro and red onion. Then servers start circulating with the Brazilian-style meat on skewers, simply prepared over hardwood mesquite, crusted generously with sea salt and not much else.

BREAKFAST
THE WATER WITCH ⑤
5519 Shore Blvd., 727/346-2444
HOURS: Tues.-Fri. 8 A.M.-2 P.M. Sat. and Sun. 8 A.M.-4 P.M., Tues.-Thurs. 5-9 P.M., until 10 P.M.Fri. and Sat.

The same couple that owns Pia's Trattoria nearby opened this not long ago to satisfy the need for healthful breakfasts in the area. Adopting a world-beat approach to the morning meal, there's France with its flaky croissant and marmalade, or a hearty Italian array of cold antipasti with a stiff espresso, puffy Belgian waffles served with a rich chocolate milk, and German *pfannkuchen*. Thinner than a pancake and thicker than a crepe, they can go sweet and they can go savory, wrapping around Nutella and powdered sugar or fresh asparagus and grilled chicken breast.

ITALIAN
PIA'S TRATTORIA ⑤⑤
3054 Beach Blvd. S., 727/327-2190
HOURS: Mon.-Sat. 11:30 A.M.-2:30 P.M. and 5-9:30 P.M.

Pia's is the kind of sweetly earnest restaurant that you'd like to think unfurls fully realized from the ground, good basic ingredients and a healthy inoculation of Italian culinary know-how nurtured by sweat and love. Its setting is a teeny bit foyer and mostly outdoor patio covered with a chickee thatch and populated by a hodgepodge of picnic tables. The menu's short, the same at lunch and dinner and weighted to crusty pressed panini and pastas topped with one of a handful of simple sauces.

SEAFOOD
BACKFIN BLUE CAFÉ ⑤⑤
2913 Beach Blvd. S., 727/343-2583,
www.backfinbluecafe.com
HOURS: Wed.-Mon. 4-9:30 P.M.

Nestled in a 1920s-era pink-and-green cottage, Backfin has the kind of front porch that's easy to settle into and hard to leave. It's renowned locally for its crab cakes, corn and crab soup, slow-roasted prime rib, and bacon-wrapped shrimp, making most publications' annual list of top restaurants. Despite the erudition in the kitchen, it's got an Old Florida vibe that's especially charming to out-of-towners.

RESTAURANTS

Clearwater and Clearwater Beach   Map 8

AMERICAN
HOOTERS ⑤
2800 Gulf-To-Bay Blvd., Clearwater, 727/797-4008,
www.hooters.com
HOURS: Sun.-Thurs. 11 A.M.-11 P.M., Fri. and Sat. until midnight

Really, you owe it to yourself and owl fans everywhere to go to the original Hooters. Now 25 years old, the original pleasant, ramshackle sports-oriented joint has spawned an international empire and short-lived airline. I've eaten here with gusto, and I was even a women's studies major. It's a family restaurant, really, with good chicken wings (order them not breaded, with the really hot sauce, but a little dry so they don't come all goopy). Only, it's a family restaurant in which all waitresses are wildly pneumatic and wearing those flesh-colored pantyhose from the 1970s under orange nylon short-shorts. The whole chain was sold in March 2008, so go quick before the new owners mess it up.

RESTAURANTS

COURTESY OF VISIT ST. PETERSBURG/CLEARWATER

The Gulf Coast communities feature restaurants specializing in local seafood.

BREAKFAST

LENNY'S RESTAURANT ⑤

21220 U.S. 19 N., Clearwater, 727/799-0402

HOURS: Daily 6 A.M.-3 P.M.

It's long been the hands-down winner for breakfast, but for the Jewish staples of blintzes, knishes, latkes. You can get an omelet here, too, if you want to look like a goy. Many of the extremely affordable breakfast combos are named for members of the owner's family. It's Lenny's kids running the joint these days, but it still has personality (goofy jokes on the ceiling, garage-sale knickknacks in lieu of décor) and if you're not afraid of carbs, the potato pancakes with sour cream eat like a meal.

JAPANESE

KIKU JAPANESE FINE DINING ⑤⑤

Pelican Walk Plaza upstairs, 483 Mandalay Ave., Clearwater Beach, 727/461-2633, www.clearwaterbeachkiku.com

HOURS: Mon.-Fri. 11:30 A.M.-2 P.M., Mon.-Thurs. 5-10 P.M., Fri. and Sat. until 11 P.M.

When you're ready to declare *omakase* (essentially, "let it rip, Chef, I'm putty in your hands"), the man behind the sushi counter at Kiku is one to trust for the freshest fish flown in from Hawaii, Seattle, Boston, California, and New York. Tatami rooms are available for when you want to be alone.

NEW AMERICAN

BELLEAIR GRILL AND WINE BAR ⑤⑤

1575 S. Fort Harrison Ave., Clearwater, 727/449-2988, www.belleairgrill.com

HOURS: Daily 11:30 A.M.-3 P.M., Sun.-Wed. 4-9 P.M., Thurs.-Sat. until 10 P.M.

A sophisticated new restaurant has emerged at the site of a beloved old-timer, with stylish sides, small- and large-plate options, certified Angus beef and sustainable seafood, and a wine list that will get you out of the humdrum chard/cab rut. Risotto gets a lot of play on the New American menu, its acme achieved with a wild mushroom and duck version, deep, earthy flavors elevated with a swirl of white truffle oil. For something lighter to start, a colorful showstopper salad

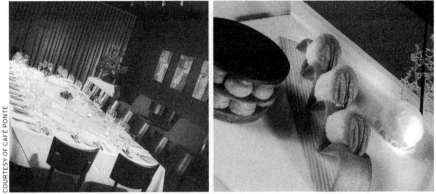

Cafe Ponte's main dining room, and their picture-postcard banana split dessert.

features marinated artichoke hearts, cherry tomatoes, olives and shaved red onion, and asiago. Entrées are simple but exacting: Grilled wild salmon brings a gorgeous piece of fish capped with frizzled leeks and married with a bacon-smoky pile of slow-cooked French lentils.

CARETTA ON THE GULF ❸❸❸

Sandpearl Resort, 500 Mandalay Ave., Clearwater Beach, 727/441-2425, www.sandpearl.com

HOURS: Daily 7 A.M.-3 P.M., Sun.-Thurs. 5:30-10 P.M., Fri. and Sat. until 11 P.M.

Sandpearl Resort, the first new resort to be built on Clearwater Beach in 25 years, does not suffer from the hotel-dining blahs. It contains a nice poolside café and a coffee shop, but the major accomplishment is Caretta on the Gulf. Named for a species of loggerhead turtle, the restaurant has all the elements that make for success: sleek and knowledgeable service, a gorgeous beach view, stunning decor, plus tasty and fairly priced food and drink. A lovely raw bar near the restaurant entrance sets the tone: ceviche, oysters on the half shell, spiny lobster and spicy tuna sushi rolls. Then the rosy glow and crackle of a wood-burning oven sends out roasted fishes, chicken, and meats that for the most part are paired with thoughtful, unusual side dishes and sauces.

PIZZA
CRISTINO'S ❸❸

1101 S. Fort Harrison Ave., Clearwater, 727/443-4900

HOURS: Mon.-Thurs. 11 A.M.-9 P.M., Fri. and Sat. until 10 P.M.

Three Italian brothers, Lenny, Marco, and Joe Cristino, opened Cristino's Coal Oven Pizza at the beginning of 2007 just south of downtown Clearwater. It's not anything fancy—a dozen or so tables done up casually, with food display cases anchoring the room. Service is friendly and unfussy; the wine list is just a handful of unspecified vinos, a few familiar beers. The big coal oven is unobtrusive, but it's the source of exactly half of the excitement here. The good stuff comes in the form of four basic pies: margherita, marinara, bianca, and quattro formaggi. Keep 'em simple and you're in for a delicious, thin-crust pizza. The other half of the excitement at Cristino's? The house gelatos are spectacular, from the vanilla stracciatella to the chocolatey-hazelnut swirl.

WINE BAR
BOBBY'S BISTRO ❸❸❸

447 Mandalay Ave., Clearwater Beach, 727/446-9463, www.bobbysbistro.com

HOURS: Nightly 5-10 P.M.

This place has been a beefy *Wine Spectator* award winner for years on the basis of its burgundies, but Bobby's Bistro is sheer lusciousness for the

Oregon and California pinot noir lover. The food is sophisticated California cuisine, and the service is top-notch.

CLEARWATER WINE COMPANY 💲
483 Mandalay Ave., Ste. 113, Clearwater Beach, 727/446-8805, www.clearwaterwinecompany.com
HOURS: Mon.-Thurs. 11:30 A.M.-10 P.M., Fri. and Sat. until 11 P.M., Sun. 4-10 P.M.

A fun place to taste more than 40 wines by the glass, Clearwater Wine Company opened in 2007. Kristi Lam and her parents orchestrate a casual, living-room atmosphere—some Friday nights with live music—offering tipples from every major wine-producing region in the world, with deep happy hour discounts between 5 and 7 P.M. (Oh, and there's a Yappy Hour the last Saturday of the month for the sophisticated dog and his owner.)

Dunedin   Map 8

CHINESE
IVORY MANDARIN BISTRO 💲💲
2192 Main St., 727/734-3998
HOURS: Sun.-Thurs. 11 A.M.-9:30 P.M., Fri. and Sat. until 10 P.M.

Around since 1993 in Dunedin, this old-timer has slowly accrued a wall's worth of accolades and Best Of awards along with its devoted, largely non-Chinese clientele. Crisp linens, Chinese floral prints, and sprays of silk orchids lend a dash of formality to the proceedings, but the menu reads like a greatest-hits list of Cantonese-American dishes. That means a workhorse hot and sour soup, juicy pork spare ribs, sweet-tangy orange beef, and nurturing pan-fried chow fun noodles.

CONTINENTAL/SEAFOOD
BON APPETIT 💲💲💲
148 Marina Plaza, 727/733-2151
HOURS: Mon.-Thurs. 11:30 A.M.-9 P.M., Fri. and Sat. until 10 P.M., Sun. 11 A.M.-8:30 P.M.

It's attached to the Best Western Yacht Harbor Inn and Suites, so there's a certain amount of that holdover Continental cuisine fanciness one associates with hotel restaurants. Owners Peter Kreuziger and Karl Heinz Riedl manage to add a definite panache to the seafood-heavy menu, whether it's a passel of garlic-heady mussels steamed in herbaceous sauvignon blanc or the season's freshest stone crabs adorned with only a squeeze of lemon and a pool of clarified butter. The thing is, you don't have to get all uppity and pay the big prices—guests can watch the dolphins play as the sun sets out on the water and not spend a bushel if they dine at the Marine Café adjacent to the restaurant. It's a different menu than the fancier sibling, but a single sheet of signature dishes from the main restaurant is available outside.

ECLECTIC
KELLY'S 💲💲
319 Main St., 727/736-5284, www.kellyschicaboom.com
HOURS: Sun.-Thurs. 8 A.M.-10 P.M., Fri. and Sat. until 11 P.M.

An ad description of Kelly's, For just about . . . Anything! isn't hyperbole, really. Super family-friendly, Kelly's has the kind of far-reaching comfort-food menu that rivals Tolstoy for reader stamina, leaving no stone unturned, from eggplant-portobello-tomato Napoleons to butternut squash ravioli. It's a kids' kind of joint, very affable and accommodating. Its **Chic-A-Boom Room** next door is more serious evidence that Dunedin has one of the most lighthearted, fun-loving communities around.

MEXICAN
CASA TINA 💲💲
365 Main St., 727/734-9226, www.casatinas.com
HOURS: Sun.-Thurs. 11 A.M.-10 P.M., Fri. and Sat. until 11 P.M.

Downtown Dunedin has been charmingly reinvigorated with restaurants and cafés in recent years. Shimmery orange and teal curtains pick up the dappled light from punched tin star lanterns and an altarlike candelabrum at the entrance. Rough-hewn wooden chairs, a wood-and-concrete floor, and an open kitchen pass-through inform your expectations: casual, affordable, fun, and Mexican. Bingo on all counts, but Casa Tina has a few tricks up its sleeves. Rice, beans, and all sauces are vegetarian, and virtually all entrées are offered in vegetarian and vegan versions that are far from perfunctory. The carnivore has the full complement of options, but it's the vegetarian or pescetarian who is most ably served.

NEW AMERICAN
THE BLACK PEARL $$$

315 Main St., 727/734-3463,
www.theblackpearlofdunedin.com
HOURS: Daily 5-9:30 P.M.

A little bit of a splurge, special-occasion restaurant, it's been here for more than 20 years with a tiny, intimate dining room that never fails to charm. Try the cedar-planked salmon or the crab imperial. It's one of those rarefied places that embody the outré word "nouvelle," meaning fairly steep prices and aesthetic aspirations, fairly low quantity on each plate. It works for me; you be the judge.

WALT'S SEASONAL CUISINE $$$
1140 Main St., 727/733-1909, www.waltscuisine.com
HOURS: Tues.-Fri. 11 A.M.-2 P.M., Tues.-Sat. 5-10 P.M.

Native son Walt Wickman takes whatever is freshest at the moment—local line-caught fish, produce trucked in from farmland nearby—and has his way with it. The daily-changing menu is short, only a handful of apps, entrées, and a couple of desserts, but the aesthetic is sophisticated and very 21st century. It's not in the charming part of downtown Dunedin: Look for the 40-seater in an unglamorous strip mall. New in 2007, it already has legion devotees.

STEAKHOUSE
SPOTOS STEAKJOINT $$$
1280 Main St., 727/734-0008,
www.spotossteakjoint2.com
HOURS: Sun.-Thurs. 4-10 P.M., Fri. and Sat. until 11 P.M.

Spotos Steakjoint sends out ably aged and prepared steaks. But get this, from a recent menu: filet of Burmese python. I kid you not. Owner Jimmy Stewart has gotten interested in wild game, importing a range of exciting options (rattlesnake, etc.) and holding occasional wine and game dinners.

Greater Pinellas County   Map 9

AMERICAN
THE HURRICANE $
807 Gulf Way, 727/360-9558 St. Pete Beach
HOURS: Sun.-Thurs. 11 A.M.-9:30 P.M., Fri. and Sat. until 10 P.M.

If you can go to just one place in the St. Pete Beach area, it's to get the blackened grouper sandwich at The Hurricane (on Pass-A-Grille Beach). I don't care if the place seems a little touristy; give me that sweet white fish, amped with red and black pepper and lots of salt, add in some tomato, lettuce, and a big swath of mayo, all on a pretty, soft roll. It's as good as it gets in Pinellas County. There's a nice bar adjacent to the restaurant and a rooftop sundeck up top for sunset scrutiny.

BREAKFAST
SKYWAY JACK'S RESTAURANT $
2795 34th St. S., 727/867-1907
HOURS: Daily 5 A.M.-3 P.M.

Skyway Jack's Restaurant has been a kitschy classic around here for more than a quarter century, moved once because it was on the approach to the Skyway Bridge and got pushed out to make room for more lanes. It still sells stuff like scrambled pork brains served with eggs, potatoes, and grits—who eats this? Stick with regular breakfast food (orange-pecan French toast or the creamed chipped beef on toast), or the smoked mullet if you're feeling bold.

MEXICAN
CARMELITA'S $

5042 E. Bay Dr., Clearwater, 727/524-8226 (also
5211 Park St. N, St. Petersburg, 727/545-2956),
www.carmelitas.net

HOURS: Sun.-Thurs. 11 A.M.-9:30 P.M.,
Fri. and Sat. until 10 P.M.

Each of the legendary locations serves up
the same luscious, zingy-spicy green enchi-
ladas to dispatch with a potent margarita.
It's the kind of extra-cheese, refried-bean,
gooey saturated-fat smorgasbord that somehow tastes just right after a long night. The
digs are comfy and family-friendly but don't
go if you're looking for cutting-edge regional
Mexican fare.

NEW AMERICAN
🄲 CAFE PONTE $$$

Off Ulmerton Road in the Icot Center, 13505 Icot Blvd.,
Clearwater, 727/538-5768, www.cafeponte.com

HOURS: Mon.-Fri. 11:30 A.M.-2 P.M., Tues.-Thurs.
5:30-10 P.M., Fri. and Sat. until 11 P.M.

In foodie circles, Cafe Ponte may be the top
dog. Chef Chris Ponte trained at Taillevent in
Paris and studied at Johnson & Wales and the
Cordon Bleu, his sophisticated restaurant in the
Icot Center a proper showcase for his luxurious
palette. (The strip-mall setting may confound
would-be diners, but a single meal will set them
straight.) The food is smart but luxurious: rich
mushroom soup with a dollop of truffle cream;
crispy whole snapper with mango, mint, and
macadamia nuts over a ginger-vanilla rum sauce;
and a supremely comforting yet vaguely exotic
braised short rib tagine. Dou of duck brings
braised thigh and pan-roasted breast with a
heady Asian spice, paired with seared foie gras,
a gingered sweet potato pancake, and an orange-
Szechuan peppercorn sauce.

NIGHTLIFE

Why do white-sand beaches seem to call out for cold beer? A question for the ages, one that can be adequately pondered in Pinellas County. Along the Gulf side of the peninsula, beach bars abound in just about every community, most sporting a grouper sandwich, a Jimmy Buffet–inspired band, or facsimile of either one. We've listed the biggies, but the truth is there are dozens of little ramshackle, sandy-floored watering holes you may just stumble into (or maybe the stumbling comes later).

Tampa is trickier. Since the downtown fairly rolls up the sidewalk at night, there's not a locus of late-night activity there. Hyde Park has its fair share of night spots, but Ybor City is the city's nightlife district, drawing 40,000 visitors on weekends. It's where people step out. During the week there are few bars with throbbing music oozing out onto the street; then it's more about sedate dining. Forget date night on the weekend; then it's a place you rove with buddies, scaring up trouble. Beyond Ybor, there are pockets of irrational exuberance near the USF campus and at Channelside and International Plaza.

But whether you rave or rhumba, after-hours entertainment in the Tampa Bay area runs the gamut from throbbing house music to demure coffeehouse poetry readings. By and large, dress is casual (dress codes are usually posted outside establishments or on websites), cover charges are generally low or nonexistent, and show prices slide well below those in bigger metro areas. Beach bars may lean a little heavily on the Jimmy Buffet oeuvre, but with a little effort all musical tastes

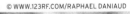

© WWW.123RF.COM/RAPHAEL DANIAUD

HIGHLIGHTS

LOOK FOR ◖ TO FIND RECOMMENDED NIGHTLIFE.

◖ **Best Place to See Big Names in a Small Venue:** Hip-hop to alt-country, **Jannus Landing** hosts visiting superstars in an indoor-outdoor tree-shaded nightclub (page 61).

◖ **Best Bar to Kick You into Vacation Mode:** It's a big, shambling, fruity-drinked

The Wave nightclub is part of the Shephard's Beach Resort.

COURTESY OF THE WAVE/NATHAN RAY

beach bar of conga lines and paper wristbands, but **Shephard's Beach Resort** offers a something-for-everyone approach with different musical genres in different rooms (page 64).

◖ **Best Tropical Brain-Freeze Cocktail:** Part pick-up bar, part waterside watering hole, **Bahama Breeze** attracts the nubile and their appreciators (page 65).

◖ **Top Place to Play Pool Shark:** It's not called **The Rack** for nothing. South Tampa's favorite pool hall actually serves decent sushi, too (page 71).

◖ **Best Bar in Which to Sing "Danny Boy":** On Thursday, Friday, and Saturday nights, **MacDinton's Irish Pub & Restaurant** in Hyde Park has lines up to a couple hundred strong. These aren't all folks of Irish descent, but they seem to know their way around a Guinness (page 72).

◖ **Closest Thing to Big-City Nightlife:** Buying in heavily to this new ultra lounge concept, Clearwater's **The Venue** is many things under one roof, each separate bar with its own sleek personality set in a huge, multistory nightclub (page 74).

◖ **Ground Zero for Local Gay Nightlife:** Central Avenue in St. Petersburg has been settled by dozens of gay business owners. Unsurprisingly, its **Detour** is the area's biggest gay bar (page 74).

can be accommodated at local nightspots. And who is tops in liquid refreshment? Neat, on the rocks, shaken not stirred-Tampa Bay's best cocktails are spread far and wide, with numerous places thronged most nights with aperitif aficionados.

Live Music

CHA CHA COCONUTS

800 2nd Ave. NE, The Pier, St. Petersburg, 727/822-6655

HOURS: Mon.-Thurs. 11 A.M.-midnight, Fri. and Sat. 11 A.M.-1 A.M., Sun. noon-10 P.M.

`Map 6`

Push the top button on the elevator at The Pier on St. Petersburg's waterfront. It opens at Cha Cha Coconuts, a good-times tropical paradise with kooky fruity drinks, conch fritters, and other standard-issue Floribbean cuisine, and live music many nights. You're not likely to see anything world class, but the views from up there on the open patio make anything sound pretty good.

⬛ JANNUS LANDING

220 1st Ave. N., St. Petersburg, 727/896-1244, www.jannuslandingconcerts.com

HOURS: Vary by performance

`Map 6`

A smaller venue for rock and contemporary acts, Jannus is supposedly the oldest outdoor concert venue in Florida. From jam bands like Medeski, Martin, and Wood, to Snoop Dogg, to Lucinda Williams—it all sounds fabu from a spot in the outdoor courtyard. It's bigger than a nightclub, with bigger acts, but there's still a cool club vibe and usually a 30s-and-up crowd. No reserved seating.

NEW WORLD BREWERY

1313 E. 8th Ave., Tampa, 813/248-4969

HOURS: Daily 3 P.M.-3 A.M.

COST: Most evenings no cover; some bands $3-5

`Map 3`

One of Ybor City's oldest and most beloved venues, with a lush tropical courtyard and a range of musical tastes from alt-rock to cool fusion jazz. There are more than 30 microbrews on tap (Dogfish Head, etc.—they don't brew their own anymore, but the owners are connoisseurs of other suds excellence) and everyone seems to be a regular.

NIGHTLIFE

You won't find a shortage of live music venues in Tampa and St. Petersburg.

COURTESY OF THE PALLADIUM/DAR WEBB

The Palladium at St. Petersburg College

ORPHEUM

1902 Ave. Republica de Cuba, Tampa, 813/248-9500
HOURS: Doors open 7 P.M. nightly, show times vary.
some shows 21 and up, some all ages
Map 3

Local acts, regional acts, and national acts take the stage regularly in this club run by the folks at the State Theater. Often an opener and a headlining act for not too much dough, it's a great sound system and a music lover's dream night out. Punk, blues, alt-country, it all plays here to a diverse crowd. Some nights it's just DJs and dancing, still fun. Be sure to call ahead —not all shows are all-ages—and be sure to check out the leopard print pool table when you get there.

THE PALLADIUM

253 5th Ave. N., St. Petersburg, 727/822-3590,
www.mypalladium.org
HOURS: Vary by performance
Map 6

Part of St. Petersburg College, this is a popular venue for visiting groups, whether it's rock, jazz, cabaret, chamber music, or Serbian folk music. No reserved seating.

PEGASUS LOUNGE

10008 N. 30th St., Tampa, 813/971-1679
HOURS: Mon.-Sat. 1 P.M.-3 A.M.
Map 4

Live bands, 28 bottled beers, big-screen TV, and darts—a recipe for collegiate happiness. USF students heft Mich Ultras while watching bands that range from folk to goth—industrial and hard-core—all of it loud. With nearly 30 bands plugging their amps in at the Pegasus every month, this little North Tampa club has become a must-see-and-be-seen for area music lovers. With a large stage, killer sound, a fair amount of seating, and even a decent burger, it's not hard to see why the lounge's reputation has grown in just this past year. The beers are the usual suspects, the drinks aren't winning any prizes, but that's no matter to the crowd busy with darts, pool, and even a good jukebox for when the band flags.

live music at Skipper's Smokehouse

SKIPPER'S SMOKEHOUSE

910 Skipper Rd., Tampa, 813/971-0666,
www.skipperssmokehouse.com
HOURS: Tues.-Fri. 11 A.M.-11 P.M., Sat. noon-11 p.m.,
Sun. 1 p.m.-11 p.m.
Map 4

Located in northern New Tampa, Skipper's is the city's beloved indoor-outdoor live blues venue. It's Tampa's best live music venue (blues, alt-rock, Tuvan throat singers, the gamut), with concerts held outdoors under the canopy of a huge, moss-festooned live oak. It has a lively 30s-and-up bar scene (a mighty fine mojito), and a ramshackle restaurant serves a wonderful blackened grouper sandwich, gator nuggets, and black beans.

STATE THEATRE

687 Central Ave, St. Petersburg, 727/895-3045
HOURS: Show times vary, generally 9 P.M.-2 A.M.
COST: $10-15
Map 6

In an historic gutted movie theater shellacked with flat black no-frills paint, this is where locals get their mosh on. The genres cycle through folk, alt rock, punk and ska, thus the audience varies wildly night to night—regardless of the show, regulars applaud the intimacy of the venue and the "real" (read grungy) quality of the space. Very limited seating, so it's largely standing-room-only (check out the balcony to take the energy, and noise, down a notch).

TAMPA THEATRE

711 Franklin St., Tampa, 813/274-8981,
www.tampatheatre.org
HOURS: Vary by show
Map 1

Built in 1926, it's a beloved downtown landmark with an acclaimed film series, concerts (Gordon Lightfoot, Keb Mo, Bright Eyes—it's a wide range), special events, and backstage tours. The creepy/fancy Basque architecture makes it an especially delicious place to see a show, almost always a sit-down affair.

Dance Clubs

CADILLAC JACK'S

6100 Gulf Blvd. (inside Howard Johnson's),
St. Pete Beach, 727/360-4575,
www.cadillacjacksonstpetebeach.com
HOURS: Thurs.-Sun. 4 P.M.-2 A.M.
Map 7

The only nightclub with dancing on Pinellas' South Gulf beaches, it's attached to Ricky T' Beach Bar, both venues boasting live music and a party-hearty crowd. Cadillac Jack's specialty is martinis, big time, with dozens of vodka flights of fancy. Music starts each night at 9:30 and the crowd is mixed ages but ready for rip-snorting fun.

CLUB PRANA

1619 E. 7th Ave., Tampa, 813/241-4139,
www.clubprana.com
COST: $10 cover, $30 bottle service
Map 3

Club Prana opened its doors in 2000 and quickly became the velvet-roped crown jewel in the Ybor scene. In 2002, the club expanded to five floors. From the main floor and mezzanine to the exclusive 3rd floor lounge, 4th-floor "club level," and 5th floor rooftop "sky bar," the space is attractive brushed stainless steel and hardwood floors. Patrons tend to be young and trendy.

CLUB SKYE

1509 E. 8th Ave., Tampa, 813/247-6606
HOURS: Mon.-Sat. 1 P.M.-3 A.M.
COST: Cover varies; Sat. no cover before 11 P.M.
Map 3

Club Skye is what's on the horizon for Tampa's party nights. Silky white curtains part to reveal the night's drama as it unfolds. What's it gonna be? Whether you're here for College Ladies' Night, International Night, Friday Night Bomb with Wild 98.7 FM broadcasting live, or Saturdays with DJ Trauma, Skye is the party to beat in Ybor. Although only certain nights are technically Naughty School Girl Nights, every night has a preponderance of slinky, sexy post-collegiate girls, especially notable when the club runs costume nights or competitions.

CZAR VODKA BAR

1420 E. 7th Ave., Tampa, 813/247-2664,
www.czarybor.com
HOURS: Wed., Fri., and Sat. 9 P.M.-3 A.M.
COST: $5 cover
Map 3

Czar is a newcomer, located in the atmospheric Pleasuredome/Tracks/El Goya building. Vodka drinks are de rigueur at Czar, with two rooms sporting dance floors, video screens, and nice booths (the side room is called Cyberia); there's also a super swank chill out room. Wednesdays also features "Crisco Disco," an old-school roller-skating extravaganza, with on-site skate rentals.

◆ SHEPHARD'S BEACH RESORT

601-619 S. Gulfview Blvd., Clearwater Beach,
727/441-6875
HOURS: Tiki bar weekdays 2-11 P.M., weekends 1 P.M.-2 A.M.; The Wave nightclub Thurs.-Sun. 9 P.M.-2 A.M.; Sunset Lounge daily 9:30 P.M.-2 A.M. Live music is performed 2-11 P.M. Mon.-Fri., 1-11 P.M. weekends
COST: $10 cover on weekends
Map 8

Before you even arrive you're immersed in its buzzy, Party Central feeling. There's the valet parking, then the cover charge, and accompanying paper wristband. Getting the lay of the land, order fruity poodle drinks with names like Shipwrecks and D Cups, heavy on the Midori, and watch the goings-on at the outdoor tiki bar. Live reggae promotes conga lines and other exuberant group dancing; inside at the Sunset Lounge, a house band called Da Jam slides through R&B numbers for a calmer crowd. Still, the center of festivities at Shephard's can be found at The Wave nightclub, with go-go dancers in big furry boots and bouncers suitably equipped with mammoth biceps and radio headsets. Just at the water's edge, the patio outside sports leather-clad beds—shades of South Beach.

COURTESY OF THE WAVE/NATHAN RAY

the Wave nightclub at Shephard's Beach Resort

STORMY'S

807 Gulf Way, St. Pete Beach, 727/367-7571
HOURS: Wed.-Sun. 5-11 P.M.
Map 9

You get your grouper sandwich downstairs at the Hurricane, a longtime institution on Passe-A-Grille beach. Digest a while, then head upstairs to Stormy's, an open-air nightclub in which to shake it a little while keeping one eye on the sun setting over the Gulf. There are happy-hour specials and occasional live performances.

Bars

ADOBE GILAS

1600 E. 8th Ave., Tampa, 813/241-8588
HOURS: Mon.-Sat. 11 A.M.-2:30 A.M., Sun. noon-2:30 A.M.
Map 3

Margarita madness and killer karaoke. Who says you have to act your age? A raucous spring-break-all-year crowd flocks to this lively Centro Ybor tequila-centric watering hole. Named for a cantankerous (and poisonous) Gila monster, it's a fun place, right at the pulsing heart of Ybor City, in which to pick your poison and let it rip. Think you can handle a 64-ounce margarita? Feel free to attempt it amongst these consummate 'rita professionals. Food runs to dips and chips, so the draw is the rustic indoor-outdoor space and abounding good cheer.

BAHAMA BREEZE

3045 N. Rocky Point Dr. E., Tampa, 813/289-7922
HOURS: Daily 4 P.M.-2 A.M.
Map 5

Located out on the Courtney Campbell Causeway (in the Rocky Point area), it's a froufrou tropical-drink singles hangout with a huge waterside deck on which you will occasionally see Rays players, Buccaneers, and large

CIGAR BASICS

Want to try a cigar but don't know the first thing? Tampa's a good place to begin. Even before you light up, a cigar's visual specifications can give clues to its character. The outer wrapper's color indicates a great deal about a cigar's flavor. A *maduro* wrapper is a rich, deep brown, imparting a cigar with deep, unctuous flavors. A *claro* wrapper, on the other hand, is a light tan and lends little additional flavor to a cigar. There are essentially six color grades. Roughly from lightest to darkest, these are: *candela* (pale green), *claro, natural* (light brown), *colorado* (reddish brown), *maduro,* and *oscuro* (almost black).

Shape is another central factor in cigar selection. Among *parejos* or straight-sided cigars, there are three basic categories. A *corona* is classically six inches long, with an open foot (the end that is lighted) and a closed head (the end that is smoked). Within this category, **Churchills** are a bit longer and thicker, *robustos* are shorter and much thicker, and a double *corona* is significantly longer. *Panetelas,* the second category, are longer and much thinner than *coronas,* and the third category, lonsdales, are thicker than panetelas and thinner and longer than *coronas.*

Figurados comprise the other class of cigar, which spans all of the irregularly shaped types. This includes torpedo shapes, braided *culebras,* and pyramid shapes that have a closed, pointed head and an open foot.

A cigar band is generally wrapped around the closed head of a cigar. Its original function was to minimize finger staining, not to identify brands. Nonetheless, on the band you will find the name a manufacturer has designated for a particular line of cigars – names like Partagas, Macanudo, Punch, and Montecristo. Keep in mind that after 1959, many cigar manufacturers fled Cuba to open shop elsewhere, taking their brand names with them. Thus, a brand name does not always betray a cigar's country of origin.

For neophytes lighting up for the first time, a milder cigar may ease you in. The Macanudo Hyde Park is a mild smoke, as is the Don Diego Playboy Robusto or Lonsdale. For a fuller-bodied cigar, the Punch Diademas and the Partagas Number 10 are both popular. If you're looking for a robust, ultra full-bodied taste, you might try the Hoyo de Monterrey Double Corona. The best way to discover your own personal tastes is to stop into a fine tobacconist or cigar-friendly restaurant and have a chat.

hand-rolled cigars

men who could have been contenders. Island-theme playground that it is, it gets top honors for the tropical drinks. Their frozen piña colada comes with swirls of strawberry ice and a float of Myers's dark rum.

BAR LOUIE
International Plaza, 2223 N. West Shore Dr., Tampa, 813/874-1919, www.barlouieamerica.com
HOURS: Daily 11 A.M.-2 A.M.
Map 5

It's got more taps going than a Savion Glover show. More than 40 beer taps line the long bar, as does a broad age range of sophisticated shoppers and partiers. An urban industrial vibe makes you feel far from the ritzy shopping of International Plaza mall. The encyclopedic array of beers can make you feel just about zippo in no time. It's a huge and echoey space, at its best when the after-work professionals swarm in for a casual nosh and a fancy brew or two. The chichi martinis seem to be the purview of the well-heeled female patrons, many of whom are surrounded by shopping bags from the day's prey.

BEAKS OLD FLORIDA
2451 Central Ave., St. Petersburg, 727/321-9100
HOURS: Tues.-Sun. appetizers 4-5 P.M., full menu 5-11 P.M.
Map 9

Beaks doesn't so much have decor as an astounding accretion of crap. It's a more-is-more motif whereby, if one plastic parrot is good, 20 plastic parrots are great. A long row of 1970s rococo chandeliers illuminates the tomato soup–red bar; fake tropical plants are everywhere; carved decoys, plastic bamboo fountains, and birdcages imprisoning fake jailbirds of a variety of species crowd in at the bar with the customers, themselves mostly attired in a cacophony of Hawaiian shirts. It's the kind of comfortable, good-time neighborhood joint that usually takes decades to create. The funky little bar/restaurant is the brainchild of partners Evelyn Powell and Jamie Farquharson, the latter the founder of The Bubble Room on Captiva back in 1978.

The culinary focus is bar-food-with-a-twist, most of these twists improvements upon the originals.

CHIC-A-BOOM ROOM
319 Main St., Dunedin, 727/736-0206
HOURS: 11 A.M.-2:30 A.M.
Map 8

A little more glamorous and hip than many bars on the Dunedin scene, it skews a little young and a little more toward the fancy-martini side. Decor is kitschy-cool 1950s diner. The same owners have Kelly's next door.

COYOTE UGLY
1722 E. 7th Ave., Tampa, 813/228-8459
HOURS: Tues.-Sat. 5 P.M.-3 A.M.
Map 3

In the center of all the action, this bar aims older, not more mature, and is often just about the biggest party in Ybor City, presided over by the most audacious bartenders to ever wield a shot glass. If you have to ask what a body shot is you're ripe for a hard life lesson from one of Coyote's devilish (and usually gorgeous) bartenders. Just like in the movie (which in turn was based on a bar in New York City), all-female bartenders drag the unsuspecting up on the bar for some raunchy drinking, dancing, and whatever. The bare-bones room is festooned with discarded brassieres from exuberant all-ages patrons.

THE GARDEN
217 Central Ave., St. Petersburg, 727/896-3800
HOURS: Daily 11:30 A.M.-2 A.M.
Map 6

Appropriately named, the garden, under the shade of a banyan, is the choicest seating. It's a cocktails kind of joint, with food as largely an afterthought (think ballast, not haute cuisine, but Mediterranean in spirit), but the 1880s building has a kind of sophistication imparted by the lovely setting, the cigars sold at the back, and the live jazz.

NIGHTLIFE

COURTESY OF VISIT FLORIDA

Stumps Supper Club

GULFPORT ON THE ROCKS
5413 Shore Blvd. S., Gulfport, 727/321-8318
HOURS: Daily 10 A.M.-2 A.M.
Map 7

Gulfport isn't beachy, but this comfy staple is just across from Williams Pier and Boca Ciega Bay. The thick fog of smoke inside is shorthand for "no food served here." There's usually live music—maybe the Edgewater Band ("back from its tour of Pinellas Park")—ably making its way through "Mustang Sally" and other crowd-pleasers. A beer-and-shots kind of comfy neighborhood bar, it features a nice pool table with straight cues—cheap and seemingly underutilized.

HOWL AT THE MOON AND STUMPS SUPPER CLUB
615 Channelside Dr., 813/226-2261, Tampa, www.stumpssupperclub.com
HOURS: Howl, Thurs.-Sat. 8 P.M.-2 A.M.; Stumps, Wed.-Thurs. 4-10 P.M., Fri. 4 P.M.-3 A.M., Sat. 3 P.M.-3 A.M., Sun. 3-9 P.M.
Map 1

Howl puts two Yamaha baby grands at the center of all the festivities at Tampa's liveliest piano bar. The staff is quick to break into song, which doesn't diminish the sense of barely contained conviviality at this waterside watering hole. The cuisine is largely pleasant and forgettable, but the drinks are stiff and the crowd is anything but. The revelers, mostly in their 20s and 30s, are locals and out-of-towners with a song in their heart.

Stumps, next door and owned by the same people, is more food-oriented, with Southern-style ribs, pulled pork, and fried chicken. It also hosts live music and house band Jimmy James and the Velvet Explosion weekends, strictly campy retro stuff (um, their website plays "The Girl from Ipanema" ad nauseum) with the occasional Outkast and Black Eyed Peas to keep things interesting.

THE HUB
719 N. Franklin St., Tampa, 813/229-1553
HOURS: Mon.-Sat. 10 A.M.-3 A.M., Sun. 1 P.M.-3 A.M.
Map 1

It's dark, it's smoky, it's cash only, and the

COURTESY OF VISIT FLORIDA

live entertainment at Howl at the Moon

it along with a little live music on the weekends at Backjack's. During the week, the sleek, vast restaurant embraces the throngs with a laudably broad wine list and a something-for-everyone culinary approach that includes pistachio-crusted red snapper, lush prime rib eye steaks and a smart array of familiar *nigiri* and *makimono* sushi rolls.

JIMMY B'S BEACH BAR

6200 Gulf Blvd., St. Pete Beach, 727/367-1902
HOURS: Daily 11 A.M.-2 A.M.
Map 7

The signature drink is something called a Hot Wet Spot, equally embarrassing to order and to drink: a piña colada with a drizzle of blueberry liqueur, all topped with a floof of whipped cream. Slightly salacious embarrassment seems to be a theme: The menu boasts the "biggest weenie on the beach" among a handful of sandwiches, bar snacks, and pizza. Alas, the kitchen gets backed up on busy nights, so you may end up eyeballing others' jalapeno poppers, grouper fingers, and onion rings. The outdoor deck is gorgeous, with a long boardwalk down to the beach illuminated by the kind of plastic flaming cauldrons one sees at Halloween superstores. Stand on the sand, listening as the band segues from Rush to Pink Floyd, then make your way back out to the front past the girl peddling Jaegermeister shots and other bad ideas.

O'KEEFE'S TAVERN AND RESTAURANT

1219 S. Fort Harrison Ave., Clearwater, 727/442-9034
HOURS: Daily 11 A.M.-2 A.M.
Map 8

O'Keefe's is the bar to beat for St. Patrick's Day. A good-times, pint-or-three shambling Irish pub, its history goes back to the 1960s when it was O'Keefe's Tap Room, a history still visible despite the many additions and remodelings. A white brick exterior gives way to a comfortable series of rooms festooned with lots of green accents and Irishobilia. The brogue-required bartenders are fast and furious with the beers (more than 100 offerings) and the all-ages crowd is unified by their affection for

drinks will grow hair on your chest. And those are all the good qualities. A beloved dive bar where no one exactly remembers why they started coming, the drink of choice is the kamikaze, but frankly they aren't particularly good until you've had your third. Under certain circumstances the jukebox is a masterful work of diabolical genius. It reads like a blue-collar bar, but many of the regular constituents are circuit court judges, lawyers, etc. lingering downtown for a grungy good time. For many Tampans, ending an evening here is a tradition.

JACKSON'S BISTRO-BAR-SUSHI

601 S. Harbour Island Blvd., Ste. 100, Tampa, 813/277-0112
HOURS: Mon.-Thurs. 11:30 A.M.-2:30 P.M. and 5-10 P.M., Fri. and Sat. 11:30 A.M.-2:30 P.M. and 5-11 P.M., Sun. 10:30 A.M.-2:30 P.M. and 5-10 P.M.
Map 2

Feeling lucky? Tempt fate with a Death by Chocolate martini at Jackson's. The chocolate-infused vodka and white and dark Godiva liqueurs are worth a little risk. You can sample

NIGHTLIFE

WINE BARS

Have grape expectations? Tampa Bay has some places to quaff a little viticultural genius. Bob Heilman's Beachcomber has been a beefy *Wine Spectator* award winner for years on the basis of its burgundies, but **Bobby's Bistro** (447 Mandalay Ave., Clearwater Beach, 727/446-9463) is sheer lusciousness for the Oregon and California pinot noir lover.

Tio Pepe, Charley's Steakhouse, the Columbia restaurant, Bern's, and **Domenic's Capri Italian Restaurant** always get major plaudits for the breadth of their lists, but often this amounts to us mere mortals looking wistfully as we turn the pages of the phonebook-thick tome. A fun place to taste more than 40 by the glass, **Clearwater Wine Company** (483 Mandalay Ave., Ste. 113, Clearwater Beach, 727/446-8805) just celebrated its first anniversary. Kristi Lam and her parents orchestrate a casual, living-room atmosphere most Friday nights with live music, offering tipples from every major wine-producing region in the world, with deep happy hour discounts be-tween 5 and 7 P.M. (Oh, and there's a "Yappy Hour" the last Saturday of the month for the sophisticated dog and his owner.)

And resurrected after a strange closure last year, **Wine Exchange** (1611 W. Swann Ave., Tampa, 813/254-9463) is back and pouring interesting flights by the glass. Too bad the movie theater next door is sunk or it would stay a little busier.

True to its name, **The Grape** (International Plaza Mall, Tampa, 813/354-9463) has cool purple club chairs that invite lengthy investigation of the more than 120 wines available by the bottle, glass, or half glass, divided into categories by relative weight, or body of the wines. Some evenings it's lively girls' night out as ladies heft glasses of pinot noir amongst a sea of shopping bags.

A nearly vegetarian wine bar new on the scene in 2008, **Pan y Vino** (369 Main St., Dunedin, 727/734-7700) is the sister restaurant to Casa Tina next door. Salads, cheese plate, and more complement an eclectic and fair-priced by-the-glass list.

COURTESY OF VISIT FLORIDA

the wine cellar at Columbia Restaurant

the place. Once known for its "seven-course Irish dinner" (that's a six pack and a potato), O'Keefe's fare is pretty good.

PEABODY'S

15333 Amberly Dr., 813/972-1725
HOURS: Daily 11 A.M.-3 A.M.
Map 4

It may not be the cutting-edge in nightlife, but Peabody's has earned a loyal clientele among New Tampa young professionals. Run by the same people who have the more youthful dance club, The Falls, next door, Peabody's appeals to a fairly mature New Tampa crowd, but one that appreciates a happy-hour-all-the-time policy (two-for-one and more). Big screen TVs, billiards, electronic darts, and NTN trivia games don't distract from the smiley, nubile staff. It's a sports bar in sheep's clothing, one where the whole family won't mind sharing lively conversation over burgers (but after 9 P.M. it's over 21 only).

(THE RACK

1809 W. Platt St., 813/250-1595
HOURS: Mon.-Fri. 4 P.M.-3 A.M.,
Sat. and Sun. noon-3 A.M.
Map 2

Head to the Rack for eight ball and *tekka maki*—a combo made in yuppie heaven. You don't see the kind of serious players who bring their own spiffy Schon or Predator cues, but there's respectable play at most of the tables in the hip, low-light, leather-couched space. The crowd is young but not too young, cool but not too cool.

SKIP'S

371 Main St., Dunedin, 727/734-9151
HOURS: Mon.-Sat. 4 P.M.-2 A.M.
Map 8

Why do I love this bar so much? The music's not too loud, everyone seems willing to chat with each other, and it's smack in the middle of good-times downtown Dunedin. Oh, and you can very easily take command of one of the dart boards. A few picnic tables out front allow you to take in the night air, and Skip

himself is a warm and inviting presence in the bar. Food is minimal.

SPLITSVILLE

615 Channelside Dr., Tampa, 813/514-2695,
www.splitsvillelanes.com
HOURS: Mon.-Thurs. 4 P.M.-1 A.M., Fri.-Sat. 11 A.M.-3 A.M.,
Sun. 11 A.M.-1 A.M.
Map 1

Spares, strikes, whatever—it's good food, a stunningly whimsical environment, and the coolest bowling shoes ever. Bowlers aren't known for their looks, so Splitsville lacks verisimilitude with its hottie waiters and equally glam clientele. The decor sets you straight with oversized "bowling pin" columns, red velvet ropes, and 12 pristine lanes. Excellent shareable bar snacks are available laneside: Sliders are deliciously messy and oniony, the bacon skins crisp and laden with fat three ways—sour cream, bacon, cheddar—and the just-from-the-oven Toll House cookies will wilt while you snarf every one. They also make a mean apple martini: Finlandia vodka, Apple Pucker, and apple Jolly Rancher, shaken and served straight up. You've never had a more delicious libation while wearing bowling shoes.

UNDERTOW BEACH BAR

3850 Gulf Blvd., St. Pete Beach, 727/368-9000
HOURS: Tues.-Sat. noon-2 A.M., Sun. 1 P.M.-midnight
Map 7

Set back from Gulf Boulevard, it's two buildings and a patio squatting right on the sand. The bar, to the left, is boisterous, with a strange running-water moat inset in the long oval-shaped bar. Cocktail waitresses wear something reminiscent of the Dallas Cowboy cheerleaders' late-70s glory years, but the bathing-suits-and-flip-flops crowd doesn't bat an eye. The outdoor patio is the place to be, weathered plywood tables amid a cluster of pillars holding up nothing (we debated, was this a Stonehenge motif or the remnants of an aborted patio roof?). Some nights there's live reggae, but others the music is canned. Opt for the very respectable rum runners and an order of wings (a generous 12 for $4).

NIGHTLIFE

Irish Pubs

DUBLINER PUB

2307 W. Azeele St., Tampa, 813/258-2257,
www.thedublineririshpub.com
HOURS: Mon.-Thurs. 3 P.M.-3 A.M.,
Fri. and Sat. noon-3 A.M.
Map 2

There's a lot of Irish zeal on and around Azeele. If you like your music—or your flirting—with a heavy brogue, head to everyone's favorite quaint Irish bar, the Dubliner. It's set in a tiny house with a nice front porch; burgers are solid and the youngish crowd is convivial.

FOUR GREEN FIELDS

205 W. Platt St., Tampa, 813/254-4444
HOURS: Mon.-Wed. 11 A.M.-1 A.M.,
Thurs.-Sun. 11 A.M.-2 A.M.
Map 1

Located one block west of the Tampa Bay Convention Center, the thatched-roof cottage is an utter anomaly. Order an Irish whiskey or a black and tan from the man with the thick brogue behind the worn wooden bar. There's an outdoor deck set amid palm trees, live Irish folk music most nights, and some say the best pint of Guinness in Tampa. The menu won't win any awards for originality, but the fry basket is piping hot and generous.

(MACDINTON'S IRISH PUB & RESTAURANT

405 S. Howard Ave., Tampa, 813/251-8999
HOURS: Mon.-Sat. 11:30 A.M.-3 A.M., Sun. 5 P.M.-3 A.M.
Map 2

Another Irish entry, with a killer black and tan, a warming Irish coffee, and a fair representation of Irish staples, from rib-sticking, mashed-potatoey shepherd's pie to respectable corned beef and cabbage. This is absolutely the biggest scene in Tampa, with lines down and around the block on weekend nights. Why? Who can say. The beer tastes just the same as it does other places.

Lounges

BLUE MARTINI

2223 N. West Shore Blvd., Tampa, 813/873-2583,
www.bluemartinilounge.com
HOURS: Mon.-Thurs. 4 P.M.-3 A.M.,
Fri. and Sat. 1 P.M.-3 A.M.
Map 5

It should come as no surprise that Blue Martini has a bevy of fabulous sillytinis that draw serious devotees. One of the most popular drinks, the purple passion, features Ketel One, Fruja raspberry liqueur, sour mix, 7Up, the pale purple delight then garnished with an orchid. A bar for full-fledged adults, Blue Martini features an elevated stage behind the bar on which to see live rock nightly. The menu leans to attractive and contemporary small plates (seared tuna, hummus and pita chips).

THE GRAPE

813/354-9463, 2223 N. West Shore Blvd., Tampa
HOURS: Mon.-Sat. 11 A.M.-10 P.M., Sun. noon -10 P.M.
Map 5

Cool purple club chairs invite lengthy investigation of the more than 120 wines available by the bottle, glass or half glass, divided into categories by relative "weight" or body of the wines. Goofy descriptions and lack of vintage years make the list a little frustrating for the serious oenophile, but a menu of cheeses, pates and spreads marries nicely with the quaffs. Some evenings it's lively girls' night out as ladies heft glasses of pinot noir amongst a sea of shopping bags. Menu high notes include a tasty spinach salad and a worth-the-extra-drycleaning chocolate fondue.

BOTTOM'S UP

Neat, on the rocks, shaken not stirred – Tampa Bay's best cocktails are anything but well-kept secrets. The following places are thronged most nights with aperitif aficionados. Here's where to go for what.

CLASSIC COCKTAILS

Good martinis abound in these parts, nearly the finest of which can be found at the **Rare Olive** (300 Central Ave., St. Petersburg, 727/898-7273). Still, special props go to **Dirty Martini** (25032 U.S. 19 N., Clearwater, 727/796-2442). Yes, an icy, be-olived glass of perfection, but there are also Naked Sushi nights to recommend the establishment.

It's hard to beat the Bloody Mary bar at **Café Alma** (260 1st Ave. S., St. Petersburg, 727/502-5002) for Saturday brunch. Ratchet it up with all the horseradish you feel is necessary, cooling it down with that miracle celery or an order of blue crab Benedict.

Where better to enjoy a classic I-double-dog-dare-you kamikaze cocktail than **The Hub** (719 N. Franklin St., Tampa, 813/229-1553), one of Tampa's most beloved dive bars? Hubsters swear by the generous pours of vodka, Rose's lime juice, and triple sec that comprise the house kamikaze.

Mojitos, the latest must-have cocktail in these parts, are best sampled at **The Table** (539 Central Ave. N., St. Petersburg, 727/823-3700), going heavy on an investigation of the watermelon version (big chunks of fresh melon) or the piquant blood orange spin.

FROUFROU COCKTAILS

After a grueling search for the city's best cosmopolitan – someone had to do it – **Side-Bern's** (2208 W. Morrison Ave., Tampa, 813/258-2233) emerges victorious. Their version of the icy, pale-pink cocktail made ubiquitous by constant flogging on Sex and the City, ain't cheap, but it's flawless. How appropriate that it's found in this urbane hot spot, home to world-beat small plates and a knockout daily-changing selection of breads.

Bellini (2832-2838 Beach Blvd., Gulfport, 727/327-4222), the sleek New York-style lounge attached to La Fogata, would make you feel hip even slurping an O'Doul's with a bendy straw. However, its cocktail list is top-notch, with items such as the Divine Goddess (Van Gogh pomegranate vodka, Cointreau, sour mix, and cranberry garnished with a flower) for all your antioxidant needs.

What better to precede Pacific Rim seafood than a bracing Asian lemon drop of SKYY citrus vodka, Zen green tea liqueur, Patron Citronge liqueur, sweet-and-sour, and ginger? No wonder the Tampa dining cognoscenti has embraced the lively and über-stylish Hawaiian-fusion **Roy's** (4342 W. Boy Scout Blvd., 813/873-7697), brainchild of celebrity chef Roy Yamaguchi. Several years in, Roy's has still got the kind of buzz that could cover a whole bunch of power tools in action.

It should come as no surprise that **Blue Martini** (2223 N. West Shore Blvd., International Plaza, Tampa, 813/873-2583) has a bevy of fabulous martinis that draw serious devotees. One of the most popular drinks, the Purple Passion, features Ketel One, Fruja raspberry liqueur, sour mix, 7Up, the pale purple delight then garnished with an orchid. An unabashed chick drink.

GUARANTEED-HANGOVER COCKTAILS

The sake bomber. First there is the cajoler, urging those weaker or more easily influenced to take the challenge. The shot glass is taken up in the left hand and dropped, in tandem with all tablemates, into the glass of beer. A moment of fizzing, small tidal waves, then the beer is hefted with the right hand and consumed in a few giant gulps. The shot glass nudging at one's lips, this is a game of speed. If those at the table are unable to say, "Geez, that was a bad idea" in Japanese, the table resorts to short whooping sounds. To find the area's best, head to Ybor City's **Samurai Blue Sushi & Sake Bar** (1600 E. 8th Ste C-208, Tampa, 813/242-6688).

And nothing says, "I'm ambivalent about adulthood" like drinking a body shot out of a cute bartender's navel while your friends holler at Ybor City's **Coyote Ugly** (1722 E. 7th Ave., Tampa, 813/228-8459).

NIGHTLIFE

PUSH ULTRA LOUNGE

128 Third St. S, St. Petersburg, 727/895-6400
HOURS: Wed.-Sun. 8 P.M.-2 A.M.
Map 6

A huge new dance club with rooftop bar and outdoor garden patio heats up the nights in downtown St. Petersburg, not surprisingly at the site of a historic fire house. Drinks lean to boutique tequilas in a range of stylish margaritas. Celebrities like Paris Hilton have been known to make a showing.

☾ THE VENUE

2675 Ulmerton Rd., Clearwater, 727/571-2202,
www.thevenuetampabay.com
HOURS: Takara, daily 4 P.M.-1:30 A.M.; Viaggio,
Sun.-Wed. 4-10 P.M., Thurs.-Sat. until 11 P.M.;
Club V opens at 10 P.M.
Map 9

The newest thing to make a splash in 2008, its 27,000 square feet of bars and restaurants are tucked, warrenlike, into the Feather Sound space that used to be Storman's Palace. Ultra lounge, martini bar, deck bar, champagne lounge, private wine room, cabana deck, VIP rooms, sushi bar, tapas restaurant. This playground is aimed at making four hours young again, heady with options and high expectations. I went expecting *Girls Gone Wild: The Next Generation,* where all the carousing had to be completed in time to relieve the babysitter. What I found was a rollicking good time, a giant petri dish of pheromones and cleavage and thundering beats. Oh, and dinner. The Venue's two restaurants are way better than they have to be.

VINTAGE ULTRA LOUNGE

16 2nd St. N., St. Petersburg, 727/735-3347
HOURS: Wed.-Sun. 8 P.M.-2 A.M.
Map 6

Fine, Paris Hilton has patronized St. Petersburg's Push Ultra Lounge, but Rihanna came and hung out at the new, super-hip Vintage. Not only that, her boyfriend got into a fight with a paparazzo (alright, really just a *St. Petersburg Times* photographer, but still). It's got all the VIP attitude of many ultra lounges, but doesn't always seem super busy. I wonder if it's here for the long haul.

Gay and Lesbian

BAXTER'S

1519 S. Dale Mabry, 813/258-8830,
www.baxterslounge.com
HOURS: Daily noon-2 A.M.
Map 5

It just keeps closing and popping up somewhere else. A friendly neighborhood meeting place, it features hot dancers Wednesday–Saturday nights, movies Thursdays, karaoke on Sunday, and more. Dimly lit, with pool table, darts, and plenty of parking.

CITY SIDE

3703 Henderson Blvd., 813/350-0600,
www.clubcityside.com
HOURS: Mon.-Sat. 5 P.M.-2 A.M.
Map 2

A weird location for a gay club (can you say strip mall, next to a sports bar?), it's an inviting lounge with pool tables, intimate dance floor, and outdoor patio. Far from a frenetic scene, it's appropriate for a little after-work conversation and relaxation.

☾ DETOUR

2612 Central Ave., St. Petersburg, 727/327-8204
HOURS: Daily 2 P.M.-2 A.M.
Map 9

Central Avenue east of about 9th has, in recent years, become where many gay-owned businesses have settled. The neighborhood is called the Grand Central District, and thus, this three-venue nightclub until recently was Grand Central Station, now Detour. In over 13,000 square feet, it's got two bars, a large dance floor, two stages to support live entertainment and karaoke, pool tables, a wide outdoor patio, Internet café, and lots of free parking. DJ Don, DJ Rossi, and DJ Luna mix up some spicy beats, and the light system will get you in the mood.

GEORGIE'S ALIBI OF ST. PETE
3100 3rd Ave. N., St. Petersburg, 727/321-2112, www.georgiesalibi.com
HOURS: Daily 11 A.M.-2 A.M.
Map 9

The sister property to the booming Wilton Manors outpost down in Fort Lauderdale (and another in Palm Springs, CA), it's settled into an unlikely strip mall. Most days it's a relaxed,

pleasant place to unwind and meet new people, but some nights it's more energetic dance parties and special events (drag bingo, anyone?).

KI KI KI
1908 W. Kennedy Blvd., Tampa, 813/241-4188
HOURS: Daily 11 A.M.-3 A.M.
Map 2

One of the most venerable gay bars in the city (much of the city's gay life used to be centered on Kennedy but now has closed up or spread out elsewhere), it's a beer-only rec-room-wood-paneled cruise spot for the working man. Corner jukebox and pool table get heavy play.

ARTS AND LEISURE

While it was the first state to be settled by Europeans, Florida might be the last state to have entered fully into modernity. It remained more or less a frontier until the 20th century, with the first paved road not until 1920. It was really World War II that changed things in the state, prompting a period of sustained growth that lasted more than 50 years.

Because of its relative youth, the Tampa Bay area has not had enough time to cultivate long-standing arts traditions and venerable cultural institutions of other American cities. Located an hour to the south of the Tampa Bay area, Sarasota is the undisputed arts capital of the Gulf Coast, having had circus impresario John Ringling lavish his adopted home town with visual and performing arts venues and concerns. St. Petersburg and Tampa don't quite reach the same heights, but downtown St. Petersburg certainly competes with the city to the south for per capita arts organizations. All along the waterfront and St. Petersburg's east-west avenues, fanning out from Central, you'll find more than a dozen arts and historical museums, galleries, and local theaters. Despite its sophistication in other arenas (like, um, sports arenas), Tampa doesn't quite measure up, with a sparser number of superlative local arts offerings.

In terms of other types of recreation—outdoor activities, spectator sports, and other diversions—Hillsborough and Pinellas counties are both an embarrassment of riches. The wealth of beaches and state parks on the Pinellas side allow for sun, sand, fishing, boating, and more low-key navel contemplation, while Hillsborough

HIGHLIGHTS

LOOK FOR (TO FIND RECOMMENDED ARTS AND ACTIVITIES.

(**Best Reason to Feel Surreal:** The famous mustachioed Spanish surrealist is honored in St. Petersburg's sleek **Salvador Dalí Museum,** a tremendous collection of his work and the work of those inspired by him (page 81).

(**Best Place to Share Popcorn with a Ghost:** The **Tampa Theatre,** elaborately decorated to resemble an open Mediterranean courtyard, features 1,446 seats, 99 stars in the auditorium ceiling, and nearly 1,000 pipes in its mighty Wurlitzer theatre organ. And the ghost of an old projectionist (page 89).

(**Best Place to Scratch a Major Retail Itch:** Anchored by Nordstrom, Neiman Marcus, Dillard's, Ballard Designs and Robb & Stucky Interiors, **International Plaza** contains more than 200 high-end specialty stores (page 93).

(**Best Place to Crack an Old Spine:** St. Petersburg's **Haslam's Book Store** is the state's largest new and used bookstore, with more than 300,000 volumes tucked into the comfy storefront (page 96).

(**Hot Spot for Canine Couture:** **Downtown Dogs** in Tampa traffics in lavish leashes and accessories for when man's best friend feels like putting on the dog (page 97).

(**Best Source for Lacy Underthings That Make a Statement:** For lingerie

you'll want to show off, head to downtown St. Petersburg's **Maison Rouge** (page 97).

(**Top Sandy Splendor:** There are some wonderful choices for sun and sand, so why settle for just one when you can opt for the double-whammy of **Caladesi and Honeymoon Islands,** a pair of white-sand barrier islands flanking Dunedin north of Clearwater. Caladesi is accessible only by ferry from Honeymoon Island (pages 98 and 101).

(**Best Way to Wander Through a Verdant Yesteryear:** It puttered along as a kitschy Old Florida attraction for years, until the City of St. Petersburg restored **Sunken Gardens,** four-acre tropical gardens, to their former glory (page 108).

(**Best Excuse to Don the Yellow Jersey:** Pinellas County's **Pinellas Trail** is one of the longest linear parks in the southeastern U.S., a 15-foot-wide bike path running from St. Petersburg up to the sponge docks of Tarpon Springs, with stops along the way for a cold drink or sightseeing (page 110).

(**Best Excuse for Peanuts and Cracker Jacks:** Tampa Bay has both the boys of summer and the boys of spring. You can see professional baseball much of the year, with the **Tampa Bay Rays** (page 116) during the regular season and the **New York Yankees Spring Training** at the end of February and in March (page 115).

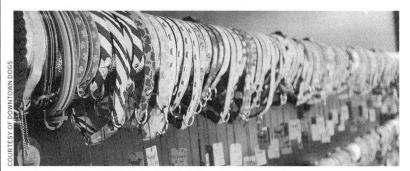

COURTESY OF DOWNTOWN DOGS

A collar to suit any dog can be found at Downtown Dogs.

has professional and college sports of all kinds. Tampa gets the nod for retail enticements, with two super-high-end malls to its name, while downtown St. Petersburg offers up a quirky afternoon of window shopping amongst the many independent boutiques and galleries.

The Arts

MUSEUMS

BEACH ART CENTER
1515 Bay Palm Blvd., Indian Rocks Beach, 727/596-4331, www.beachartcenter.org
HOURS: Mon.-Thurs. 9 A.M.-4 P.M., Fri. 9 A.M.-noon
COST: Free admission
Map 9

A sweet nonprofit arts center, it offers classes for locals in fine arts and crafts. It also has two small galleries set up in the old American Legion Hall.

DUNEDIN FINE ARTS CENTER & CHILDREN'S ART MUSEUM
1143 Michigan Blvd., Dunedin, 727/298-3322, www.dfac.org
HOURS: Mon.-Fri. 10 A.M.-5 P.M., Sat. 10 A.M.-2 P.M., Sun. 1-4 P.M.
COST: Free admission
Map 9

The center has four galleries, studio classrooms, the David L. Mason Children's Art Museum, the Palm Cafe, and gallery gift shop. The exhibits are often the work of students. The children's museum provides hands-on activities that assist families in understanding and appreciating the work of Florida artists exhibited in the galleries. Even if you spend your time in the art center and not the children's museum, the scale is such that it's not intimidating or boring for kids.

FLORIDA HOLOCAUST MUSEUM
55 5th St. S., St. Petersburg, 727/820-0100, www.flholocaustmuseum.org
HOURS: Daily 10 A.M.-5 P.M.
COST: $12 adults, seniors, and college students, $6 students under one
Map 6

The fourth largest of its kind in the United States, some of the museum is devoted to the memory of millions of innocent people who suffered, struggled, and died in the Shoah. Recent exhibits have included an examination of the Jehovah's Witnesses persecution during World War II as well as a look at Pope John Paul II's relationship with the Jewish people. But it also showcases only loosely linked exhibits such as the lush, life-affirming work of Czech artist Charles Pachner (who lost his whole family during the war), or the mixed-media paintings, sculptures, and installations of contemporary French artist Marc Ash.

FLORIDA INTERNATIONAL MUSEUM
244 2nd St. N., St. Petersburg, 727/341-7901, www.floridamuseum.org
HOURS: Mon.-Sat. 9 A.M.-6 P.M., Sun. noon-6 P.M.
COST: $20 adults, $17 seniors, $13 children 6-12, free for children under 6
Map 6

This is an exciting time to stop in for a visit at the Florida International Museum, which is just finishing up as the first stop on the North American tour of Vatican Splendors, one of the largest collections of art, documents, and historically significant objects from the Vatican, some of which has never been seen outside the Vatican. The museum has a permanent exhibition called The Cuban Missile Crisis, which explores the 13 most frightening days of the Cold War when the world teetered precariously close to all-out nuclear conflict. It includes a fully stocked fallout shelter and a circa 1960s living room from which you can see President Kennedy's October 1962 speech on an old RCA set.

The Florida Holocaust Museum is the fourth largest of its kind in the United States.

FLORIDA MUSEUM OF PHOTOGRAPHIC ARTS

200 N. Tampa St., Ste. 130, Tampa, 813/221-2222, www.fmopa.org
HOURS: Tues.-Sat. 10 A.M.-5 P.M.
COST: Suggested donation $4
Map 1

This small photography museum is fairly new on the scene (2001), collecting, preserving, and exhibiting historic and contemporary works by nationally and internationally known photographic artists. Recent exhibits have included the camera obscura work of Abelardo Morell and an array of lovely 40-inch-long Cirkut camera landscapes taken between 1904 and 1943 by Al and Jean Burgert of Burgert Brothers Commercial Photography Studio in Tampa. The museum also offers photographic programs and workshops to the community.

GREAT EXPLORATIONS

1925 4th St. N., St. Petersburg, 727/821-8992, www.greatexplorations.org
HOURS: Mon.-Sat. 10 A.M.-4:30 P.M., Sun. noon-4:30 P.M.
COST: $9 general admission, $8 seniors, free for children one and under
Map 9

After spending time at Sunken Gardens, give the kids their due next door at Great Explorations. The hands-on science center had a much-needed cash infusion a few years back, with lots of slick educational exhibits on things like the hydrologic cycle or ecosystem of the estuary. Many of the exhibits are best appreciated by late elementary-aged kids (let's say kids up to about 11), but exhibits such as Gears and the Laser Harp have appeal even to little kids. If your family enjoys hands-on science museums, head over to Tampa's MOSI for a bigger dose. This makes a fun afternoon, though, especially when capped by an ice cream at Coldstone Creamery, craftily located on the premises.

GULF COAST MUSEUM OF ART

12211 Walsingham Rd., Largo, 727/518-6833
HOURS: Tues.-Sat. 10 A.M.-4 P.M., Sun. noon-4 P.M.
COST: $8 adults, $7 seniors, $4 students, free for children under 12
Map 9

In the Pinewood Cultural Park, it features contemporary art by Floridian artists from 1960 on. The center also offers classes and workshops for children and adults in ceramics, metalworking, painting, sculpture, photography, and drawing.

HENRY B. PLANT MUSEUM

401 W. Kennedy Blvd., Tampa, 813/254-1891
HOURS: Tues.-Sat. 10 A.M.-4 P.M., Sun. noon-4 P.M.
COST: $5 adults, $2 children under 12
Map 1

Looking regal yet totally out of place with its minarets, keyhole arches, and ornate Moorish revival architecture, the Henry B. Plant Museum is housed in the dramatic hotel railroad baron Henry B. Plant built in 1891

ARTS AND LEISURE

COURTESY OF TAMPA BAY & CO

The Henry B. Plant Museum is housed in the south wing of Plant Hall, the former Tampa Bay Hotel.

at a cost of $2.5 million, with an additional $500,000 for furnishings. Its 511 rooms were the first in Florida to be outfitted with electricity. It operated as a hotel until 1930 and now houses the University of Tampa. The museum consists of opulent restored rooms with original furnishings that provide a window on America's Gilded Age, Tampa's history, and the life and work of Henry Plant. The best time to see it is at Christmastime, when the rooms are bedecked for the season with elaborately trimmed trees, lush greenery, antique toys, and Victorian-era ornaments.

HERITAGE VILLAGE
11909 125th St. N., Largo, 727/582-2123,
www.pinellascounty.org
HOURS: Tues.-Sat. 10 A.M.-4 P.M., Sun. 1-4 P.M.
COST: Free admission
Map 9

The history buff can visit the restored homes and buildings of Heritage Village. It's a living history kind of thing with people roaming around purposefully in period costume, spinning, weaving, and whatnot. Most of the 25 structures date back to the late 19th century. If you go to Heritage Village, make a day of it and visit the work-in-progress **Florida Botanical Gardens at Pinewood Cultural Park** nearby.

KID CITY
7550 North Blvd., Tampa, 813/935-8441,
www.flachildrensmuseum.com
HOURS: Wed. and Fri. 9:30 A.M.-2 P.M.,
Sat. 9:30 A.M.-4 P.M.
COST: $5
Map 5

Very young children will be suited to an afternoon at Kid City. In kind of a miniature outdoor city, it has 16 exhibit buildings with hands-on exhibits about different kinds of work (a firehouse, a bank, a grocery store, etc.) and their necessary skills. Find out what you should be when you grow up.

MOSI
4801 E. Fowler Ave., Tampa, 813/987-6300,
www.mosi.org
HOURS: Mon.-Fri. 9 A.M.-5 P.M.,
Sat. and Sun. 9 A.M.-6 P.M.
COST: $20.95 adults, $18.95 seniors,
$16.95 children 2-12
Map 4

Tampa's Museum of Science & Industry is a wonderful resource for local schools, family vacationers, or local parents when they're just out of bullets (not literally). It's a sprawling modern structure that contains 450 hands-on activities grouped into learning areas. There's some goofy stuff (the Gulf Coast Hurricane Chamber, which really just blows a bunch of loud air), but ignore that and head to the High Wire Bicycle, the longest high-wire bike in a museum, which allows visitors to pedal while balanced on a one-inch steel cable suspended 30 feet above ground. The exhibit The Amazing You teaches all about the human body. The museum has an IMAX dome and hosts traveling exhibits as well. The center hosted a compelling *Titanic* exhibit that actually mirrored

COURTESY OF ST. PETERSBURG/CLEARWATER AREA CVB

The Museum of Fine Arts in St. Petersburg, widely recognized for its varied collection, including an impressive array of French Impressionist works, opened a new wing in February 2008.

the experience of riding the ship (you assume the identity of a passenger and then find out if you lived or died), and currently has a lovely exhibit called *MAGIC: The Science of Illusion* designed around four main magical illusions. Through interactive exhibits, film, and immersion experiences, guests explore the principles of simple mechanics, optics, electromagnetism, math, and psychology.

If you time your visit to allow some cooler temperatures, the free-flying butterfly garden is a treat, with microscope viewing, magnifying glasses, and chemistry stations.

MUSEUM OF FINE ARTS

255 Beach Dr. NE, St. Petersburg, 727/896-2667, www.fine-arts.org

HOURS: Tues.-Sat. 10 A.M.-5 P.M., Sun. 1-5 P.M.

COST: $8 adults, $7 seniors and students, $4 kids 7-18, free for children 6 and under

Map 6

Near the beginning of 2008, the Museum of Fine Arts unveiled its much-anticipated Hazel Hough Wing. It started with a gangbuster exhibition of works that have been rarely on view or in some cases, never before displayed at the MFA. Featuring works by such noted artists as Renoir, Leger, Pissarro, Matisse, Faberge, Chuck Close, and James Rosenquist, it showcased just how marvelous the museum's collection is. Right on the waterfront adjacent to Straub Park, the museum contains the full gamut of art from antiquity to the present day. The collection of 4,000 objects includes significant works by Cézanne, Monet, Gauguin, Renoir, Rodin, Henri, Bellows, and O'Keeffe. Its permanent collection's strength is 17th- and 18th-century European art, and the museum has a lovely garden as well.

◀ SALVADOR DALÍ MUSEUM

1000 3rd St. S., St. Petersburg, 727/823-3767, www.salvadordalimuseum.org

HOURS: Mon.-Wed. and Sat. 9:30 A.M.-5:30 P.M., Thurs. until 8 P.M., Fri. until 6:30 P.M., Sun. noon-5:30 P.M.

COST: $15 general, $13.50 seniors, $10 students, $4 children 5-9, free for children 4 and under

Map 6

Perhaps the most lauded art museum in Pinellas County, it's the world's most

ARTS AND LEISURE

comprehensive collection of permanent works by the famous Spanish surrealist master, with other exhibits relating to Dalí. The museum has a number of his important surrealist works, what he described as a "spontaneous method of irrational knowledge based on the critical and systematic objectivation of delirious associations and interpretations." Although he's identified strongly with the movement, in 1934 Dalí was formally expelled from the surrealist Group of Paris with a mock trial (some of the reason for his expulsion had to do with an unsavory enthusiasm for Adolf Hitler). But after he came to the U.S. (a trip paid for by Picasso), he embarked on his classical period, characterized by what he called nuclear mysticism.

The museum is wonderful—a great space, the work elegantly annotated and curated. What's not to love? Melting clocks, elephants with spiders' legs—I'll say one thing for him, no one's ever stood in front of his work and said, "Man, I coulda done that one."

ST. PETERSBURG MUSEUM OF HISTORY

335 2nd Ave. NE, St. Petersburg, 727/894-1052, www.spmoh.org
HOURS: Mon.-Sat. 10 A.M.-5 P.M.
COST: $12 general, $9 seniors and students, $7 children 7-17
Map 6

It is one of the oldest historical museums in the state, with family-friendly displays and exhibits depicting St. Petersburg's past. It had a recent remodel and enlargement, with a local history exhibit that contains a Native American dugout canoe, a cannonball fired by Union sailors at the home of a Confederate resident, an exact replica of the world's first scheduled commercial airliner (it flew out of St. Petersburg), and lots of other cool stuff. If it's still there, the visiting exhibit called *Royalty . . . Triumphs and Tragedies* is rich, displaying artifacts of Diana, Queen Elizabeth II, The Queen Mother, the Duke and Duchess of Windsor (King Edward VIII and Mrs. Wallace Simpson), Prince Charles, and other royals. Not sure what it has to do with St. Petersburg, but still nice.

TAMPA BAY AUTO MUSEUM

3301 Gateway Centre Blvd., Pinellas Park, 727/579-8226, www.tbauto.org
HOURS: Mon. and Wed.-Sat. 10 A.M.-4 P.M., Sun. noon-4 P.M.
COST: $8 adults, $5 seniors and students, free for children under six
Map 9

Opened in 2005, this 12,000-square-foot space showcases a unique collection of vintage cars and vehicles that demonstrate special creativity and imagination in their history and engineering. They include pioneering front-wheel-drive and rear-engine cars from the 1920s and 1930s, and each vehicle was chosen based on the engineering achievements that made it an important part of the evolution of the automobile.

TAMPA BAY HISTORY CENTER

Administrative Office 225 S. Franklin St., Tampa, 813/228-0097
Map 1

The Tampa Bay History Center's new 60,000-square-foot home in the Channelside district was Hillsborough County's $17 million effort to celebrate the Tampa Bay area's history in the larger context. The permanent exhibits explores 500 years of recorded history and 12,000 years of human habitation in the region. Native Americans and Spanish conquistadors, pioneer settlers and cigar workers, immigrants and cowboys, military and sports heroes all get their 15 minutes in the two floors of exhibit space and the lobby-level gallery and theater.

TAMPA MUSEUM OF ART

2306 North Howard Ave., Tampa, 813/274-8130, www.tampagov.net
HOURS: Tues.-Sat. 10 A.M.-5 P.M., Sun. 11 A.M.-5 P.M., the third Thurs. of the month until 8 P.M.
COST: $8 adults, $6 seniors, $3 students and children over six, children under six free
Map 1

You wouldn't think a midsized city art museum could spark so much controversy. And it's not the good kind of controversy: an exhibit of Robert Mapplethorpe's provocative photos, say, or Jeff Koons' Cicciolina sculptures or anything else that used to get Jesse Helms hot under the collar. For years, the Tampa Museum of Art has been poised to go somewhere and no one seems to agree on its destination. Several plans have been scrapped entirely, but in 2007 there was a breakthrough. Everyone agreed on a site: in Curtis Hixon Park, adjacent to the Poe Garage overlooking the Hillsborough River. And they agreed on an architect: Stanley Saitowitz from San Francisco. And they agreed on a plan: a 120,000-square-foot complex, with phase one consisting of 60,000 square feet.

The opening of the new facility is expected in fall 2009—but until construction is robustly underway art lovers and community leaders may be waiting for the other shoe to drop. Meanwhile, the Tampa Museum of Art continues doing what it does best in a temporary space, hosting changing exhibitions ranging from contemporary to classical, and elegantly showcasing its permanent collection of Greek and Roman antiquities, 20th- and 21st-century sculpture, paintings, photography, and works on paper.

TAMPA POLICE MUSEUM

411 N. Franklin St., Tampa, 813/276-3392,
www.tampabayhistorycenter.org
HOURS: Mon.-Fri. 10 A.M.-3 P.M.
COST: Free admission
Map 1

Located next to the Tampa Police Department headquarters, it's a sweet little museum that honors fallen officers and preserves historically important records, books, uniforms, guns, and other police equipment. It's especially poignant for visiting law enforcement folks, but kids of all stripes will enjoy the on-site police car, motorcycle, and helicopter.

UNIVERSITY OF SOUTH FLORIDA CONTEMPORARY ART MUSEUM

4202 E. Fowler Ave., Tampa, 813/974-2849,
www.usfcam.usf.edu
HOURS: Mon.-Fri. 10 A.M.-5 P.M., Sat. 1-4 P.M.
COST: Free admission
Map 4

University of South Florida is an enormous institution, casting its imposing shadow on the cultural scene of Tampa. The visitor, however, may have little reason to walk around the less-than-picturesque campus. A visit to the Contemporary is a good excuse to drive around the university before parking at the small gallery. USFCAM maintains the university's art collection, comprised of more than 5,000 art works. There are exceptional holdings in graphics and sculpture multiples by internationally acclaimed artists, such as Roy Lichtenstein, Robert Rauschenberg, and James Rosenquist, who have worked at USF's Graphicstudio. Contemporary photography and African art are also important areas of the collection. The museum also hosts USF student art shows and oversees sight-specific public art projects on campus.

YBOR CITY STATE MUSEUM

1818 E. 9th Ave., Ybor City, 813/247-6323.
www.ybormuseum.org
HOURS: Daily 9 A.M.-5 P.M.
COST: $3, free children six and under
Map 3

The Ybor City Museum State Park is a state historic park consisting of the Ybor City Museum, housed in the Ferlita Bakery building (a neighborhood bakery operated by the Ferlita family, Italian immigrants who established the business at that location in 1896), the casita (an old cigar worker home), and the garden. The park contains permanent exhibits on Vicente Martinez Ybor, the founding and early history of Ybor City, the cigar industry, the social clubs of the city, and the Ferlita Bakery itself. Watch a cigar-rolling demonstration (Fri.-Sun. 11 A.M.-1 P.M.). The Saturday 10:30 A.M. walking tour includes admission to the museum and casitas and is $6 on a first-come basis.

GALLERIES
THE ARTS CENTER

719 Central Ave., St. Petersburg, 727/822-7872,
www.theartscenter.org
HOURS: Tues.-Sat. 10 A.M.-5 P.M.
COST: Free admission
Map 6

A long-standing focus for work by area artists as well as many out-of-town names, sometimes international. Its 5,000-square-feet of gallery space is divided up into six small galleries, plus classroom space for ceramics, painting, drawing, digital imaging, photography, printmaking, jewelry-making, metalworking, and sculpture classes.

BAISDEN GALLERY

442 W. Grand Central Ave., No. 100, Tampa, 813/250-1511, www.baisdengallery.com
HOURS: Tues.-Thurs. noon-4 P.M., Fri. 11 A.M.-3 P.M., Sat. noon-4 P.M.
COST: Free admission
Map 2

Located right next to Mise en Place, one of the area's nicest restaurants, this 2,000-square-foot space features three galleries of rotating exhibits, focusing most strongly on influential contemporary glass art (Dale Chihuly and his increasing hoards of imitators) as well as contemporary paintings and photography.

BLEU ACIER

109 W. Columbus Dr., Tampa, 813/272-9746, www.bleuacier.com
HOURS: Sat. 1-5 P.M. and by appointment
COST: Free admission
Map 5

While Bleu Acier exhibits works in all media, it specializes in mid-career European artists and emerging American artists. Owner Erika Greenberg-Schneider has a special interest in intaglio, photogravure, lithography, photolithography, relief, and monotype, acting as a publisher to produce limited editions and multiples of artists' work.

CRAFTSMAN HOUSE

2955 Central Ave., St. Petersburg, 727/323-ARTS, www.craftsmanhousegallery.com
HOURS: Mon.-Sat. 10 A.M.-6 P.M., Sun. 11 A.M.-4 P.M.
COST: Free admission
Map 9

Set in a charming arts and crafts bungalow, the gallery features a selection of fine craft and artwork from over 150 national and local artisans in clay, blown glass, jewelry, and wooden handcrafted furniture. Visitors can observe artists

at work in the converted carriage house pottery studio, explore the garden art courtyard, or have a nibble in the café.

FINN GALLERY

176 4th Ave. NE, St. Petersburg, 727/894-2899, www.finngallery.com
HOURS: Mon.-Fri. 10 A.M.-6 P.M., Sat. 10 A.M.-5 P.M.
COST: Free admission
Map 6

Located along the waterfront near the Museum of Fine Arts, this gallery shows originals, reproductions, and limited editions of P. Buckley Moss as well as work by several other accomplished artists.

FLORIDA CRAFTSMEN GALLERY

501 Central Ave., St. Petersburg, 727/821-7391, www.floridacraftsmen.net
HOURS: Mon.-Sat. 10 A.M.-5:30 P.M.
COST: Free admission
Map 6

For the past 53 years, it's Florida's only statewide nonprofit organization representing thousands of Florida's established and emerging fine craft artists. The small gallery space hosts exhibitions, workshops, and educational programs, and is especially delightful around the winter holidays, with seasonal crafts of all kinds.

GALLERY AIA

200 N. Tampa St., Suite 100, Tampa, 813/229-3411, www.aiatampabay.com
HOURS: Mon.-Fri. 9 A.M.-5 P.M.
COST: Free admission
Map 1

The regional chapter of The American Institute of Architects exhibits work by local and regional architect/artists including photography, paintings, sculpture, and furniture. Its aim is to promote awareness, interest, and understanding of the architecture profession in the Bay Area; call to make sure an exhibit is going on.

GLASS CANVAS GALLERY AND CROATIAN NATIVE ART GALLERY

146 2nd St.. N., St. Petersburg, 727/821-6767
HOURS: Mon.-Sat. 10 A.M.-5 P.M.
COST: Free admission
Map 6

This contemporary gallery represents more than 350 glass artists from around the world. From sculptures, vases, perfumes, platters, paperweights to glass fish, all signed pieces are handcrafted and one-of-a-kind. The Croatian artists produce unusual original wall art of reverse oil paintings on glass.

NESTOR HAVERLY GALLERY

25 2nd St. N., St. Petersburg, 727/822-4800,
www.nestorhaverlygallery.com
HOURS: Wed.-Sat. 11 A.M.-5 P.M.
COST: Free admission
Map 6

The Nestor Haverly Gallery specializes in modern and contemporary paintings, drawings, and prints. Maura Haverly, director of the gallery, has been involved in the art world for many years. Director of the New York art fair, Art Expo, for some years, she was also a European director of Petersburg Galleries, based in London. Ms. Haverly has worked as a private dealer for the last few years, in Paris and in St. Petersburg, working with an international roster of private and public clients.

SCARFONE/HARTLEY GALLERIES AT UNIVERSITY OF TAMPA

310 N. Boulevard, Tampa, 813/253-6217,
www.utampa.edu
HOURS: Tues.-Fri. 10 A.M.-4 P.M., Sat. 1-4 P.M.
COST: Free admission
Map 1

A university teaching gallery, the Scarfone/ Hartley functions as an extension of the classroom in all media. The galleries provide an opportunity to meet artists and view and study original works created by contemporary national, international, and regional artists including students and faculty.

SECOND SATURDAY GALLERY WALK

Downtown St. Petersburg, 727/418-8887,
www.stpetearts.org
HOURS: Second Sat. of each month, 5:30 P.M.-9 P.M.
COST: Free admission
Map 6

St. Petersburg Downtown Arts Association, representing more than 30 art galleries and other downtown businesses, hosts a monthly event to give the public the chance to view art (sometimes first showings) after hours and meet with some of the artists.

THE STUDIO@620

620 1st Ave. S., St. Petersburg, 727/895-6620,
www.thestudioat620.com
HOURS: Vary by performance
COST: Varies by performance
Map 6

Brainchild of artistic directors David Ellis and Bob Devin Jones, this tiny yet ambitious space plays host to performance art, visual art exhibitions, theater, music and special events—some of the more avant-garde arts happenings in the Tampa Bay area. From spoken-word open-mike nights to socially-conscious documentary films, refugee youth photography exhibits, and shows of local printmakers, the city of St. Petersburg is that much more sophisticated for having 620 in its midst. It's small, but packs a punch.

THEATER

AMERICAN STAGE THEATRE

211 3rd St. S., St. Petersburg, 727/823-7529,
www.americanstage.org
HOURS: Curtain usually Tues-Thurs. 7:30 P.M., Fri. and Sat. 8 P.M., weekend matinees 3 P.M.
COST: Tickets $22-35
Map 6

At the top of the dramatic arts heap in Pinellas County, American Stage is Tampa Bay's oldest professional theater, with a six-play mainstage season, children's theater, educational outreach, and the annual Shakespeare in the Park festival.

In its 29th year in 2007, American Stage announced that it had entered into a partnership with St. Petersburg College to build a brand new state-of-the-art building in the heart of downtown St. Petersburg, facing Williams Park. The new **American Stage Theatre Company at the Raymond James Theatre** is expected to be completed by January 2009.

The mainstage season shows breadth, reaching from August Wilson's *Gem of the Ocean*, to the classic whodunit *Sleuth*, and Shakespeare's greatest tragedy, *Hamlet*. The Family Series is a good deal, with single tickets $7. Until the new theater opens, American Stage productions are performed at the midsize, 800-seat **Palladium Theater** (253 5th Ave. N., St. Petersburg, 727/822-3590).

CATHERINE HICKMAN THEATER

5501 27th Ave. S., Gulfport, 727/893-1070
HOURS: Vary by performance
COST: Varies by performance
Map 7

In the little town of Gulfport on Boca Ciega Bay, the fairly new 178-seat Catherine Hickman Theater, owned by the city of Gulfport, hosts Gulfport Community Players community theater productions and Pinellas Park Civic Orchestra concerts. While the theater is not gorgeous to look at from the outside, it's an intimate size with sloped flooring for better viewing and an interior courtyard that's a lovely place to while away intermission.

DAVID FALK THEATRE

428 W. Kennedy Blvd., Tampa, 813/253-6243
HOURS: Vary by performance
COST: $17-30
Map 1

Student theatrical productions take place in a fully-equipped, 1,000-seat theater built in 1928. There is no seniority; freshmen are allowed to audition for all productions in their first semester, so there's no telling what might happen. For instance: a Jane Austen musical.

FRANCIS WILSON PLAYHOUSE

302 Seminole St., Clearwater, 727/446-1360,
www.franciswilsonplayhouse.org
HOURS: Curtain 8 P.M. and matinees 2 P.M.
COST: Musicals $18, nonmusicals $14
Map 8

Francis Wilson Playhouse is a more venerable community playhouse, having opened in 1930. The intimate, 182-seat theater showcases eight comedies and musicals *(Sweet Charity, Auntie Mame)* per season and a family-oriented program in December.

MAHAFFEY THEATER AT THE PROGRESS ENERGY CENTER

400 1st St. S., St. Petersburg, 727/892-5767,
www.mahaffeytheater.com
HOURS: Vary by performance
COST: Vary by performance
Map 6

The Mahaffey changed entirely in 2004 when it was determined that its Bayfront Center Arena was no longer viable in the marketplace. The arena was demolished at the end of that year, opening up space for the current Mahaffey Theater renovation. The $20 million project more than doubled lobby size, adding guest amenities and expanding ballroom capacity and versatility. The signature component of the renovated theater is a three-story glass curtain wall and glass enclosed atrium that overlooks the city's beautiful downtown waterfront. A lovely theater, it hosts the Broadway Across America Series, many performances of the Florida Orchestra, jazz, ballet, opera, the circus, and contemporary performers as well. The Mahaffey is directly on the waterfront, within walking distance of shopping, some of the area's finest restaurants, and many of the downtown's museums.

THE PALLADIUM

253 5th Ave., N., St. Petersburg, 727/822-3590,
www.mypalladium.org
HOURS: Vary by performance
COST: Varies by performance
Map 6

Located in what once was a church built in 1925 in the Romanesque revival style and now providing a range of community theater offerings, it's under the umbrella of St. Petersburg College. It hosts college functions but also acts as a community theater, with St. Petersburg Opera Company and other local performing arts agencies using the space. It's also used for musical acts from rock to jazz, chamber music to cabaret. No reserved seating.

COURTESY OF TAMPA BAY & CO

The Tampa Bay Performing Arts Center is located downtown, on a nine-acre site along the east bank of the Hillsborough River.

RUTH ECKERD HALL

1111 McMullen Booth Rd. N., Clearwater, 727/791-7000, www.rutheckerdhall.com

HOURS: Vary by performance
COST: Vary by performance
Map 8

Ruth Eckerd Hall is the locus for much of the area's lively arts activity. The 2,200-seat space was designed by the Frank Lloyd Wright Foundation 25 years ago and the space still looks fresh, the sound still full and lush (acoustically, it had a fairly recent overhaul). It's home to the **Florida Orchestra** (mailing address 244 2nd Ave. N., #421, St. Petersburg, FL 33701, 813/286-2403), which is the top regional orchestra, performing more than 130 concerts annually here, at the Mahaffey Theater, and elsewhere. Beyond symphonic music, Ruth Eckerd hosts pop acts, visiting theater, and other performing arts. (Its educational wing, the Marcia P. Hoffman Performing Arts Institute, features a 182-seat Murray Studio Theatre, three studio classrooms, four private teaching studios, a dance studio and rehearsal space, and an arts resource library.)

ST. PETERSBURG LITTLE THEATRE

4025 31st St. S., St. Petersburg, 727/866-1973, www.splt.info

HOURS: Curtain 8 P.M. and matinees 2 P.M.
COST: $20 Musicals, $18 nonmusicals, $10 students
Map 7

Throughout its 83 years as Florida's oldest continuously operating community theater, St. Petersburg Little Theatre has presented up to six community productions per season, split fairly evenly between musicals, comedies, and dramas. It's usually crowd-pleasers like *Noises Off* or Neil Simon's *Brighton Beach Memoirs*.

TAMPA BAY PERFORMING ARTS CENTER

1010 N. W.C. MacInnes Pl., Tampa, 813/229-7827 or 800/955-1045, www.tbpac.org

HOURS: Vary by performance
COST: Varies by performance
Map 1

Just about the only game in town for performing arts, it's a huge arts complex housing four distinct theaters, in which audiences can see Opera Tampa (the resident company), the Florida Orchestra, comedies, dramas, cabaret, dance,

ARTS AND LEISURE

music, alternative theater, children's theater, and an annual Broadway series. Most local arts series and events find a home at the performing arts center—Arte 2005, Tampa Bay's Festival of Latin American art, Patel Conservatory's Tampa Bay Youth Orchestra Spring Concert—you name it, the curtain goes up here.

CONCERT VENUES

Tampa Bay Performing Arts Center, Mahaffey Theater at the Progress Energy Center, and **Ruth Eckerd Hall,** listed in the *Theater* section, are all regular hosts to touring national and regional musical acts. **Tampa Theatre,** listed in Cinema, and **St. Pete Times Forum,** listed in Spectator Sports, also host concerts. Consult their websites or Ticketmaster.com for a list of upcoming shows.

COLISEUM
535 4th Ave. N., St. Petersburg, 727/892-5202
HOURS: Vary by performance
COST: Varies by performance; $4 parking area on left
Map 6

The historic Coliseum was built in 1924 and purchased by the city of St. Petersburg in 1989. They've gussied up the gorgeous space and reopened it as a multiuse facility, hosting a range of things from Florida Orchestra pops concerts to the Toronto All Star Big Band to an exotic bird show.

FORD AMPHITHEATRE
4802 U.S. 301 N., Tampa, 813/740-2446,
www.livenation.com
HOURS: Vary by performance
COST: Varies by performance
Map 5

A few years ago, Tampa welcomed the Ford Amphitheatre, a state-of-the-art venue for 30–40 big-league music concerts a year. At an expense of $23 million, the outdoor open-air theater was constructed with huge video screens, a 7,200-square-foot stage, 9,900 reserved seats, and room for 10,500 more on the lawn (to which, shortly afterward, big space-age sound shields were erected to the relief of the neighbors). It's gorgeous, like a huge circus

tent mated with the *Millennium Falcon.* There are enough bathrooms and lots of fairly tasty food options.

But I'm leading up to a big gripe, and it's not really the amphitheater's fault. The idea was that it would host the myriad big-ticket acts that travel around the U.S. each year—Dave Matthews, Tim McGraw, or all those endless tours of Chicago or Earth, Wind and Fire. That's all fine and good, but the problem is that all those big acts gear up to do outdoor stadium and amphitheater shows in *the summer.* You do not want to go to an all-day Oz Fest show in Tampa in the middle of July. You could hurt something. The venue literature sports all this talk about how the plastic cover on top shields the amphitheater from the sun and keeps it cool. No dice. Get 10,000 sweaty bodies grooving to Jimmy Buffet in 90°F heat at 90 percent humidity, and someone's going to pass out.

USF SUN DOME
4202 E. Fowler Ave., 800/462-8557
HOURS: Vary by performance
COST: Varies by performance
Map 5

This 55,000-square-foot multipurpose entertainment/sports facility on the campus of the University of South Florida hosts 300 events each year, many of them USF Bulls men's and women's basketball and volleyball teams, but also lectures and political rallies (I saw Desmond Tutu and John Kerry, not on the same bill, both somewhat underattended), rock concerts, tae kwon do tournaments, garden shows, wrestling, and more.

CINEMA
AMC VETERANS 24
9302 Anderson Rd., Tampa, 813/243-4955,
www.amctheatres.com
HOURS: Vary by show
COST: Tickets $6-9.50
Map 5

Most AMC Theater locations feature mainstream first-run movies served up in clean multiplexes with acceptable popcorn. The

Veterans location tends to show more cerebral, art-house movies. For more mainstream film options try AMC's other locations at **AMC Westshore Plaza** (210 Westshore Plaza, Tampa, 813/243-4955) and **AMC Tri-City Plaza 8** (5140 East Bay Dr., Clearwater, 727/531-2882). Tickets can be purchased in advance via AMC's website.

BEACH THEATRE
315 Corey Ave., St. Pete Beach, 727/360-6697, www.beachtheatre.com
HOURS: Vary by show
COST: Varies by show
Map 7

The St. Pete Beach Theatre is a historic landmark built in 1939 for about $50,000 by Boston financier Stephen Girard. Since then, it's operated continuously under a succession of owners (except briefly when German U-boats were spotted off the coast and a blackout was ordered that shut down the theater for about 18 months). Now it's owned by screenwriter Michael France and hosts an opera series, lectures, art-house movies, mainstream first-run flicks, and films about music (with an appropriate accompanying band).

CHANNELSIDE CINEMAS & IMAX
615 Channelside Dr., Tampa, 813/221-0700, www.channelsidetampa.com
HOURS: Vary by show
COST: Tickets $6-9.50
Map 1

Located next to Florida Aquarium in the portside shopping/dining complex of Channelside, it's a big, mainstream multiplex with the area's only 3-D IMAX screen.

MUVICO THEATERS
Muvico Centro Ybor 20, 1600 E. 8th Ave., Tampa, 813/242-0664, www.muvico.com
HOURS: Vary by show
COST: $9 adults, $7 seniors, $6 children, $7 matinees
Map 3

Muvico Theaters offer mainstream first-run movies served up in clean multiplexes with acceptable popcorn. Tickets can be purchased

in advance via the website. Other locations include the **Starlight 20** (18002 Highwood Preserve Pkwy., Tampa, 813/558-9755), and the **BayWalk 20 and IMAX** (151 2nd Ave. N., St. Petersburg, 727/502-0965).

TAMPA PITCHER SHOW AND THE TAKE 2 LOUNGE
14416 N. Dale Mabry Hwy., Tampa, 813/963-0578, www.tampapitchershow.net
HOURS: Vary by show
COST: $7 adults, $6 children
Map 5

The idea is superb. Eat real food—as opposed to Milk Duds and Jordan Almonds, although I may be the only person I know who actually likes those babies—in the dark while watching a first-run movie. With beer and wine. It's like what we do at home but with a few improvements: a) you don't have to shop, prepare, serve, or clean up the food, and b) the screen is much bigger. Still, the Tampa Pitcher Show has logistical problems. First off, if you're seated at a normal round or square table, someone is facing away from the screen. You have to sit in a line, but then the table isn't equally accessible for all. Really, you need those individual TV trays to make it all work. Second, you know how when you spill your M&Ms the whole floor at the movies is filled with a satisfying pinging noise and then a little crunchiness underfoot? Doesn't work as well with steak or mashed potatoes. The 26-year-old cinema was on the brink of closure, but has been newly renovated and an upscale lounge with full liquor and dining service added.

TAMPA THEATRE
711 Franklin St., Tampa, 813/274-8981, www.tampatheatre.org
HOURS: Vary by show
COST: $8 movies
Map 1

Tampa has its share of multiplexes, but eschew the 20-screeners in favor of two hours in the dark at the Tampa Theatre. Built in 1926, it's a beloved downtown landmark with an acclaimed film series, concerts (Gordon

COURTESY OF TAMPA BAY & CO

The Tampa Theatre is a restored gem showing modern independent and classic films with pre-show Wurlitzer organ concerts.

Lightfoot, Keb Mo, Bright Eyes—it's a wide range), special events, and backstage tours. They say the grand motion picture palace's decor is something called Florida Mediterranean, but to me it's vintage creepy rococo, with statues and gargoyles and intricately carved doors. Speaking of creepiness, many believe that the theater is haunted by the ghost of Foster Finley, who spent 20 years as the theater's projectionist. So if you feel a hand in your popcorn, it may not be your seatmate's. Sometimes the films shown are classics, complete with Wurlitzer, other times it's more indie; look online at the schedule. Theater concessions include excellent popcorn, sophisticated candies, and beer and wine. Interesting fact: It was the first public building in Tampa to be equipped with air-conditioning.

Festivals and Events

WINTER
GASPARILLA FILM FESTIVAL
Ybor City , 813/514-9962,
www.gasparillafilmfestival.com
Map 2

In in the past few years there's been "reel" big news in February with the launch of the Gasparilla Film Festival in 2006. Tampa's always had its share of wonderful, smaller film festivals—Tampa International Gay and Lesbian Film Festival in October, the Independent Film Festival in September, even the Ybor Festival of the Moving Image—but Tampa remained the largest city in the country without a big annual film festival. The new festival takes place the end of February at venues in and around Ybor City. Over five days more than 40 films are screened in a variety of genres—what they are calling Latin Panorama (films with a Latin twist), New Horizons (films that directly focus on the arts), Fun and Fear (a mix of comedies and horrors), short films, and special screenings of featured American indie films. Then spice it all up with a handful of industry panel discussions, VIP parties, glamorous dinners, and celebrity sightings. For the festival schedule, visit the festival's website.

GASPARILLA PIRATE FEST
Ybor City and Downtown Tampa,
www.gasparillapiratefest.com
Map 1

The biggest party in Tampa comes at the beginning of February with the Gasparilla Pirate Fest, a kooky celebration over 100 years old in honor of legendary pirate José Gaspar, "last of the Buccaneers," who terrorized the coastal waters of West Florida during the late 18th and early 19th centuries. The weekend festivities get underway when 1,000 ersatz pirates sail into downtown on a fully rigged pirate ship, a replica of an 18th-century craft that is 165 feet long by 35 feet across the beam, with three masts standing 100 feet tall. The ship is met by a flotilla of hundreds of pleasure crafts intent on "defending the city." The upshot is that pirates take over Tampa for a while, like Mardi Gras, only with more "argh, me matey" and eye patches accompanying the beads and buried treasure. The length of Bayshore Boulevard is lined with bleachers for the occasion, musical acts sprout on stages all over town, and there's general merriment and carousing.

HOLIDAY BOAT PARADE
Downtown St. Petersburg
727/821-6443
Map 9

The first weekend each December boats from around Pinellas put on the dog. Come out to the North Straub Park, Vinoy Park, or the Pier for a view of this annual illuminated festival which travels from Harborage Marina, through Bayboro Harbor and on to the Vinoy Yacht Basin. Live music and broadcasts by a local radio station accompany the parade.

FLORIDA STATE FAIR
4800 U.S. 301 N., Tampa, 813/621-7821,
www.floridastatefair.com
Map 5

Also in mid-February is the Florida State Fair, a 12-day salute to the state's best in agriculture, industry, entertainment, and foods on a stick. It's been going strong since 1904, with more than 100 rides and shows spread across a 325-acre site. Recent additions include a ridiculously campy Las Vegas-style review, deep-fried fudge and something called a walking taco (um, really nacho chips in a bag with all the gunk tossed in), and an interactive livestock show called "Ag Venture." That's all fine and good, but the real draw is the nostalgic feel of 4-H youngsters showing off their prized chickens and such, or maybe the Elvis impersonation contest.

FLORIDA STRAWBERRY FESTIVAL
2202 West Reynolds St., Plant City, 813/752-9194,
www.flstrawberryfestival.com
February is a busy month, also holding the

ARTS AND LEISURE

COURTESY OF TAMPA BAY & CO

Thousands of paradegoers line Bayshore Boulevard for the annual Gasparilla Pirate Fest.

county fair–like Florida Strawberry Festival, with a huge midway, national country acts, and lots of strawberry cookoffs. Plant City is known as the "Winter Strawberry Capital of the World," and these sweet babies are delicious. More than 5,000 acres of strawberries are planted annually. With an annual value of over $400 million, Hillsborough county is one of the largest agricultural counties in the nation, producing—beyond strawberries—citrus, tomatoes, cucumbers, eggplant, squash, okra, peppers, beans, dairy products, eggs, ornamental horticulture, tropical fish, beef cattle, swine, and more.)

SPRING
AIRFEST AT MACDILL AIR FORCE BASE
8415 Bayshore Blvd., 813/828-3866
Map 5

One of the largest air shows in the Department of Defense, AirFest, usually held mid-April, features the U.S. Air Force Air Demonstration Squadron (the Thunderbirds) performing aerial maneuvers in their F-16 Fighting Falcons.

BAY AREA RENAISSANCE FESTIVAL
Central Park, Largo, 727/586-5423
Map 9

Jugglers, jousters, sorcerers, ladies with their boobs pushed up precariously in their bodices, and turkey legs, lots of turkey legs. Mid-March to mid-April, the annual Renaissance fair gives people ample time to dress like goofballs before hot weather sets in.

GRAND PRIX OF ST. PETERSBURG
Downtown St. Petersburg, 888/34-SPEED, www.gpstpete.com
Map 6

At the end of March, beginning of April, live concerts, family events, and a variety of sports exhibitions complement this race-car road race through the streets of St. Petersburg.

MAINSAIL ARTS FESTIVAL
North Straub Park, downtown St. Petersburg, 727/892-5885
Map 6

Along the waterfront of downtown St. Petersburg, one of the most respected arts festivals in the country is held towards the end of April, with participants from all over the country exhibiting their work.

SUMMER
TASTE OF PINELLAS
Vinoy Park, St. Petersburg, 727/892-4193
Map 6

During the first weekend in June, Vinoy Park in downtown St. Petersburg is filled with the county's best food vendors, national and regional music, arts, artists, and craftspeople representing the best in Pinellas County. The annual event benefits All Children's Hospital.

FALL
CLEARWATER JAZZ HOLIDAY
Coachman Park, Clearwater, 727/461-5200, www.clearwaterjazz.com
Map 8

Each year more than 50,000 visitors come to Coachman Park in downtown Clearwater during the third week of October to enjoy four days and nights of free jazz by some of today's greats. Now in its 30th year, the festival started as a 10-day music jam held in the back of a flatbed truck.

GUAVAWEEN
Yobr City, www.cc-events.org/gw
`Map 3`

Tampa's second biggest party is not unlike Gasparilla for its focus on wild costumes and wilder revelry. Guavaween is the city's Cuban-style Halloween celebration, held around October 30. Riffing on the fact that Tampa was nicknamed "The Big Guava," the celebration features the Mama Guava, who has sworn to take the "bore" out of Ybor (EE-bore) City.

Really, after the parade is over, it's a big excuse to drink too much and wander the streets of Ybor City in preposterous attire.

STONE CRAB FESTIVAL
Frenchy's Restaurants, Clearwater, frenchysonline.com
`Map 8`

Stone crab season opens mid-October, celebrated each year with a Stone Crab weekend in which visitors and locals plow through 10,000 pounds of claws (you eat only one of each beast's claws because fisherfolk haul 'em up, yank off one claw, and throw them back to grow another). Eat them like the locals, chilled (it's gauche to ask for them hot) with mustard sauce.

Shops

SHOPPING MALLS AND CENTERS

BAYWALK
125 2nd Ave. N., St. Petersburg, 727/895-9277, www.yourbaywalk.com
HOURS: Vary by store
`Map 6`

Baywalk is the upscale tourists' shopping destination in St. Petersburg. It's right downtown, with an indoor-outdoor array of shops (some independents, some like Ann Taylor and Chico's), fairly fancy restaurants with a number of cuisines represented, and outdoor entertainment on the Mainstage. It also has a 20-screen movie theater—stop in before or after at Grill 121 for a decent martini.

BEACH DRIVE NORTHEAST
Along the city's waterfront on Beach Dr., from Central Ave. to 5th St. N., St. Petersburg
HOURS: Vary by store
`Map 6`

The area across from the Museum of Fine Arts offers a scenic view of the bay with a side order of trendy boutiques and shops. They are located almost exclusively along the west side of the street, then wrap around slightly onto

each avenue. A must is a stop into Paciugo (pa-CHU-go) for fortifying gelato.

CHANNELSIDE BAY PLAZA
615 Channelside Dr., Tampa, www.channelsidetampa.com
HOURS: Vary by store
`Map 1`

The recent-vintage entertainment center on Tampa's downtown waterfront adjacent to the Florida Aquarium and the cruise terminal, has just a few stores worth investigating—a wine shop, Antonio's Cigars, Qachbal's Chocolatier, Wine Design Wine Shop, Sports City sportswear, and a couple of galleries.

◖ INTERNATIONAL PLAZA
2223 N. West Shore Blvd., 813/342-3790, www.shopinternationalplaza.com
HOURS: Mon.-Sat. 10 A.M.-9 P.M., Sun. noon-6 P.M.
`Map 5`

With anchor stores Neiman Marcus and Nordstrom, International Plaza, opened in 2001, gets the nod for fanciest shopping. A handful of usual mall stores (J. Crew, Banana Republic, Ann Taylor) are spiffed up by their proximity to 200 other specialty shops like Tiffany &

International Plaza in Tampa

COURTESY OF INTERNATIONAL PLAZA

Co., Jos. A. Bank, Louis Vuitton, Montblanc, Gucci, and Coach. Really, it's the poshest assembly of stores in any shopping center on the Gulf Coast, served by an open-air village of restaurants called Bay Street, all in a location minutes from the airport and downtown. The Christmas decorations in the Neiman Marcus store alone are worth the drive.

JOHN'S PASS VILLAGE AND BOARDWALK

150 John's Pass Boardwalk, Madeira Beach, 727/393-8230, www.johnspass.com
HOURS: Vary by store
Map 9

A catch-all, part touristy shopping/dining destination, and part locus of fishing activity. This is where to hook up with the local fishing fleet, cruise lines, boat rentals, parasailing, and Jet Skiing. But it's also nice for a stroll and a little window shopping along the giftware, resortwear, swimsuit stores, and galleries clustered together. More than 100 merchants have set up shop here, most geared toward visitors.

OLD HYDE PARK VILLAGE

West Swann Ave., South Dakota Ave., and Snow Ave., Tampa, 813/251-3500
HOURS: Vary by store
Map 2

The outdoor shopping area along Hyde Park's West Swann Avenue, South Dakota Avenue, and Snow Avenue is the most appealing shopping destination in town, especially when the weather's nice. There's a large covered parking lot, free to shoppers, and a lovely landscaped plaza at the center. Pottery Barn and Williams-Sonoma are among the bigger stores, with Ann Taylor, Brooks Brothers, Anthropologie, Talbots, and Tommy Bahama.

PRIME OUTLETS

5461 Factory Shops Blvd., Ellenton, 941/723-1150
HOURS: Mon.-Sat. 10 A.M.-9 P.M., Sun. noon-6 P.M.
Map 9

If you want to roll up your sleeves and get serious about retail, you need to drive south on I-75 for 40 minutes until you reach the Prime Outlets in Ellenton north of Bradenton. There,

ARTS AND LEISURE

Prime Outlets offer outlet shopping in a relaxing atmosphere.

you'll find 175 stores like Bose, Ann Taylor, Nine West, Samsonite, DKNY, Black & Decker, Villeroy & Boch, Nike, Sak's Off Fifth, Wilson Leather, Polo Ralph Lauren, and Waterford/Wedgewood—all offering deep, deep discounts. It's an outdoor shopping center, with enough variety and decent food concessions to make for a pleasant full day of shopping.

THE PIER

800 2nd Ave. NE, St. Petersburg, 727/821-6443, www.stpetepier.com

HOURS: Mon.-Thurs. 10 A.M.-9 P.M., Fri. and Sat. 10 A.M.-10 P.M., Sun. 11 A.M.-7 P.M.

Map 6

The Pier is really the heart and soul of visitor activity in St. Petersburg, looking like an inverted pyramid, or the good guys' home base in a sci-fi movie. You can rent bikes, grab a rental rod and reel and fish off the end, depart from the Pier on a sightseeing boat charter, see a flick at the 20-screen movie theater, visit the little aquarium, dine in the family-friendly food court, or browse the complex's many shops. It's not high-end stuff,

more touristy—there's a pet accouterment store, a entertainment-celebrity collectibles shop, candle store, T-shirt stores, that kind of thing.

TYRONE SQUARE MALL

6901 Tyrone Square, St. Petersburg, 727/347-3889, www.simon.com

HOURS: Mon.-Sat. 11 A.M.-9 P.M., Sun. 11 A.M.-7 P.M.

Map 9

It's a standard-issue 170-store indoor mall, mostly geared toward serving the local community. Dillards, JC Penney, Sears, and Macy's are the anchors, with all the familiar filler stores (Sunglass Hut, Brookstone, Hollister, Jos. A. Bank). The food court has some adequate contenders.

UNIVERSITY MALL

2200 E. Fowler Ave., Tampa, 813/971-3465, www.universitymalltampa.com

HOURS: Mon.-Sat. 10 A.M.-9 P.M., Sun. noon-6 P.M.

Map 4

Located across the street from USF (in fact, USF holds some of its large lecture classes here

ARTS AND LEISURE

in the movie theater; no word on whether you can order popcorn), University Mall is a garden-variety indoor shopping center, not very well maintained, with sullen teenagers talking on cell phones, mostly familiar mall stores, a 16-screen movie theater, and a fairly decent food court.

WESTFIELD SHOPPING TOWN
8021 Citrus Park Town Center, Citrus Park, 813/926-4644
HOURS: Mon.-Sat. 10 A.M.-9 P.M., Sun. noon-6 P.M.
Map 5

Westfield Malls dot the Florida landscape, most of them pleasant indoor shopping centers with the full gamut (Abercrombie to Zales) of small shops and anchors, mostly serving the local community. Fairly far from where most visitors stay, the Citrus Park location is a nice example of the breed, with a 20-screen Regal Cinema and a BJ's Restaurant and Brewhouse which proffers decent salads, pizzas, and house beers.

WESTSHORE PLAZA
250 Westshore Plaza, Tampa, 813/286-0790, www.westshoreplaza.com
HOURS: Mon.-Sat. 10 A.M.-9 P.M., Sun. noon-6 P.M.
Map 5

About a minute from International Plaza, Westshore features more than 100 similarly fancy specialty shops and four major department stores, including a lovely Saks Fifth Avenue. It contains a 14-screen AMC Theater and restaurants like Maggiano's Little Italy, P.F. Chang's, and The Palm.

YBOR CITY
7th and 8th avenues, between 14th and 22nd streets
HOURS: Vary by store
Map 3

Shopping along 7th Avenue in Ybor City, Tampa's Latin quarter, will yield some interesting finds. It's a little gritty, with a few vintage clothing shops, a fair amount of racy lingerie, GBX Fashion Shoes, and a funky Urban Outfitters. It's where to go if you get a hankering for a tattoo or piercing.

ANTIQUES
CENTRAL AVENUE ANTIQUE MARKETPLACE
2541 Central Ave., St. Petersburg, 727/321-1576, www.centralavenueantiques.com
HOURS: Mon.-Sat 10 A.M.-6 P.M., Sun. 11 A.M.-5 P.M.
Map 6

A 3,000-square-foot showcase for a wide spectrum of antiques, from art and furnishings to jewelry and pottery. In January and October, it hosts three-day Sunshine City Antiques & Collectibles Shows.

GAS PLANT ANTIQUE ARCADE
1246 Central Ave., St. Petersburg, 727/895-0368
HOURS: Mon.-Fri. 10 A.M.-5 P.M., Sat. 10 A.M.-6 P.M., Sun. noon-4 P.M.
Map 6

Some say it's the largest antiques mall on the Gulf Coast. Not sure about that, but it's four floors arrayed with the wares of 100 dealers. It features American and European antiques and collectibles and worldwide shipping is available.

PATTY & FRIENDS ANTIQUE MALL
1225 9th St. N., St. Petersburg, 727/821-2106, www.pattyandfriends.com
HOURS: Daily 10 A.M.-5 P.M.
Map 6

Fine, Gas Plant can be the largest, but Patty & Friends is the oldest in the state. Really an association representing 60 dealers, it's located near a number of other local antiques outposts. Furniture, silver, porcelain, pottery, and collectibles are packed into two remodeled houses. The shop also accepts consignment and Internet sales.

BOOKSTORES
HASLAM'S BOOK STORE
2025 Central Ave., St. Petersburg, 727/822-8616, www.haslams.com
HOURS: Mon.-Sat. 10 A.M.-6:30 P.M.
Map 6

Florida's largest new and used bookstore merits a couple of hours of browsing, especially if the weather is inclement (a rarity). Haslam's Book Store is now owned by the third generation of

COURTESY OF VISIT FLORIDA

Tampa has antique shopping aplenty.

the same family, with more than 300,000 volumes. In a world populated increasingly by Borders and Barnes & Noble (hey, I'm a frequenter of both), it's refreshing sometimes to hang out in an independently owned bookstore. Haslam's has a large number of rare books, and they seem to be really into science fiction.

INKWOOD BOOKS

216 S. Armenia Ave., Tampa, 813/253-2638, www.inkwoodbooks.com
HOURS: Mon.-Fri. 10 A.M.-7 P.M., Thurs. until 9 P.M., Sat. until 6 P.M., Sun. 1-5 P.M.
Map 2

Tampa has its share of mainstream bookstores, but Inkwood is the city's only independent bookstore. The two women who own it are a wealth of information on fiction, children's, biography, poetry, cookbooks, and Floridiana books, and whiling away an afternoon or evening in the little 1920s bungalow is a real treat. There's an extensive schedule of readings and book club events.

ZBOOKZ NEW & USED BOOKS

7901 46th Ave. N., St. Petersburg, 727/698-4669, www.zbookz.com
Map 9

Started in 1984, it's now more primarily an online resource for rare volumes. But there's a brick-and-mortar store too, with a fireplace and a comfy reading room. With 2,000–3,000 new titles at any time, it's still most impressive as a used bookstore. The SparkleSpot bead shop is also on-site.

SPECIALTY STORES
DOWNTOWN DOGS

1604 W. Snow Ave., Tampa, 813/250-3647, www.shopdowntowndogs.com
HOURS: Mon.-Sat. 10 A.M.-7 P.M., Sun. noon-5 P.M.
Map 2

Located in the posh Old Hyde Park Village area, Downtown Dogs is devoted to carrying only the most coveted, hard-to-find accessories (those so dear they verge on ridiculous) for your pooch on the planet. You can find an imaginative selection of lavish collars, leashes, apparel, bedding, and whimsical toys for the canine in your life.

KABLOOM OF ST. PETERSBURG

300 Beach Dr. NE, St. Petersburg, 727/362-1623
HOURS: Mon.-Sat. 9 A.M.-6 P.M.
Map 6

Kabloom has the kind of breathtaking bouquets that win you a place in anyone's heart. The teeny shop's real strong suit is the bold juxtaposition of different species of flowers; also funky giftware and tabletop accouterments. They deliver and do weddings.

MAISON ROUGE

300 Beach Dr. NE, Ste. 125, St. Petersburg, 727/898-8400
HOURS: Mon.-Thurs. 10 A.M.-8 P.M., Fri. and Sat. 10 A.M.-10 P.M., Sun. 10 A.M.-5 P.M.
Map 6

This is the thinking woman's lingerie shop. Sure, plenty of little pink fripperies one might find at Victoria's place, but really luscious undergarments in lovely fabrics with superior workmanship can only be found at Maison Rouge.

ARTS AND LEISURE

Downtown Dogs' staff pooch will gladly help you make a selection.

COURTESY OF DOWNTOWN DOGS/RENE NEFF

MILAGROS
1104 Central Ave., St. Petersburg, 727/821-7555,
www.sisteragnes.com
HOURS: Mon.-Sat. 10 A.M.-6 P.M.
Map 6

Glycerin soaps are handmade daily by Sister

Agnes in whimsical and fragrant designs. In addition to candles, soaps, and bath salts, the funky shop imports Latin American religious art, *milagros,* and statuary.

Sports and Recreation

BEACHES
◖ CALADESI ISLAND
Directly to the south of Honeymoon Island, it is accessible only by boat, hourly ferry service available from Honeymoon, 727/469-5918
HOURS: 8 A.M.-sunset daily
COST: $9 adults, $5.50 children
Map 9

Of Honeymoon and Caladesi, Caladesi is the wilder of the two islands. There's the state park marina and swim beach right near where the ferry lets you off, but the rest of the island remains undeveloped. The Gulf side of the island

has three miles of white-sand beach (this is the part that always makes the top rankings of beaches), and the bay side has a mangrove shoreline and sea grass flats. So, Gulf side for swimming and beach lolling, the bay side for birding and wildlife watching. You'll see lots of beautiful creatures, but the most entertaining are the armadillos, which are so myopic as to walk right over your shoe if you're very still. Like a bunch of befuddled, yet armored, Mr. Magoos.

If you're a strong kayaker or sailor, there are kayak and sailboat rentals on the causeway near Honeymoon Island. Once on Caladesi,

Caladesi Island is one of the few undeveloped barrier islands left in the state.

there's a 3.5-mile canoe trail starting and ending at the south end of the marina that leads paddlers through mangrove canals and tunnels and along sea grass flats on the bay side of the island.

Two cautions about Caladesi: Don't miss the last ferry or you'll be in a real pickle. And if you have brought a dog over to the dog beach at Honeymoon, it's a shame but Caladesi doesn't allow pets on the ferry (if you go by private boat, pets are invited on leash).

CLEARWATER BEACH
West on Hwy. 60
HOURS: Year-round lifeguards daily 9:30 A.M.-4:30 P.M.
Map 8

When you conjure in your mind a Florida Gulf Coast beach, it's Clearwater you're imagining. These are textbook stretches of white sand and clear, warm Gulf water, with lots of comfy beachside hotels and waterside amenities for families. The area is home to a couple of world-class beach destinations, the kinds of places that often make Dr. Stephen Leatherman's

("Dr. Beach" has been ranking America's beaches for 12 years) annual top-10 list.

A fairly urban city beach, Clearwater Beach, the only Pinellas County beach with year-round lifeguards, is a long, wide stretch offering showers, restrooms, concessions, cabanas, umbrella rentals, volleyball, and metered parking. **Pier 60,** where the beach meets the causeway, is the locus of lots of local revelry and activity—during the day it's a heavily trafficked fishing pier, while at night the focus is Sunsets at Pier 60, a festival that runs nightly two hours before sunset to two hours past sunset, with crafts, magicians, and musicians all vying for your attention with the ostentatious sunset display over the Gulf of Mexico. Pier 60 also contains a covered playground for the little ones, who will also like catching the bright red Jolley Trolley ($1.25 to ride) from Clearwater Beach and heading back to your hotel, downtown, or to Sand Key.

Clearwater Beach has a few rules to follow: No alcohol on the beach. Swim within the "safe bathing limit" area, extending 300 feet west of the high water line and clearly marked by buoys or pilings. Jet Skis and boats are not allowed within this line. Clearwater Beach is a good beach if you just have a couple of hours to spend; many of the area's other best beaches require more of a commitment and are more of a full-day adventure.

EGMONT KEY STATE PARK
At the mouth of Tampa Bay, southwest of Fort de Soto Beach, St. Petersburg, 727/893-2627, www.floridastateparks.org
HOURS: Daily 8 A.M.-sundown
COST: Free admission
Map 9

Accessible only by ferry or private boat, Egmont Key State Wildlife Preserve makes a great day trip. There aren't a lot of facilities on the island, which is wild except for the ruins of historic Fort Dade and brick paths that remain from when it was an active community with 300 residents. You'll see the 150-year-old working lighthouse (constructed in 1858 to "withstand any storm" after a first one was savaged by two

THE STINGRAY SHUFFLE

It's not a dance, exactly.

Pinellas County beaches have their share of flat, seafloor-living stingrays. Visitors occasionally step on these creatures, their winglike fins hidden in the sandy shallows. When trod upon, a stingray flips up its tail in self-defense and delivers a nasty stinging puncture with its barb. To avoid this, drag your feet along the sandy bottom (as opposed to stepping up and down). The "shuffle" may not look too swift, but it alerts stingrays to your approach. They are just hanging around the shallows to catch shellfish and crustaceans and they'd rather not waste their time on stinging you.

If you are unlucky enough to be stung, it's important that you clean the wound with freshwater immediately (other bacteria in seawater can infect the area). As soon as you can, soak the wound in the hottest water you can stand for up to 90 minutes to neutralize the venom. The pain can be severe, often accompanied by weakness, vomiting, headache, fainting, shortness of breath, paralysis, and collapse in people who are allergic to the venom. You may want to see a doctor, who might add insult to injury with a tetanus shot.

Always report stingray injuries to the lifeguard on duty.

hurricanes in 1848 and 1852), gun batteries built in 1898, a pretty stretch of beach, and lots of gopher tortoises and hummingbirds. There is no camping on Egmont Key.

FORT DE SOTO STATE PARK

3500 Pinellas Bayway S., Tierra Verde, 727/582-2267, www.fortdesoto.com

HOURS: Daylight hours

COST: Free admission

Map 9

South of St. Petersburg, Fort de Soto Park is an embarrassment of riches, with 1,136 unspoiled acres, seven miles of beaches, two fishing piers, picnic and camping areas, a small history museum, and a 2,000-foot barrier-free nature trail for guests with disabilities, set on five little, interconnected islands. The fort itself is in the southwest corner of Mullet Key, and there's a toll ($0.85) on the bridges leading into the park. The islands were once inhabited by the Tocobaga and visited by Spanish explorers. It was surveyed by Robert E. Lee before the Civil War, and during the war Union troops had a detachment on both Egmont and Mullet Keys. The fort was built in 1898 to protect Tampa Bay during the Spanish-American War and is listed on the National Register of Historic Places. And during World War II, the island was used for bombing practice by the pilot who dropped the bomb

on Hiroshima. But you thought we were talking about beaches, right?

Well, exploring the old fort is part of what makes this experience special (hey, it was named top beach by TripAdvisor in 2008 and also by Dr. Beach), drawing more than 2.7 million visitors annually. After fondling the four 12-inch seacoast rifled mortars (the only ones of their kind in the U.S.), head on to one of the two swim centers, the better of which is the North Beach Swim Center (it has concessions). At the beach, you're likely to see laughing gulls, ibis, and ospreys, as well as beach sunflowers and beach morning glories peeking out from the sea oats. Fishing enthusiasts can choose between the 500-foot-long pier on the Tampa Bay side or the 1,000-foot-long pier on the Gulf side. Each has a food and bait concession.

Once in the park, take a right at the stop sign, go one mile, and on the right look for **Topwater Kayak** (3500 Pinellas Bayway S., Tierra Verde, 727/864-1991, daily 9 A.M.–5 P.M., last rental at 3:30 P.M., single kayaks $23 for one hour, $29 for two hours; canoes $30 for one hour, $40 for two hours; bike rentals are available inside the park, $6 per hour, $20 per day, cash only). It also issues maps of the area. Numbered signs along the shore mark a 2.25-mile kayak trail through Mullet Key Bayou.

Fort de Soto Park has the best camping in

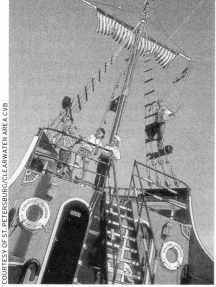

COURTESY OF ST. PETERSBURG/CLEARWATER AREA CVB

Avast ye matey, this is Captain Memo's Pirate Cruise sailing from the Clearwater Marina.

the area, with campsites directly on the Gulf. Camping is $34 per night (RV spots $40), but here's the rub for visitors. Most of the 235 campsites require reservations, which must be made far in advance. There are a handful of walk-in campsites available, but they are hot commodities. All sites have water and electrical hookups, and there are modern restrooms, dump stations, a camp store, washers/dryers, and grills. Pets are allowed in Area 2 and some of the spots are directly on the water. Be advised, the resident raccoons are more dexterous than most, able to pick cooler locks and unwrap lunch meat with aplomb.

◖ HONEYMOON ISLAND STATE RECREATION AREA

1 Causeway Blvd., at the extreme west end of Hwy. 586, Dunedin, 727/469-5942
HOURS: Daily 8 A.M.–sunset
COST: Admission $5 for up to eight people per car, $3 single driver, $1 pedestrians and bicyclists
Map 9

Honeymoon Island and Caladesi Island are

more of a double-whammy, perfectly suited for visiting back to back. In fact, the two islands were once part of a single larger barrier island split in half during a savage hurricane in 1921. Together, they offer nearly 1,000 acres of mostly undeveloped land, not too changed from how it looked when Spanish explorers surveyed the coast in the mid-1500s.

The Tocobaga were the first known residents of Honeymoon Island, with ventures in more recent centuries having been quashed by deadly hurricanes. First known as Sand Island, then more inelegantly as Hog Island, it got its current name in the 1940s when marketing folks tried to pitch it as a retreat for newlyweds, with little palm-thatched bungalows and cottages. It didn't quite take, stymied also by World War II, and the island went through several changes of hands before becoming a state park.

After a huge beach renourishment project in 2007, Honeymoon Island offers visitors all kinds of fun activities, but especially good is the fishing—you're likely to catch flounder, snook, trout, redfish, snapper, whiting, sheepshead, and, occasionally, tarpon. The island is home to 208 species of plants and a wealth of shore and wading birds, including a few endangered bird species. As per the beaches, my favorite part is the pet beach. It is where I learned that my dog sinks like a stone when immersed. If you subscribe to the hypothesis that people look like their pets, this is prime observation opportunity, as both pets and owners are scantily clad as they cavort in the warm water.

PASS-A-GRILLE BEACH

1000 Pass-a-Grille Way, Pass-a-Grille, 727/363-9247
HOURS: Always open
COST: Metered parking $1.25 per hour or $5 per day
Map 7

Pass-A-Grille Beach is at the southern end of the string of barrier islands, at the tip of the beach communities. It was one of the first public beaches on Florida's west coast and the area's first resort, dating from the late 1800s. It's still considered one of the loveliest. Small shops, snack bars, and restaurants are located along the coast, making this a pleasant place

ARTS AND LEISURE

WALKING AND OTHER ON-LAND TOURS

Get spooked during **Downtown St. Petersburg Ghost Tours** (119 2nd St. N., next to Starbucks, St. Petersburg, 727/894-4678, www.ghost-tour.net, daily at 8 P.M., $15 adults, $8 ages 4-12), a 90-minute, candlelit walking tour of the city's most haunted places, led by a guide in a creepy, Halloween-appropriate costume.

Bayside Tours (at the foot of The Pier, 335 2nd Ave. NE, St. Petersburg, 727/896-3640, www.gyroglides.com, $30-50) offers 60- and 90-minute tours of the city on Segways. The two side-by-side wheels (as opposed to a bike or motorcycle, in which the two wheels are in a line) are self-balancing, and you stand above the wheels on a little platform and steer the electric-powered vehicle with the handlebars. With speeds of up to 12 mph, they can be used in pedestrian areas and are a perfect way to cover serious ground at a pace slow enough to really appreciate things. Plus, you look really cool. Headgear is provided.

You can rent a bicycle, tricycle, or other stylin' wheeled vehicle for a jaunt around downtown St. Petersburg from **Wheel Fun Rentals** (800 2nd Ave. NE, St. Petersburg, 727/820-0375, www.wheelfunrentals.com), but guided tours are also available.

to catch some rays and have a refreshing drink in the shade when the sun gets too hot. From here there's shuttle service out to unspoiled Shell Key.

ST. PETE BEACH
Four miles along Gulf Blvd. in the town of St. Pete Beach
HOURS: Always open
COST: Metered parking
Map 7

St. Pete Beach has a lot of low-rise pastel motels and an easy, laid-back lack of civic planning. Sprawling and unfussy, its only organizing principle is "the beach is over there." For some reason you'll run into a lot of European travelers here—thus, by implication, those disconcertingly smaller bathing suits on men—especially the British. It's a livelier vibe than many Gulf Coast beaches, but not quite a spring break magnitude of sybaritic indulgers. The hammered and the Girls Gone Wild boob-flashers go elsewhere, although my friend and I were once asked by young baseball-capped men to "show us your boobs." The beach itself is long and renourished, sand-wise. There are concessions, picnic tables, lots of parking, showers, and restrooms. In all, a very nice day at the beach.

To the north of St. Pete Beach along Gulf Boulevard, there are a number of other good beaches along the barrier island of **Sand Key**, which contains the eight communities between St. Pete Beach and Clearwater Pass. **John's Pass Beach** at the southern end of Sand Key and north for a couple of miles in **Madeira Beach** is beautiful sand and good fishing. Going north, the beaches in **Redington Beach** have limited public access but are pretty. Still farther north, **Indian Rocks Beach** has good public access and a party vibe (lively beach bars). Bypass the beaches in **Belleair**, as access and amenities are very limited, in favor of an afternoon at **Sand Key County Park** (north end of Gulf Blvd. at Clearwater Pass, 727/595-7677), which has lifeguards, playgrounds, cabana rentals, and lots of wide, white-sand beach.

PARKS
ANCLOTE KEY PRESERVE STATE PARK
1 Causeway Blvd., Dunedin, 727/469-5942
HOURS: Daily 8 A.M.-sundown
COST: Free admission
Map 9

You've got to want it, but this unbridged island, accessible only by private boat or ferry, is a treat. More than 43 species of bird call it home, or at least temporary asylum, and there's a lovely 1887 lighthouse standing around on the southern end of the island not doing much of anything. Camping overnight is free, there are grilling and picnic facilities, and the fish (snook, sea trout, and mullet) in these waters seem eager to please. For ferry service, contact **SunLine Cruises** out of Tarpon Springs at 727/944-4468, **Island Time Adventures** out of Clearwater at 727/447-0969, or **Sponge-O-Rama** out of Tarpon Springs at 727/943-2164.

BOYD HILL NATURE PRESERVE

1101 Country Club Way S., St. Petersburg, 727/893-7326
HOURS: Tues.-Thurs. 9 A.M.-8 P.M., Fri. and Sat. 9 A.M.-6 P.M., Sun. 11 A.M.-6 P.M.
COST: $3 adults, $1.50 children
Map 9

It's 245 acres of pristine Florida wilderness, with five distinct ecosystems—hardwood hammocks, sand pine scrub, pine flatwoods, willow marsh, and the Lake Maggiore shoreline. This may be my favorite, as it is incredibly convenient, just minutes from downtown, but it nonetheless feels far from the maddening crowds. Precious green space in an urban landscape, it is an important stopover on the Atlantic flyway—165 bird species have been observed here. You can camp at Boyd and there's a small educational center with exhibits on the five ecosystems.

BROOKER CREEK PRESERVE

1001 Lora Ln., Tarpon Springs, 727/943-4000, www.friendsofbrookercreekpreserve.org
HOURS: Trail open daily sunrise-sunset
COST: Free admission
Map 9

For a rough-and-ready nature experience, drive up to Brooker Creek Preserve, an 8,500-acre wilderness in the northern section of the county near Tarpon Springs. Currently, its environmental education center offers four miles of self-guided hiking trails at the southern end of Lora Lane off of Keystone Road, about one-half mile east of East Lake Road. The preserve also offers guided hikes every Saturday (reservation required, 727/453-6800), and it hosts the annual **Run in the Woods** in April, the area's only walk/run that is completely cross-country through beautiful backwood pinelands and prairies.

HILLSBOROUGH RIVER STATE PARK

15402 U.S. 301 N., Thonotosassa, 813/987-6771
HOURS: Daily 8 A.M.-sundown
COST: $4 for up to eight people per car, $20 camping
Map 5

One of Florida's original state parks, built in 1936 by the Civilian Conservation Corp, the park's Fort Foster, a replica of an original Second Seminole War military fort, is open for guided tours on Saturdays and Sundays. The Fort Foster Visitor Station houses a display of artifacts from the time period and provides the visitor with information about the operation of the fort. The park's Rapids Nature Trail meanders through oak hammocks to the edge of the Hillsborough River at the point where an outcropping of limestone rocks has created rapids—a popular spot for photographers. The park rents canoes and offers 112 campsites, picnic areas, a swimming pool, pavilions, and the Spirit of the Woods Pool Side Café and Gift Shop.

LETTUCE LAKE PARK

6920 E. Fletcher Ave., Tampa, 813/987-6204
HOURS: Daily 8 A.M.-6 P.M.
COST: Free admission
Map 4

For a bit of unmediated nature that's close to civilization, head to Lettuce Lake Park, just east of the University of South Tampa. It's a stone's throw from urban sprawl, but don't hold that against it. The dense wilderness shelters a 3,500-foot-long raised boardwalk and a recently rebuilt tower overlooking the Hillsborough River, a perfect place from which to spy on tall wading birds, gators lurking amongst cypress knees in the swamp or even delicate orchids and other epiphytes nestled in the trees' crooks. Rent a canoe for a closer look at the creatures that call this tannin-tinged water home, hike the fully accessible boardwalk or dirt trails (no dogs on the boardwalks), then settle in for a picnic at one of the waterfront shelters, equipped with barbecues. A children's playground, restrooms, and water fountains make this swath of nature very civilized indeed.

ARTS AND LEISURE

BOATING AND FISHING TOURS

Bilgewater Bill, Mad Dog Mike, Gangplank Gary, and the other pirates will greet you with an "argh, me matey" on the deck of **Captain Memo's Original Pirate Cruise** (25 Causeway Blvd., Dock 3, Clearwater Beach, 727/446-2587, daily 10 A.M., 2 P.M., and sunset cruises, $35 adults, $30 seniors, $25 children), a two-hour pirate cruise on a fancy bright red pirate ship. In a similar vein, **John's Pass Village & Boardwalk** (12901 Gulf Blvd. E., just between Madeira Beach and Treasure Island, 727/423-7824, www.thepirateshipatjohnspass.com, daily 11 A.M., 2 P.M., and sunset, $30 adults, $20 for children 2-20, free for children under 2) offers a **Pirates at the Pass** cruise on a fully kitted out pirate ship. You'll engage in water pistol battles and treasure hunts and listen to pirate stories.

John's Pass Village is home to a large commercial and charter fishing fleet, as well as art galleries, restaurants, and boutiques along a waterfront boardwalk. Families also seem to enjoy the dolphin tours out of John's Pass and into scenic Boca Ciega Bay. A couple of companies offer these – **Hubbard's Sea Adventures** (departs from John's Pass boardwalk, 727/393-1947, www.hubbardsmarina.com, daily 1 P.M., 3 P.M., and 5 P.M., $17 adults, $9 children 11 and under) brings you face-to-face with the bay's breadth of wildlife.

Farther south, **Dolphin Landings** (4737 Gulf Blvd., behind the Dolphin Village Shopping Center, St. Pete Beach, 727/367-4488, www.charterboatescape.com, sailing times vary, $25-35) conducts two-hour dolphin-watch cruises and longer three- to four-hour trips to Shell Key, an undeveloped barrier island. The scheduled trips and private charters are conducted on one of 40 locally owned sailboats, pontoon boats, and deep-sea fishing yachts.

Dolphin Queen (800 2nd Ave. NE, St. Petersburg, 727/647-1538, www.pierdolphincruises.net) offers 90-minute cruises of Tampa Bay on a 44-foot catamaran. Tours at 11:30 A.M. and 1, 3, and 5 P.M. cost $20 adults, $17 seniors, $12 children ages 3-12. And **Shell Key Shuttle** (Merry Pier, 801 Pass-a-Grille Way, St. Pete Beach, 727/360-1348, www.shellkeyshuttle.com, $22 adults, $11 children 12 and under) leads low-impact ecotours on the unspoiled small barrier island preserve on Shell Key. Guests enjoy shelling, sunbathing, swimming, and bird- and dolphin-watching. Take a picnic lunch and rent beach umbrellas and snorkel gear. There are three departure and return times.

Sweetwater Kayaks (10000 Gandy Blvd., St. Petersburg, 727/570-4844) does full- and half-day wildlife tours via kayak. Scoot through mangrove tunnels right by big lurking gators. Sweetwater also arranges custom adventure tours for groups and multiday outings.

Offshore Sailing School (The Harborage at Bayboro, 1110 3rd St. S., St. Petersburg, 800/221-4326, www.offshore-sailing.com, tuition starts at $895) is a tremendous amount of fun, three days on the water with an instructor and three other students, plus hours of classroom time learning all the sailing jargon, parts of the boat, points of sail, etc. At the end of the class you take a fairly difficult 80-question test, and you get out and show your sailing chops to your teacher, complete with man-overboard demonstrations and doing a quick stop by "shooting" into the wind. You learn on a midsize day sailer, a Colgate 26, designed specifically for training and chosen by the U.S. Naval Academy to replace their training fleet. Courses are for beginners, racers, and cruisers; there's also a basic keelboating class.

SAWGRASS LAKE PARK

7400 25th St. N., immediately west of I-275 in Pinellas
Park, St. Petersburg, 727/217-7256, environmental
center 727/526-3020

HOURS: Daily 7 A.M.–sunset

COST: Free admission

Map 9

A spot on the Great Florida Birding Trail,
also lauded by the National Audubon Society,
Sawgrass sees thousands of birds migrate
through the park during the fall and spring. A
one-mile elevated boardwalk winds through a
maple swamp and oak hammock. There's an observation tower with views of the park's swamps,
canals, and lake, where you're likely to see wood
storks, herons, egrets, and ibis in addition to
gators and turtles. The park has naturalist-led
nature tours and field trips, and its Anderson
Environmental Center contains a large freshwater aquarium and exhibits on the area. My only
caution is that during the wet months it can get
a bit flooded in this park.

If you find an injured bird in your wandering, call **Suncoast Seabird Sanctuary**
(18328 Gulf Blvd., Indian Shores, 727/
391-6211), one of the country's largest nonprofit hospitals for wild birds. With a new
hospital facility, the sanctuary rescues and
releases hundreds of birds each year into the
wild. The sanctuary also offers a free tour every
Wednesday and Sunday at 2 P.M., meeting at
the beachfront deck.

SNEAD ISLAND AND
EMERSON POINT PARK

Take Business 41 into Palmetto, turn right on
10th St. W. and follow signs to island, 941/776-2295

HOURS: Daily 8 A.M.–sundown

COST: Free admission

Map 9

Owned by the State of Florida and maintained
by the Manatee County Conservation Lands
Management team, Snead Island is just east
of Egmont Key (south of Pinellas County), a
good excuse to tramp around in nature—15
miles of it bordering shoreline along the Gulf
and the lovely Manatee River. The park is fa-
vored by hikers because of its variety of trails

The Hillsborough River threads 55 miles
through Central Florida and Tampa to empty
in Hillsborough Bay.

COURTESY OF VISIT FLORIDA

and loops, with occasional boardwalks hugging
the waterways.

Snead Island is home to Emerson Point
Park, worth tacking on to your adventure—the
park's 195 acres of salt marshes, beaches, mangrove swamp, lagoons, grass flats, hardwood
hammocks, and semi-upland wooded areas are
viewable from a well-maintained eight-foot-
wide shell path as well as more rustic walking
and biking paths. Manatee County has poured
money into this park in recent years such that
master gardeners convene here regularly for
guided walking tours of the varied plant and
animal life. Call 941/722-4524 to find out the
tour schedule.

Of special note to Native American his-
torians, Emerson Point Park is home to the
Portavant Temple Mound (east end of 17th
Street W.), an impressive mound complex.
Walkways and boardwalks take you over and
around a huge 150-foot flat-top temple mound
and several horseshoe-shaped shell middens.
Interpretive markers explicate the site.

ARTS AND LEISURE

ALLIGATORS

In his excellent memoir, *Totch, A Life in the Everglades,* Totch Brown describes a gator's sounds:

> Gators make three different sounds. One is the "grunt" used by young gators in distress to call their mothers. When you pick up a baby gator it'll start grunting every time. The mother will come to this sound right away. (With practice, you can imitate this "grunt" and often fool a grown gator into coming to you.)
>
> Then there's a blowing sound gators make when they're more or less hemmed up, or cornered and are good and mad.
>
> The third sound is the gator bellow — a bloodcurdling sound that can be heard for miles across the Everglades. When one gator bellows, usually another will answer.... When a 12-foot gator bellows, he raises his head up as high as possible, his mouth wide open, and with a full breath, lets out his air. It's a sight to be seen! The bellowing is generally in mating season, the late spring, when the rains are about to start. The gators seem to be asking Mother Nature for a drink of water."

I've seen a gator bellow, right at the edge of my backyard pond, his head tipped way back. To me he didn't seem like he was asking anybody for anything other than to buzz off. It's a monster noise, deeply unsettling, apt to have the kind of effect that everyone's first viewing of *Jaws* did back in 1975.

Alligators were first listed as an endangered species in 1967, their numbers threatened by hunting and habitat loss. Then the American alligator was removed from the endangered species list in 1987 after the U.S. Fish and Wildlife Service pronounced a complete recovery of the species. Conservative estimates put the population at around a million in Florida, Louisiana, Texas, and Georgia. Because they can tolerate brackish water as well as freshwater, they can be found in rivers, swamps, bogs, lakes, ponds, creeks, canals, swimming pools, and lots of Florida golf courses.

The American alligator is the largest reptile in North America (distinguished from the American crocodile by its short, rounded snout and black color). They can live 35-50 years in the wild, 60-80 years in captivity. The average adult male is 13 feet in length (half of the length taken up by the tail), although they can grow up to 18 feet long. Bulls are generally larger than females, weighing 450-600 pounds.

They're everywhere in Florida, and they eat just about anything. Usually that means lizards, fish, snakes, turtles, even little gators, but they'll also enjoy bologna sandwiches and schnauzer.

Florida residents have heretofore learned to be blasé about gators. They're an everyday part of living in this subtropical climate. But things are changing. Sanibel Island may be leading the way for a new stance on gators in the state. In the past six years several people have died in alligator attacks across the state, with several in Sanibel. It's hard to be as sanguine about gator-human relations when women are getting chomped while pruning their gardens.

The problems are not just a function of large numbers — people feed the gators and thus the alligators have gotten chummy and less fearful of humans, and vice versa.

So now new policies are being put in place. In many spots along the Gulf Coast, if gators get large (over eight feet) they are taken away and "processed" (not a good euphemism). Smaller ones get relocated. The jury is out on this interspecies relationship.

STAY SAFE

Alligators are cold-blooded (literally, maybe figuratively). It's a good survival tactic because they don't need to eat as much or as often as their warm-blooded counterparts. In fact, they can't eat unless their internal body temperature is 90 degrees. Thus, they don't eat all winter, and in the spring can be seen in the midmorning basking on the banks in a sunny spot. They're hungry and horny in April and May – a good time to steer especially clear. In the summer, the females lay their eggs in a nest (up to 70 eggs) and cover them over, then the eggs incubate for 65 days. (As a cool aside, alligators lack sexual chromosomes, so that sex is determined by the temperature at which eggs incubate. Between 90 and 93 degrees they're all male, between 87 and 89 degrees they're female.) The mom stays close, carrying the freshly hatched babies to the water. Even after they're swimming around, mama is protective for up to the first two years (supposedly she can hear their cry for help up to a mile away). Still, it's said only 1 in 10 alligators lives through the first year.

So, to review:

- Don't feed the gators. And if you see others doing so, give them a hard time.

- Don't bother the babies or come between a mother and her young.

- Don't bug them during their cranky spring mating season.

- Closely supervise kids playing in or near fresh or brackish water. Never allow little kids to play by water unattended. The same goes for pets. In fact, just don't let your dog swim in fresh or brackish water in Florida, period.

- Alligators feed most actively at dusk and dawn, so schedule your lake or river swim for another time.

- They don't make good pets. They are not tamed in captivity, and it's illegal besides.

- If you are bitten, seek medical attention, even if it seems minor. Their mouths harbor very infectious bacteria.

- If you see a big one that seems inordinately interested in humans, call the local police nonemergency number.

- Don't throw your fish scraps and guts back into the water when fishing. This encourages gators to hang around boats and docks.

A LITTLE FLORIDA GATOR HUMOR

An old codger in Florida owned a large farm with a big pond in the back. He had it fixed up pretty nicely, with a picnic table, a shady fruit orchard, a little fishing dock.

One evening the farmer decided to go down to the pond and have a look around. He grabbed an old five-gallon bucket to bring back some fruit.

As he neared the pond, he heard voices, with shouting and laughter. As he came closer he saw it was a bunch of young women skinny-dipping in his pond. He made the women aware of his presence and they all went to the deep end.

One of the women shouted to him, "Sir, we're not coming out until you leave!"

The old man frowned. "I didn't come down here to spy on you ladies swimming naked." Holding up the bucket, he said, "I'm here to feed the alligator."

Moral: Old men can still think fast.

◗ SUNKEN GARDENS

1825 4th St. N., St. Petersburg, 727/551-3102,
www.stpete.org/sunken
HOURS: Mon.-Sat. 10 A.M.-4:30 P.M., Sun. noon-4:30 P.M.
COST: $8 adults, $6 seniors, $4 children 2-11
Map 9

Sunken Gardens was snatched from the jaws
of death in 1999, nursed back to health under
the careful ministrations of the city of St.
Petersburg. Nothing a little nurturing and $3
mill couldn't fix. It's a four-acre plot of land,
much of it 100 years old and counting. There
are 50,000 tropical plants and flowers, demonstration gardens, a 200-year-old oak tree, cas-
cading waterfalls, flamingos, etc.

It's more than a garden, though—it's St.
Petersburg's most beloved Old Florida attraction. In 1903, a plumber named George
Turner, Sr. bought the property, which contained a large sinkhole and a shallow lake.
By dint of effort and a huge maze of clay
tile, he drained the lake and prepared the
soil for gardening. He sold tropical fruit that
he grew here at a roadside stand, but folks
liked walking through the tranquil greenery
so much that he started charging admission.
By 1935, the garden was officially opened
as Turner's Sunken Gardens (because of the
former lake and sinkhole, the whole thing
sits down low in a basin), attracting approximately 300,000 visitors per year. It was followed by some other attractions of dubious
taste: the World's Largest Gift Shop and the
King of Kings Wax Museum. It was one of
those places that had loud, modestly liter-
ate billboards on the southbound highway
up through a couple of states.

But, as is common for these kinds of Florida
attractions, its business fell off as more glitz
was mandated by ever more sophisticated patrons. It drizzled along until the city felt com-
pelled to help, also restoring the gift shop/wax
museum space to its former Mediterranean
revival glory (it's where **Great Explorations,
the Children's Museum** is housed). I know
I'm painting a picture of hard times and empty
pockets, but Sunken Gardens is beautiful, ever
so slightly campy, and a definite slice of local

history. A must if you can tear yourself away
from the beach.

WEEDON ISLAND PRESERVE CULTURAL AND NATURAL HISTORY CENTER

1800 Weedon Island Dr., St. Petersburg,
727/453-6500, www.weedonislandcenter.org
HOURS: Preserve open daily sunrise-sunset,
cultural center open Wed.-Sun. 10 A.M.-4 P.M.
COST: Free admission
Map 9

Extending along the west side of Tampa Bay
in Pinellas County, Weedon Island Preserve is
an odd bird, an attraction hard to classify exactly. It's a group of low-lying islands in north
St. Petersburg that as long as 10,000 years or so
ago was home to Timucuans and Manasotas.
The largest estuarine preserve in the county, it
is also home to a large shell midden and burial
mound complex. Visitors to the cultural center
can see artifacts excavated from the site by the
Smithsonian in the 1920s in exhibits designed
collaboratively by anthropologists, historians,
and Native Americans.

But you can't spend all your time at the
cultural center watching videos about the art
and history of the early peoples of Weedon
Island—the park has a four-mile canoe trail
loop, a boardwalk and observation tower,
three gentle miles of hiking trails, a fishing pier (snook, redfish, spotted trout), and
waterfront picnic facilities. Weedon
Island Preserve Center offers guided nature
hikes every Saturday and regularly scheduled guided canoe excursions (registration
727/453-6506).

BIKING
FLATWOODS PRESERVE

Main entrance about five miles north of I-75 on Morris
Bridge Rd., second entrance 3.5 miles north of I-75 on
Bruce B. Downs Blvd.
HOURS: Daylight hours
COST: $1 suggested donation
Map 4

This is my ride. I leave my front door on the
bike, kitted out with all the proper gear (well,
maybe a couple years out of date, but that's the

TEE TIME

GOLFING IN TAMPA

Tampa has a couple of dozen public and semi-private courses for the visitor to try. Many of them are open to the public but located in Tampa's swankier northeast residential developments. Here are a handful of the area's top public courses:

Babe Zaharias Golf Club (11412 Forest Hills Dr., 813/631-4374, www.babezahariasgc.com) 18 holes, 6,244 yards, par 70, course rating 68.9, slope 121, greens fee $15–42.

University of South Florida Golf Course (also called "The Claw") (4202 E. Fowler Ave., 813/632-6893) 18 holes, 6,863 yards, par 71, course rating 74.2, slope 132, greens fee $25–54.

Rocky Point Golf Course (4151 Dana Shores Dr., 813/673-4316, www.rockypointgc.com) 18 holes, 6,444 yards, par 71, course rating 71.7, slope 122, greens fee $19–38.

Rogers Park Golf Course (7910 N. Willie Black Dr., 813/356-1670, www.rogersparkgc.com) 18 holes, 6,802 yards, par 71, course rating 72.3, slope 125, greens fee $15–42.

Heritage Isles Golf & Country Club (10630 Plantation Bay Dr., 813/907-7447) 18 holes, 6,976 yards, par 72, course rating 73.2, slope 132, greens fees $25–47.

Westchase Golf Course (10307 Radcliffe Dr., 813/854-2331) 18 holes, par 72, 6,699 yards, course rating 72.6, slope 131, greens fee $25–89.

TPC Tampa Bay (5300 West Lutz Lake Fern Rd., Lutz, 813/949-0091) 18 holes, par 71, 6,898 yards, course rating 73.6, slope 135, greens fees $59–132.

If you are thinking about picking up the sport, the **Arnold Palmer Golf Academy** at the Saddlebrook Resort (5700 Saddlebrook Way, Wesley Chapel, 800/729-8383) teaches golfers of all skill levels. Classes combine classroom and practice time with course play. The New Player Academy and all their other packages include accommodations, 18 holes of golf a day, instruction, meals, and use of resort facilities. There are two 18-hole Palmer-designed championship courses on the property, as well as 45 tennis courts in the four Grand Slam surfaces (the resort is also home to the **Hopman Tennis Program.**

About 25 miles south of Tampa, the **Ben Sutton Golf School** (809 N. Pebble Beach Blvd., Sun City Center, 800/225-6923) was the first American school devoted to golf instruction. There are two-, three-, four-, and six-day courses.

GOLFING IN ST. PETERSBURG

Mangrove Bay and **Cypress Links** (875 62nd Ave. NE, St. Petersburg, 727/893-7800, www.stpete.org/golf, Pro shop open 6:30 A.M.–5 P.M., driving range 6:30 A.M.–7 P.M.) are two city-owned courses that sit right beside one another. Mangrove Bay is the better course – an 18-hole, par-72 facility that also includes a lighted practice range, pro shop, and lessons. Cypress Links is a nine-hole, par-three course, but it still has its share of challenges – including lots of water.

You'll find plenty of tee time options in Tampa.

COURTESY OF ST. PETERSBURG/CLEARWATER AREA CVB

way I roll). I ride four miles up Bruce B. Downs, harrowing in its entirety—Tampa is not a bike-friendly town—and then I enter Flatwoods, an 11-mile loop that takes me by baby feral pigs, armadillos, side-winding snakes, big red grasshoppers with carapaces like lobsters, and sometimes suave blue birds that I think are indigo buntings. Walk it, hike it, skate it, but watch out for me and my big grin. This 5,400-acre pine flatwoods and cypress swamp make up one of the five parks that comprise the Wilderness Park system (the others are Trout Creek, Dead River, Morris Bridge, and John B. Sargeant Memorial Park). For more great rides in Tampa, visit oliverscycles.com—it's a local bike shop that unfortunately doesn't rent bikes (Tampa, apparently, is a bring-your-own-bike town. Many bike shops but no rentals).

OLD GANDY BRIDGE AND FRIENDSHIP TRAIL BRIDGE

From I-275 in St. Petersburg, take "old" Exit 15 to Gandy Boulevard (U.S. 92) and go east to Gandy Bridge. See a small brown Friendship Trail Bridge sign prior to going onto the bridge, directing you to turn left or north to a short approach to the parking lot at the west end of the bridge.

HOURS: Daily dawn-dusk
COST: Free admission
Map 9

The best way to get oriented in the greater Tampa Bay area is to take a bike ride: The Old Gandy Bridge, which spans the bay to the south of I-275, recently underwent a $7 million transformation into an all-recreation park called the Friendship Trail Bridge. The 2.6-mile trail is open for all types of nonmotorized activities including biking, walking, running, inline skating, and fishing. Saved from the wrecking ball, it's the world's largest over-the-water recreational trail (the cool fishing catwalks that flank the bridge are open 24 hours).

Now you just need to rent a bike. **Northeast Cycles** (1062 4th St., St. Petersburg, 727/898-2453, $15 per day, nice road bikes $25 per day) will rent you bikes, and a rack for an additional $10 so you can load them up and take them over to the bridge parking lot, as will

The 37-mile Pinellas Trail provides a safe environment for bicycling, walking, jogging, and in-line skating.

COURTESY OF ST. PETERSBURG/CLEARWATER AREA CVB

Chainwheel Drive, with two locations (1770 Drew St., Clearwater, 727/441-2444; and 32796 U.S. 19 N., in Palm Lake Plaza, Palm Harbor, 727/786-3883, Mon.–Fri. 10 A.M.–7 P.M., Sat. 10 A.M.–5 P.M., $20 for four hours for hybrids, $26 for four hours for road bikes).

(PINELLAS TRAIL

Ranger 727/549-6099
HOURS: Daylight hours
COST: Free admission
Map 9

Now that you've got the bikes, you may want to avail yourself of one of the other local beauties, the 37-mile-long Pinellas Trail, one of the longest linear parks in the southeastern U.S., running essentially from St. Petersburg up to the sponge docks of Tarpon Springs. A rails-to-trails kind of deal, the original rail track was home to the first Orange Belt Railroad train in 1888, and is now a well-maintained, 15-foot-wide trail through parks and coastal areas for bikers, inline skaters, joggers, etc.

SCALING NEW HEIGHTS

John Gill is said to be the father of modern bouldering. Congrats to the proud papa, you say, if only you knew what bouldering was. It used to be that serious rock climbers would, on occasion, undertake a climb without a rope. Considered more a mental exercise in problem solving, this ropes-free style of climbing gained purchase in the 1950s, legitimized as a sport by Gill and others. As the name implies, these climbs might be practiced on large boulders or rock faces, but just as easily indoors at a climbing center. Reflecting the focus of an individual, these kinds of climbs are often referred to as "problems."

So then I guess you could say that **Vertical Ventures** (5402 Pioneer Park Blvd., Tampa, 813/884-7625, www.verticalventures.com, Tues.-Thurs. 2-10 P.M., Fri. until midnight, Sat. and Sun. 10 A.M.-6 P.M.) is here to help you solve your problems.

"People are into minimalist things these days, so bouldering is the rage now," says Christian Tartaglia, co-owner of Florida's first climbing gym and Tampa's only indoor rock-climbing facility. "Bouldering tends to be a more gymnastic or dynamic style of climbing. There are no ropes or gear, so even the beginner can start off bouldering. It doesn't go quite as high."

The 6,000 square feet of professionally-designed climbing surface focuses on both of the two main kinds of climbing: bouldering, but also "top roping," a two-person climbing system that includes a belayer down below.

Despite all the fancy technical terms, either style can be quickly understood by the rookie climber. While the former has very little gear associated with it, top roping requires a few essentials: shoes ($5 rentals), harness ($4 rentals), and chalk ($2).

For the newcomer, a beginning belay class ($30) teaches the basics, with 15 or 20 minutes devoted to how to safely manage the ropes and belay a climber – this is a safety system that ensures a falling climber can be quickly assisted. For the person on the ground, a beginning class covers basic knots, tying in to the rope, and how to catch a falling climber. For the climber, you learn climbing commands necessary for top roped climbing and basic climbing techniques. Then you're on your own for climb time: you, your partner, ropes, and a whole lot of wall.

There is a free guide to the Pinellas Trail, available at the trail office, area libraries, and the Pinellas County Courthouse Information Desk (it can also be downloaded at www.pinellascounty.org/trailgd). It lists rest stops, service stations, restaurants, pay phones, bike shops, and park areas along the trail.

CANOEING
CANOE ESCAPE

9335 E. Fowler Ave., Tampa, 813/986-2067, www.canoeescape.com

COST: Self-guided rentals are $22.50-$32.50 per paddler for a tandem canoe or kayak depending on the trip (a child under 12 can usually fit as a center passenger). A solo kayak ranges $42-52, depending on the trip. Prices include shuttle fee, paddles, and life vests.

Map 5

You want to see big gators? Great blue herons the size of the Wright brothers' first plane? River otters, turtles, families of wild pigs? Paddle down the gently flowing Hillsborough River in a 16,000-acre wildlife preserve called Wilderness Park. You can rent canoes or kayaks and head out on your own, choosing from six different self-guided day-trip combos. All paddling adventures start at Canoe Escape. Whether you go on a guided tour or on your own, call ahead, then drive to their building. Staff will equip you, give you maps and paddling pointers, then take you over to your debarkation point (all paddles are downstream), and establish a pickup time.

The Sargeant Park to Morris Bridge Park is a two-hour paddle, 4.5 miles long, with 70 percent shade and alternating sun and shade. Morris Bridge Park to Trout Creek Park is a

ARTS AND LEISURE

WALKING TREES

This area's waterfront is in many places fringed with mangrove trees. They are often called walking trees because they hover above the water, their arching prop roots resembling so many spindly legs. The mangrove is one of only a handful of tree species on planet Earth that can withstand having its roots sitting in ocean water, immersed daily by rising tides, and that thrives in little soil and high levels of sulfides. The mangrove's hardiness is just one among many of its idiosyncrasies, however.

Mangroves are natural land builders. Seed tubules about the heft and length of an excellent Cuban cigar sprout on the parent tree, drop off, and bob in the brackish water until they lodge on an oyster bar or a snag in the shallows. There, the seed begins to grow into a tree, its leaves dropping and getting trapped along with seaweed and other plant debris. This organic slurry is the bottom of the food chain, supplying food, breeding area, and sanctuary to countless tiny marine creatures. In addition, it is the foundation upon which a little island or "key" begins to take

shape, this buildup of sediment and debris creating a thick layer of organic peat upon which other plant species begin to grow. This first tree drops more seed tubules, which get stuck in the soft mud around the base of the parent tree and begin to grow. Soon, it's an impenetrable tangle of trees and roots extravagant enough to support birdlife and other animals.

Red mangrove forms a wide band of trees on the outermost part of each island, facing the open sea. The red mangrove encircles the black mangrove, which in turn encircles the white mangrove at the highest, driest part of each mangrove island (they are the least tolerant of having their roots sitting in saltwater). The mangroves' leathery evergreen leaves fall and stain the water a tobacco-colored tannic brown, but in fact the mangroves and all of the species dependent upon them do much to keep the waters clean and pure.

For all these reasons, mangrove trees are protected by federal, state, and local laws. Do not injure, spindle, mutilate, or even taunt a mangrove or face steep penalties.

two-hour, four-mile paddle, with 80 percent shade and a little full sun at the end. From Trout Creek Park to Rotary Park it's five miles of full-sun paddling, about two hours, whereas Sargeant Park to Trout Creek Park is a longer, 8.5-mile paddle with the first 75 percent in the shade. Morris Bridge Park to Rotary Park is a long, 9-mile route, and Sargeant Park to Rotary Park is for experienced paddlers only, with 14 miles of river to paddle.

If solo paddling seems daunting, Canoe Escape offers a 4.5-mile interpreted guided tour for $75 per person. I'd recommend this for the newcomer to the area because the guides' vast knowledge of the local flora and fauna enrich the trip immeasurably.

FISHING
SUNSHINE SKYWAY FISHING PIERS
To get there, head south on I-275 toward Bradenton. The North Pier (727/865-0668) is about a mile past the toll ($1). To reach the South Pier (941/729-0117), continue over the bridge and follow the signs.

HOURS: 24 hours

COST: $3 per vehicle, plus $2 general admission, $1.50 seniors, $1 children 6-11, free for children under 6.

Map 9

It must have been a sight to see. In 1990, Hardaway Constructors of Tampa and a demolition team from Baltimore joined forces to perform the largest bridge demolition in Florida history. They were doing away with the old Sunshine Skyway Bridge opened in 1954, a 15-mile crossing from St. Petersburg to Bradenton. From a long causeway on both sides, the steel bridge had a steep cantilever truss, 750 feet wide and with 150 feet of clearance above the water.

It wasn't enough clearance.

There had been some indication of this—at least five freighters or barges were roughed up by this bridge, most of them with minor damage (the Coast Guard cutter USS *Blackthorn* met with disaster, but it was just west of the bridge and it was weather related).

But it was during a violent storm on May 9, 1980, at 7:38 A.M., when Captain John Lerro's visibility was nil, that empty phosphate freighter *Summit Venture* slammed into the No. 2 south pier of the southbound span. It knocked 1,261 feet out of the center span, the cantilever, and part of the roadway into Tampa Bay. Thirty-five people on the bridge at the time perished, most of them in a Greyhound bus headed for Miami. The only victim who survived had his truck fortuitously land on the deck of the *Summit Venture.*

One of the worst bridge disasters in history, it prompted the design, funding, and building of the new Sunshine Skyway Bridge. At a cost of $245 million, it's the world's longest cable-stayed bridge, with a main span of 1,200 feet and a vertical clearance of 193 feet. The four-mile bridge opened for business in April 1987, equipped with a bridge protection system involving 36 large concrete bumpers (oddly, called dolphins) built to withstand an impact from rogue freighters and tankers up to 87,000 tons traveling at 10 knots.

So, you probably think I'm leading up to saying, "It's a gorgeous bridge, a real local landmark, you gotta drive over this thing." It's all true, but it's only a part of the story. After the construction of the new bridge, the old bridge spans were demolished like I said, by Hardaway Constructors and that demo team from Baltimore, except they preserved portions of it as fishing piers, piling the rubble alongside to form fish-friendly artificial reefs.

Since the original bridge span was built, fisherfolk have been bragging about the variety of game they catch: shark, tarpon, goliath grouper, kingfish, Spanish mackerel, grouper, sea bass. It's anomalous, because usually you have to be in a boat in order to have water deep enough for many of these species. Anglers

Pinellas County offers world-class deep-sea and flats fishing.

have caught 1,000-pound tiger sharks from the bridge, traffic honking behind them. And now, with the artificial reefs adding extra enticement to the fish, the Sunshine Skyway Fishing Piers are killer fishing spots.

There's a 0.75-mile-long North Pier and a 1.5-mile-long South Pier—together said to be the world's longest fishing pier. You can drive your car onto the pier and park it right next to your fishing spot, parallel parking on the left lane, with room for cars to drive and walkways on either side of the span. There are restrooms on both piers, and bait shops sell live and frozen bait, tackle, drinks, and snacks. They also rent rods. The North Pier has a large picnic area next to the bait shop.

So, yeah, drive over the new bridge—its bright yellow paint freshened in 2007—but, more importantly, wet a line on the remnants of the old one. You don't need a fishing license to fish off the piers.

FISHING CHARTERS
Map 9

Inshore trips may yield snook, tarpon, Spanish

SMOKIN'

Here's a tricky scenario. You're on a great Gulf Coast vacation, the weather's perfect, you're feeling relaxed, so you decide to do a little charter fishing. You're out on the boat, you feel a yank, and there's a 40-pound greater amberjack on your line. You work a while and haul in a couple more of those and a whole mess of 20-inch Spanish mackerel. What a great day. My question: Now what? Are you going to take that fish cooler back to the Radisson and have them stink up the joint?

Here's what to do. You go to **Ted Peters Famous Smoked Fish** (1350 Pasadena Ave., South Pasadena, 727/381-7931, Wed.-Mon. 11:30 A.M.-7:30 P.M., $10-20, no credit cards) and they'll smoke them for you for $1.50 per pound. They can even make kingfish taste good, and that's saying something. They fillet them, throw them over a smoldering red oak fire in the smokehouse, then package them up

for you to take. (The smoked fish keeps for 4-5 days in the fridge.)

And if you don't have fish to smoke, still go to Ted Peters. It's been an institution for more than 50 years in Pinellas County, prized for its laid-back style and inviting picnic tables. Heck, even the Food Network got all moony-eyed about this place in 2006. The main attraction is obviously the smoked fish – the smoked fish spread with saltines is good, the salmon is excellent, the mullet is an intensely fishy acquired taste – but Ted Peters also produces some fabled cheeseburgers and German potato salad that is balanced precariously between the zing of vinegar and the smoke of bacon. Perfect, a good thing because you can't have fries with your burger – no Fryolator. This is a beer-drinking establishment, it gets fairly busy, and it closes early.

mackerel, king mackerel, cobia, sheepshead, red snapper, and others. Offshore you're more likely to catch gag or black grouper, amberjack, sea bass, triggerfish, red snapper, and gray snapper. Offshore, bottom, inshore, or even surf-casting—there are lots of people around here with enormous experience willing to take you out on a saltwater charter or just hook you up with gear. Oh, and the area's rivers offer decent freshwater fishing for catfish, bass, and bream. And many restaurants in the area are amenable to cooking up your fresh catch.

The price of a private charter averages $150–165 per hour (inflated gas prices are hiking that up), for up to six people. Many boats only accommodate six people, so make clear how many people are in your party. You can also sign up for a group charter, pooling with other people who are looking to go out (the prices are the same, you just split it between all the people on the boat). Obviously, you have to find others who are simpatico, in terms of what they're fishing for and how long they want to be out. Rod, reel, bait, and fishing license are usually

included, but bring your own drinks and lunch. **Hubbards's Marina** (150 John's Pass, Boardwalk, Madeira Beach, 727/393-1947, www.hubbardsmarina.com) is one of the reliable companies, offering daily half- and full-day deep-sea charters, with a meal ticket option available. Reservations are required and prices start at $50 per person. For something much more low key **The Pier Baithouse** (800 2nd Ave. N., on The Pier, St. Petersburg, 727/821-3750, daily 8 A.M.–10 P.M.) rents poles, bait, and buckets for fishing from The Pier. The staff can also arrange private fishing charters.

SPECTATOR SPORTS
DOG RACING
Derby Lane, 10490 Gandy Blvd. N., St. Petersburg. 727/576-1361, www.derbylane.com

HOURS: Mon., Wed. and Sat., gates open at 11:30 A.M. with 12:30 P.M. post time

COST: $1, free on Tuesdays

Map 9

This gaming complex offers live greyhound action year-round, simulcast wagering, and a poker

The Buccaneers play at Raymond James Stadium, not far from Tampa International Airport.

room. Races also run daily in the evenings. Poker room opens at noon Monday–Saturday.

◖ NEW YORK YANKEES
SPRING TRAINING

Legends Field, 1 Steinbrenner Dr., off N. Dale Mabry, 813/879-2244
HOURS: Vary by game
COST: $15-31
Map 5

Along much of the Gulf Coast, the Grapefruit League's spring training is a serious draw for sports fans each March. Since 1988, the New York Yankees have based their minor league operation, spring training, and year-round headquarters for player development in Tampa. Modeled after the original Yankee Stadium in the Bronx, Legends Field has been the Yankees' home since 1996. The complex houses a 10,000-seat stadium with 13 swanky luxury suites, a community-use field, and a major league practice field. It's also the home of the Florida State League Champion Tampa Yankees (New York Yankees–Florida State League Single "A" Affiliate) and the Hillsborough Community College Hawks baseball team.

PHILADELPHIA PHILLIES
SPRING TRAINING

Bright House Networks Field, 601 Old Coachman Rd., Clearwater, 727/442-8496
HOURS: Game days vary, times usually 1:05 or 7:05 P.M.
COST: $15-32
Map 8

The Philadelphia Phillies have been training in Clearwater since 1948. The Bright House Networks Field is a a great venue, with a tiki-hut pavilion in left field, a kids' play area, group picnic areas, party suites, and club seats.

TAMPA BAY BUCCANEERS

Raymond James Stadium, 4201 N. Dale Mabry Hwy., Tampa, 813/879-2827, www.buccaneers.com
HOURS: Vary by game
COST: Tickets for the 16 regular-season games Sept.-Dec. are $31 for general admission, one of the lowest ticket prices in the NFL; special seats range from $75 on down.
Map 5

Locals are gearing up for Super Bowl XLIII in 2009. Even if your tickets are not for that game, Raymond James is a wonderful venue in which to see Tampa's beloved Buccaneers

ARTS AND LEISURE

play. Raymond James Stadium, completed in 1998, holds more than 66,000 fans—52,000 in general seating—but tickets sell out for the season opener and other big games. Tickets for individual games are sold in person at TicketMaster outlets, via 813/287-8844, and by visiting www.ticketmaster.com, not at the stadium or the Bucs' ticket office. The $168.5 million stadium features Buccaneer Cove, a 20,000-square-foot replica of an early 1800s seaport village, complete with a 103-foot-long, 43-ton pirate ship that blasts its cannons (confetti and foam footballs) every time the Bucs score. Well, six times for a touchdown, once for an extra point, twice for a safety or two-point conversion, and three times for a field goal.

Raymond James Stadium also plays host every New Year's Day to the **Outback Bowl** (813/287-8844, 11 A.M. kickoff, $65). The game matches the third-pick team from the SEC and the third-pick team from the Big Ten Conference and is the culmination of a week-long festival in Tampa.

TAMPA BAY LIGHTNING

St. Pete Times Forum, 401 Channelside Dr., 813/301-6600, http://lightning.nhl.com
HOURS: Vary by game
COST: Tickets $15-349
Map 1

The 21,000-seat, $153 million Forum on Tampa's downtown waterfront, is home to Tampa's professional hockey team, the Tampa Bay Lightning. Stanley Cup champions in 2004, the team is a relative newcomer to the ice. Its season runs October–April.

◖ TAMPA BAY RAYS

Tropicana Field, 1 Tropicana Dr., St. Petersburg, 888/326-7297
HOURS: Game days vary, times usually 2:15 or 7:15 P.M.
COST: $5-32 tickets
Map 6

Tropicana Field is currently home to the Tampa Bay Rays (formerly the Devil Rays, but old Satan has been summarily excised), but a new ballpark is in the work for the next few years. The Rays played their first season here in 1998,

and since then it has been named the second most fan-friendly stadium in the major leagues, according to a fan survey by Sports Travel, Inc. On the other hand, loads of people grouse about it: As a concession to summer temperatures and humidity in these parts, the ballpark has a dome roof (which is lit orange when the Devil Rays win at home) and artificial turf. Out of season, Tropicana Field hosts other athletic events, conventions, trade shows, concerts, and other entertainment, with a seating capacity of 60,000.

For spring training, though, the Rays until 2008 played locally at **Progress Energy Park, Home of Al Lang Field.** From this point forward, the Rays will relocate each spring to Port Charlotte a couple hours to the south. Don't fret, though, because there's other spring training action nearby. Spring training games are all month in March, and tickets usually go on sale January 15.

TAMPA BAY STORM

St. Pete Times Forum, 401 Channelside Dr., 813/301-6600, www.tampabaystorm.com
HOURS: Vary by game
COST: $9-35 for upper level tickets, $35-150 for lower level
Map 1

The local Tampa Bay Storm arena football team, five-time ArenaBowl champs, plays at the Forum, adjacent to Channelside. Arena football is played on an indoor padded surface 85 feet wide and 50 yards long with eight-yard end zones. There are eight players on the field at a time, and everyone plays both offense and defense, with the exception of the kicker, quarterback, offensive specialist, and two defensive specialists. It's a dynamic game in a more intimate space, and the Storm provides a good introduction to the game, having made it to the playoffs for 16 consecutive seasons.

TORONTO BLUE JAYS SPRING TRAINING

311 Douglas Ave., Dunedin, 727/733-0429
HOURS: Game days vary, times usually 1:05 P.M.
COST: $13-24
Map 8

The Toronto Blue Jays also have spring training

in the area, playing at Knology Park, formerly Dunedin Stadium. Built in 1990, it's a serviceable little ballpark in a fairly residential area (you end up paying almost as much for parking as for your ticket). There are upper and lower sections, the upper section having a slight overhang, which can be cooling during warm day games.

USF BULLS
Raymond James Stadium, 4201 N. Dale Mabry Hwy., 800/462-8557
HOURS: Vary by game
COST: $20–31 tickets
Map 5

The powers that be at University of South Florida have made a judgment call in the past few years. They want the university to be big league, no longer a workhorse state school with a preponderance of commuting students. They've thrown money into the effort, constructing state-of-the-art academic buildings and housing, hiring prestigious senior faculty and promising junior profs. But maybe the single biggest indicator is the football team: The USF Bulls have gone from nonexistence to Division I-AA Independent to I-A to Conference USA, and into the Big East Conference in 2005. For the spectator, this means real college football is played during the fall at Raymond James Stadium.

The community has been quick to embrace this shift, amping up attendance drastically. In 2007, the Bulls averaged 53,170 fans per game at Raymond James, the largest increase of any major college football team. The Bulls broke their existing attendance record of 49,212 four times in the 2007 season, culminating in 67,018 people attending the USF–West Virginia game, the largest non–Super Bowl crowd the stadium has ever seen.

ARTS AND LEISURE

HOTELS

Tampa's hotel scene is stymied by one thing: Tampa has no beaches. Although it's on the water—with the active Port of Tampa and waterside residential communities like Davis and Harbour Islands—there is no possibility for a luxury resort hotel or charming bed-and-breakfast just steps from the waters of Hillsborough Bay. For that kind of experience you must head over the bay to St. Pete or Clearwater.

Still, Tampa has a preponderance of pleasant, fairly priced accommodations, spread around the greater Bay Area, from the Latin Quarter of Ybor City to the Westshore business district or the Tampa Convention Center, to near Busch Gardens and the University of South Florida.

St. Petersburg and Pinellas County, on the other hand, give you lots of accommodations options. The city of St. Petersburg lies on the bay side of the peninsula. It has more history, more of a sense of place and sophistication than the beach towns along the Gulf side. There are romantic bed-and-breakfasts, fine restaurants, cultural attractions.

Clearwater Beach and St. Pete Beach on the Gulf side have the densest concentrations of beachside accommodations—in Clearwater this often means tall resort hotels and condos right on the beach; in St. Pete Beach it's low-rise motels that date back a few decades. The communities in between these two—Belleair and Belleair Beach; Indian Rocks Beach and Indian Shores; Redington Shores, North Redington Beach, and Redington Beach; Madeira Beach; and Treasure Island—are fairly residential, but with pockets of beachside hotels, motels, and rentals.

COURTESY OF VISIT FLORIDA

HIGHLIGHTS

LOOK FOR  TO FIND
RECOMMENDED HOTELS.

 **Conventioneer's Dream Hotel:** The 27-story **Marriott Waterside** is a dramatic presence in the downtown district, aiming largely for corporate groups and conferences. A full-service marina makes it ideal for visiting boaters (page 121).

 **Best Place for Sumptuous Retail Therapy:** Attached to Tampa's swishiest mall, the grand **Renaissance Tampa Hotel International Plaza** is in the middle of the Westshore business district (page 123).

 **Best Place to Roll the Dice Before Bed:** Tampa's **Seminole Hard Rock Hotel and Casino** is a rock 'n' roll memorabilia-addled gaming complex and four-diamond hotel just east of downtown. It is a 24-hour

venue, with a nightclub that is open until 6 A.M. (page 123).

 **Easiest Access to St. Petersburg's Museums and Culture:** The historic **Ponce de Leon Hotel** is dead-center in St. Petersburg's cosmopolitan downtown, with 80 recently renovated rooms (page 124).

 **Loveliest Piece of Local History:** Listed on the National Register of Historic Places, the **Renaissance Vinoy Resort & Golf Club** was built by wealthy oilman Aymer Vinoy Laughner in 1925 (page 124).

 **Most Luxurious Beachside Stay:** New in 2007, the **Sandpearl Resort** features 700 feet of white-sand beach, just a quarter-mile from shopping and dining at Pier 60 (page 127).

COURTESY OF VISIT ST. PETERSBURG/CLEARWATER

the Renaissance Vinoy Resort & Golf Club

HOTELS

CHOOSING A HOTEL

Where you stay depends on your priorities. Beach lovers will obviously opt for either the low-rise (and affordable) hotels and motels in the area of St. Pete Beach and the string of communities along Sand Key, or the more high-rise (and, generally, pricier) options to the north in Clearwater. Culture hounds my choose accommodations downtown in St. Petersburg, or downtown in Tampa in one of the large chain properties near the Tampa Bay Performing Arts Center and the convention center.

At this point, nearly every property has a website with photos. Find the best rate available online, then call the property in question

PRICE KEY

💲 Under $100
💲💲 $100-250
💲💲💲 Over $250

to see if you can negotiate a better one. Military affiliation, AAA or AARP membership, and professional affiliations may sweeten the deal. As with all metro areas in Florida, rates vary wildly by season. If affordability is of paramount importance, consider traveling in the off season (summer and fall).

Downtown Tampa and Channelside   Map 1

EMBASSY SUITES TAMPA, DOWNTOWN CONVENTION CENTER 💲💲

513 S. Florida Ave., 813/769-8300,
http://embassysuites1.hilton.com

Located adjacent to the convention center and seven miles from Tampa International Airport, this large hotel boasts an outdoor swim spa and sun deck located on the 3rd floor of the hotel, a Starbuck's in the atrium, a free fitness center, and a full business center. All accommodations are spacious two-room suites, and room rates include cooked-to-order breakfast and a nightly manager's reception.

HYATT REGENCY TAMPA 💲💲

211 N. Tampa St., 813/225-1234,
http://tamparegency.hyatt.com

Despite the fact that this is one of the most business friendly hotels downtown (generous work space, wireless Internet, 30,000 square feet of meeting space), it's still a luxurious getaway possibility. Its 521 rooms have recently been overhauled (granite and marble baths, those cool iPod docking stations); there are jogging paths, a rooftop deck with outdoor whirlpool, 24-hour fitness and

business centers, and a huge outdoor heated pool. The Hyatt also boasts a very competent Italian restaurant.

COURTESY OF VISIT FLORIDA

the Marriott Waterside

◖ MARRIOTT WATERSIDE $$

700 S. Florida Ave., 813/221-4900, www.marriott.com

Part of the Channel Riverwalk, with two cafés front and center for Port of Tampa viewing action, the hotel has 681 nicely appointed guest rooms and 36 suites, most with balconies or views that look over Hillsborough Bay. It's a huge meetings hotel, with 50,000 well-thought-out feet of renovated space. Added allures include a full-service spa and an array of competent on-site restaurants. It's adjacent to the Tampa Convention Center, thus an obvious choice for business travelers, but a 32-slip full-service marina makes it suitable for leisure boat travel.

SHERATON TAMPA RIVERWALK HOTEL $$$

200 N. Ashley Dr., 813/223-2222, www.sheratontampariverwalk.com

Right on the Hillsborough River as part of Mayor Pam Iorio's elaborate Riverwalk vision for downtown (still a work in progress), the Sheraton has 277 recently renovated guest rooms and 16 suites. Out back there's a 500-foot riverfront pool deck with a lovely swimming pool. For business meetings, the hotel has eight meeting rooms, with over 12,000 square feet of meeting space (heavy on the weddings). From here it's an easy Rollerblade along Bayshore Boulevard or over to the convention center.

WESTIN TAMPA HARBOUR ISLAND $$

725 S. Harbour Island Blvd., 813/229-5000, www.starwoodhotels.com

Harbour Island is connected to downtown via a causeway. It still has a neat island-away-from-it-all appeal while being just adjacent to the Tampa Convention Center and just two blocks from St. Pete Times Forum. Thus, this property seems fairly split between business and leisure travelers. It's got the signature Heavenly Beds, mmm, an outdoor pool, and full-service business center. There are 13 flexible meeting rooms, many with nice harbor views. Dogs up to 15 pounds are allowed with a $50 nonrefundable cleaning fee.

Ybor City   Map 3

DON VICENTE DE YBOR HISTORIC INN $$

1915 Avenida Republica de Cuba, 813/241-4545, www.donvicenteinn.com

For an experience steeped in history, head to the Don Vicente, constructed in 1895 by Cuban patriot Vicente Martinez Ybor. The boutique hotel's 16 guest rooms contain genteel flourishes like four-poster beds but also offer broadband, voicemail, and in-room desks. Even if you don't stay here, the opulent grand salon is worth peeking at.

COURTESY OF DON VICENTE INN

Don Vicente de Ybor Historic Inn

Busch Gardens and North Tampa   Map 4

EMBASSY SUITES $$
3705 Spectrum Blvd., 813/977-7066,
www.embassysuites.com

The USF hotel of choice is this tall, suites-only hotel with a soaring atrium. Rooms are pretty, with spacious living rooms and private bedrooms with either a king or two double beds. There are two TVs in every room, a weird superabundance, but nice if the kids want to watch something execrable in the next room. Although the rooms are a little more, included in the price is a very nice daily cooked-to-order breakfast buffet and the manager's reception, where you get a free cocktail and some chips in the early evening.

LA QUINTA INN TAMPA
NEAR BUSCH GARDENS $
9202 N. 30th St., 813/930-6900

This familiar chain is adjacent to the Busch Gardens entrance, with 144 nicely appointed rooms with roomy bathrooms, good lighting, large desks, and computer-friendly dataport telephones. There's also a good-sized pool.

Greater Tampa   Map 5

GRAM'S PLACE $
3109 N. Ola Ave., 813/221-0596,
www.grams-inn-tampa.com

For when you're looking for a wild experience at a tame price, Gram's Place will surely fit the bill. It's eccentric, with a different music theme (jazz, blues, rock) in each of the private suites and youth hostel–style bunks. All rooms come with a "music menu" of CDs. The hostel part looks like a railroad car fashioned around a 100-year-old train depot. The rooms are set in two circa 1945 cottages and share an oversized in-ground whirlpool tub, a BYOB bar in the courtyard, and a 16 multitrack recording studio. Lest you are imagining some cool old Grandma jamming in the recording studio with a bunch of longhairs, the "Gram" in question is Gram Parsons, once member of the Byrds and the Flying Burrito Brothers, the deceased musician responsible for the heartbreakingly beautiful song, "Grievous Angel," which Emmylou Harris made famous.

GRAND HYATT $$$
2900 Bayport Dr., 813/874-1234,
www.grandtampabay.hyatt.com

One of the big kahuna hotels in these parts, the Grand Hyatt is a large hotel near the airport that caters mainly to the corporate traveler.

There are 445 deluxe guest rooms and suites, including 38 Spanish-style casita rooms and 7 casita suites in a secluded area at the south end of the property, which is set in a 35-acre wildlife preserve on the shores of Tampa Bay. The Hyatt contains two of the best restaurants in town, Armani's and Oystercatchers.

INTERCONTINENTAL TAMPA $$$
4860 W. Kennedy Blvd., 813/286-4400,
www.intercontampa.com

This newcomer is a business traveler's dream. The 323 rooms, 17 junior suites (a handful of which are business suites), and two presidential suites feature fresh decor, feather-top mattresses with luxurious linens, functional working areas, flatscreen TVs and iPod docking stations. The hotel offers 21,000 square feet of flexible meeting space, wireless high-speed Internet throughout the entire hotel, a fitness center, a full-service concierge program, as well as a rooftop pool with views of the bay and city. The hotel also has a Shula's Steak House and Shula's No Name Lounge.

QUORUM HOTEL TAMPA $$$
700 N. Westshore Blvd., 813/289-8200,
www.quorumtampa.com

Located in the heart of the Westshore business

SADDLEBROOK RESORT

Men and women have enjoyed body pampering for thousands of years in many areas of the world. The Romans bathed and socialized in gigantic bathhouses that could hold up to 6,000 people. The Japanese took their entire families to soak in bubbling hot springs. The Turks added steam, massages, and oil to the bathing experience, followed by an après-bath relaxation period where coffee was served. And the Finns have long considered a weekly sauna part of their culture.

None of this is news to the **Saddlebrook Resort & Spa** (5700 Saddlebrook Way, 800/729-8383, $$$). It's really Tampa's nicest four-star resort hotel, only it's in the sleepy town of Wesley Chapel. It has 800 guest rooms, all gorgeous, pools, tennis, the Palmer and the Saddlebrook golf courses (and the Arnold Palmer Golf Academy), and a variety of dining options (if you eat on the patio of the Cypress Restaurant you can see nesting wood storks). But the real attraction is when you step through the Terrace Garden into the haven that is the Spa at Saddlebrook Resort, where you can indulge in massage therapy, hydrotherapy, herbal and seaweed body wraps, moor mud treatments, and aromatherapy.

district, the Quorum Hotel Tampa is just two miles from Tampa International Airport and Raymond James Stadium and sits squarely between Westshore Plaza and International Plaza shopping centers. The largely business-oriented property offers 272 spacious guest rooms, including four junior suites and two executive suites. The executive club level, consisting of 26 rooms on the 11th floor, features a comfortable private lounge with complimentary continental breakfast, evening cocktails, and hors d'oeuvres.

◀ RENAISSANCE TAMPA HOTEL INTERNATIONAL PLAZA ❸❸❸
4200 Jim Walter Blvd., 813/877-9200, www.marriott.com

One of Tampa's nicest luxury hotels is the fairly new Renaissance Tampa Hotel International Plaza near the Westshore business district at the International Plaza mall. The lush decor is reminiscent of a Mediterranean villa, an illusion bolstered by things like the jewel-toned, high-style Pelagia Trattoria at its center. The hotel's not small—with 293 guest rooms on eight floors—but the service is personal and attentive, and it seems especially geared to the repeat-business, high-end business traveler.

SAILPORT WATERFRONT SUITES ❸❸
2506 N. Rocky Point Dr., 813/281-9599,

For a more independent approach amongst the many chain names in the Rocky Point area, try Sailport, a four-story, all-suites hotel (all rooms have a queen sleeper sofa in the living room, convenient for families) with full-sized kitchens, barbecue grills, outdoor heated pool, lighted tennis court, and fishing pier.

◀ SEMINOLE HARD ROCK HOTEL AND CASINO ❸❸❸
5223 Orient Rd., 866/502-7529, www.hardrockhotelcasinotampa.com

The What Is This Doing Here(?!) Award goes to the Hard Rock. This huge luminous purple tower rises up in the middle of nowhere off of I-75 (well, it's not totally in the middle of nowhere, as the Ford Amphitheatre is just across the highway from it) like a mirage. With an illuminated 12-story tower that shifts colors, the signature huge guitar at the entrance, a 90,000-square-foot casino, and see-and-be-seen restaurants like Floyd's and Council Oak, it's like a little piece of Vegas right here in Tampa. The complex opened in 2004 and has been swamped with casino and overnight guests ever since. The 250 guest rooms and suites have a hipster art deco design, with unique extras like Tivoli stereo and CD systems and ultraluxury beds. The most luxurious part is the pool area, with cascading fountains and cool private cabanas with televisions and refrigerators. The state of Florida has green-lighted all kinds of expansion for the Hard Rock, so the gambling options will be myriad in 2008 and beyond.

TAHITIAN INN ❸

601 S. Dale Mabry Hwy., 813/877-6721,
www.tahitianinn.com

If you find yourself in the north Tampa residential area called Carrollwood and you prefer

independently owned hotels, the Tahitian Inn is a lovely two-story family-run motel that had a huge remodel in 2003, yielding 60 Tahitian-theme (dark wood, tropical accessories) moderately priced rooms and 20 executive suites, a lovely pool with tiki huts and hammocks, and the Serenity Spa with massage and Tahitian hot stone treatments. There's also a lovely little on-site café with patio seating near a koi pond. The location is close to I-275 and lots of commerce.

Downtown St. Petersburg   Map 6

LA VERANDA BED AND BREAKFAST ❸❸

111 5th Ave. N., St. Petersburg, 727/824-9997

Especially for romance seekers, La Veranda Bed and Breakfast is wonderful for couples as it's right near the heart of downtown St. Petersburg, but still quiet and romantic. It's set in a 1910 mansion girdled by wide wrap-around porches and sweet tropical gardens, its suites decorated with canopy beds, antiques, and Oriental rugs. Each suite opens directly onto the large veranda, ergo the name.

MANSION HOUSE BED AND BREAKFAST ❸❸

105 5th Ave. NE, St. Petersburg, 727/821-9391,
www.mansionbandb.com

Just up the block from another small B&B called La Veranda, in a residential neighborhood just off of downtown is a tiny inn called, rather grandly, Mansion House Bed and Breakfast. There are 12 pretty rooms set in two Craftsman-style houses, one of which is thought to have been built in between 1901 and 1904 by St. Petersburg's first mayor, David Mofett. A court-yard in between the houses is perfect for a little reading or down time. Also, there's a pool.

◖ PONCE DE LEON HOTEL ❸❸

95 Central Ave., St. Petersburg, 727/550-9300,
www.poncedeleonhotel.com

Right in the thick of things downtown, this

was one of St. Petersburg's first hotels. Opened in 1922 and hosting many of the city's most famous visitors, it's got charm and a real sense of place (without having a superabundance of amenities). Its restaurant, Ceviche, is one of the biggest draws downtown, with great tapas and live music (ask for a top floor if music and street noise will bother you), and the tiny Pincho y Pincho café serves up fabulous coffees and Spanish-style snacks and breakfast. Weekly rates available.

◖ RENAISSANCE VINOY RESORT & GOLF CLUB ❸❸❸

501 5th Ave. NE, St. Petersburg, 727/894-1000,
www.renaissancehotels.com

Some of this area's greatest landmarks are grand old hotels. In order to feel comfortable with the splurge, tell yourself it's like the price of the hotel plus the admission to a local historical attraction. A historical attraction with room service. The Renaissance Vinoy Resort & Golf Club was built by Pennsylvania oil-man Aymer Vinoy Laughner in 1925. At $3.5 million, the Mediterranean revival–style hotel was the largest construction project in Florida's history. Exquisitely restored in 1992 at a cost of $93 million, the resort exudes the kind of rarefied glamour that helps put life's quotidian woes behind you. There are 360 guest rooms and 15 suites, many with views of the marina. The hotel also has a spa, a lovely pool with a waterfall, five restaurants, tennis courts, an 18-hole golf course designed by Ron Garl, and its own marina. Again, it's the kind of hotel that was frequented by people like Calvin Coolidge, Babe Ruth, and Herbert Hoover, and is listed on the National Register of Historic Places.

St. Pete Beach   Map 7

ALDEN BEACH RESORT $$
5900 Gulf Blvd., St. Pete Beach, 727/360-7081,
www.aldenbeachresort.com

Very near the Sirata Beach Resort, the Alden is an attentively staffed, family-owned beach resort of 149 suites, especially beloved by kids. It has tennis, volleyball, two pools (a little far from the beach, so the walk back and forth takes time for little ones), and a video game room. Rooms on the pool side are significantly cheaper than on the Gulf side.

DON CESAR BEACH
RESORT & SPA $$$
400 Gulf Blvd., St. Pete Beach, 727/363-1881,
www.doncesar.com

The huge, Pepto Bismol–pink Don CeSar is a landmark in St. Pete and a longtime point of reference on maritime navigation charts. Named after a character in the opera *Maritana,* the Don CeSar has hosted F. Scott Fitzgerald and wife Zelda, Clarence Darrow, Al Capone, Lou Gehrig, and countless other celebrities. Originally opened in 1928, the property was commandeered by the military during World War II and eventually abandoned. These days, it's a Loews hotel, with 340 lovely rooms, fishing, golfing, tennis, and the soothing Beach Club & Spa. If it's too rich for your blood, take the tour and stop in for ice cream at its old-fashioned ice cream parlor (get the coffee flavor).

COURTESY OF VISIT ST. PETERSBURG/CLEARWATER

A longtime point of reference on maritime navigation charts, the Don CeSar Beach Resort is known as the "Pink Palace" and features Mediterranean and Moorish architecture.

SIRATA BEACH RESORT $$

5300 Gulf Blvd., St. Pete Beach, 727/363-5100, www.sirata.com

Sirata Beach Resort used to be connected to the TradeWinds but is now an independent, family-run midsize hotel, with a range of children's programs and activities. It's the kind of place that locals in Tampa take their brood for a weekend of R&R, with 13 unspoiled acres of beachfront. Its three pools are open daily 9 A.M.–10 P.M., the two on-site beach bars (Harry's and Rumrunner's) are hopping, and there's a Durango's Steak House attached. A beach services kiosk will set you up with parasailing, Wave Runners, Jet Skis, or a dinner sunset cruise.

TRADEWINDS ISLAND RESORTS $$

5500 Gulf Blvd., St. Pete Beach, 727/367-6461, www.tradewindsresort.com

For families, blow with the TradeWinds. It's had a recent and enormous overhaul, and offers families a bunch of accommodation choices with nary a clinker among them. The resort, supposedly the largest on the Gulf Coast, comprises the TradeWinds Island Grand ($168–457) and the Sandpiper Hotel and Suites ($149–226), and whichever one you choose includes playtime privileges at the other. The Island Grand is the fancier, a four-diamond property with soaring palms, a grand lobby, and really lovely rooms. Sandpiper would be my choice with little ones. The whole complex offers multiple pools, something like a dozen places to eat and drink, multiple fitness centers, tennis courts everywhere, a paddleboat canal meandering through the grounds, and a wide, private expanse of beach. Right out the back of the properties you can rent equipment for snorkeling or fishing, and try your hand at parasailing, waterskiing, and water scooters. The children's program (KONK, Kids Only, No Kidding!) is tremendous, with seasonal offerings like the Swashbucklin' By the Sea pirate package in which you get to meet Redbeard and walk the plank.

COURTESY OF VISIT FLORIDA

TradeWinds Island Resorts

Clearwater and Clearwater Beach   Map 8

BELLEVIEW BILTMORE
RESORT & SPA $$$

25 Belleview Blvd., Clearwater, 727/373-3000,
www.belleviewbiltmore.com

Built in 1897 by railroad magnate and west-central Florida pioneer Henry Plant, the 292-room Belleview Biltmore is reputed to be the largest continuously occupied wooden structure in the world (its roof is 2.5 acres). On the National Register of Historic Places (there are tours daily, even if you're not staying here), it's a historical retreat from the beach bustle of Clearwater, situated high on a coastal bluff, where it's easy to unwind and indulge in a little golf or the gamut of spa treatments. How's this for an eclectic host: Its guests have included Thomas Edison, Henry Ford, the Duke of Windsor, and Bob Dylan. Legg Mason Real Estate Investors recently purchased the Belleview Biltmore with plans to fully restore the property beginning in May of 2009.

SANDPEARL RESORT $$$

500 Mandalay Ave., Clearwater, 727/441-2425,
www.sandpearl.com

It's brand new, the first new resort to be built on Clearwater Beach in 25 years, and it is absolutely spectacular. The combined resort and condominium project features a 253-room hotel, a full-service spa, upscale dining, state-of-the-art meeting and event space, 117 condominium units, and 700 feet of gorgeous Gulf of

COURTESY OF VISIT ST. PETERSBURG/CLEARWATER

Built in 1897, the 292-room Belleview Biltmore Resort & Spa holds an honored position on the National Register of Historic Places.

Mexico beachfront. Rooms have an open, airy feel with balconies and high ceilings and each includes elegant, yet comfortable furnishings, fixtures, and rich textured fabrics. Fifty suites, located on the top two floors of the resort, offer one- and two-bedroom floor plans.

Greater Pinellas County

Map 9

SAFETY HARBOR RESORT AND SPA $$

105 N. Bayshore Dr., Safety Harbor, 888/237-8772, www.safetyharborspa.com

A piece of local history I'm not sure I'm buying is claimed by Safety Harbor Resort and Spa. About a zillion places along the Gulf Coast profess to be what Spanish explorer Hernando de Soto identified as the Fountain of Youth. Is it the mineral pools here at this 50,000-square-foot spa and tennis academy? Got to give you a dunno on that one. The waters are mighty nice either way, filling three pools and used in the spa treatments. The resort is also home to a tennis academy, a fairly sophisticated restaurant called 105 North, and a fancy-pants salon. The 189 guest rooms and four suites are spacious and offer nice views of Tampa Bay.

WESTIN INNISBROOK GOLF RESORT $$

36750 U.S. 19 N., Palm Harbor, 800/456-2000, www.westin-innisbrook.com

Golfers will appreciate Westin Innisbrook, a 900-acre property just north of Clearwater. It has four top-ranked golf courses, 11 tennis courts, six swimming pools (including the super, kids-oriented Loch Ness Monster Pool), a children's recreation center, several restaurants, and 60 acres with a series of jogging and cycling trails. Rooms are all suites, with nice working kitchens. Its Copperhead Golf Course stretches more than 7,300 yards long and is home to the PGA Tour's PODS Championship.

EXCURSIONS FROM TAMPA AND ST. PETERSBURG

Pick a point on the compass. An hour due north from Tampa and St. Petersburg and you run smack into what's called the Nature Coast, complete with manatee viewing, fishing, and tramping around in the palmetto-festooned flatwoods. An hour due south, it's all the sophisticated and effete cultural allures in the city of Sarasota and its barrier islands. An hour northeast? That's where you throw your hands in the air and scream during the triple inversion. It's Walt Disney World Resort, Universal, and all the theme park madness that is Orlando.

PLANNING YOUR TIME

Your whim decides which way you head for an excursion from the home base of Tampa and St. Petersburg. Well, your whim, your wallet, and your wardrobe. The Nature Coast's allures are inexpensive and casual, with enough to entertain you for two or three days (the hardcore angler, however, will be endlessly amused). Everything in Orlando requires deep pockets and comfortable shoes; jacket not required but those mouse ears help. Orlando, like the universe, seems to be ever expanding, with more and greater attractions added all the time. You might easily add a day or a week to your trip, depending on your stamina for theme parks. (To be fair, downtown Orlando and Winter Park are destinations in their own right, free of theme parks and rich with culture.)

Sarasota, on the other hand, would make a pleasant outing for dinner and a show (its theater, opera, and other arts efforts beat those

HIGHLIGHTS

LOOK FOR 【 TO FIND RECOMMENDED SIGHTS, ACTIVITIES, DINING, AND LODGING.

【 **Best Place to Scream and Throw Your Hands in the Air:** Opened officially in April 2006 at a reported cost of more than $100 million, Expedition Everest is the Number One ride to Fast Pass when you get to Disney's Animal Kingdom, at the **Walt Disney World Resort.** Disney Imagineers have built a somewhat scaled-down Mount Everest (now the tallest mountain in Florida) upon which they have re-created a small Himalayan village and a state-of-the-art thrill ride (page 132).

【 **Best Art within Driving Distance of Orlando's Theme Parks: Downtown Orlando** is the cultural hotspot of the area. This is where you'll find the stunning Charles Hosmer Morse Museum of American Art, a Winter Park destination that now houses Tiffany jewelry, lamps, pottery, paintings, art glass, leaded-glass windows, and the chapel designed for the 1893 World's Columbian Exposition in Chicago (page 134).

【 **Best Place to See Large Animals:** Find out why Rodale's Scuba Diving awards the area this title. The manatee is the goliath in question, and you can see it up close in the underwater "fishbowl" at **Homosassa Springs State Wildlife Park** on the Nature Coast (page 146).

【 **Best Place to Wet Your Line:** Roughly 62 miles of Gulf Coast, 106 miles of rivers, and 19,111 acres of lakes, and that's just in Citrus County alone. The Nature Coast is fishing country. Thanks to bag limits, closed seasons, and catch-and-release indoctrination, there seem to be more fish than ever, enlivening a day of **Offshore Fishing** in Steinhatchee (page 147).

【 **Weirdest Plants You'll Ever Fall in Love With:** You don't have to be a master gardener or panting horticulturalist to enjoy a day at **Marie Selby Botanical Gardens** in Sarasota. In 11 bayfront acres, the open-air and under-glass museum has more than 6,000 orchids and more than 20,000 other plants, many of which have been collected in the wild by the gardens' research staff. Most impressive is the vast array of otherworldly epiphytes, or air plants (page 149).

【 **Best Rainy-Day Way to Lose Yourself:** The **John and Mable Ringling Museum of Art** in Sarasota is a must-see for fans of Flemish and Italian baroque art, with room after room of breathtaking canvasses, the most impressive of which is a series by Peter Paul Rubens known collectively as *The Triumph of the Eucharist* (page 149).

Against the coral reef background in the Epcot pavillion, at the Walt Disney World Resort, the characters from *Finding Nemo* appear to be swimming with the live fishes.

COURTESY OF ORLANDO ORANGE COUNTY CVB

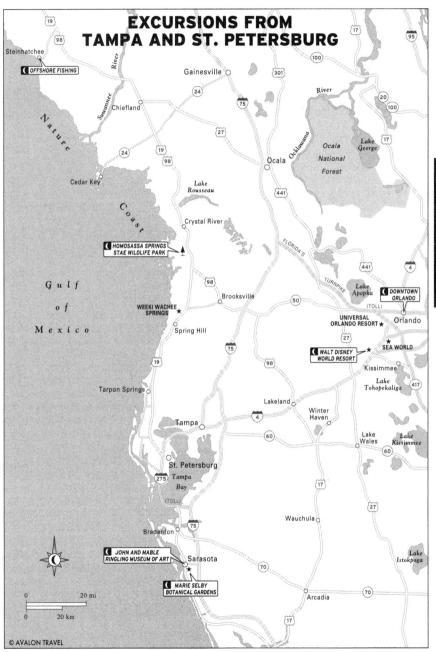

EXCURSIONS FROM TAMPA AND ST. PETERSBURG

Steinhatchee

OFFSHORE FISHING

Gainesville

Suwannee River

Chiefland

River

Ocklawaha

Nature

Cedar Key

Ocala

Ocala National Forest

Lake George

Lake Rousseau

Coast

Crystal River

HOMOSASSA SPRINGS STAE WILDLIFE PARK

Gulf

FLORIDA'S TURNPIKE

of

Brooksville

WEEKI WACHEE SPRINGS

Mexico

Spring Hill

Lake Apopka

DOWNTOWN ORLANDO

Orlando

UNIVERSAL ORLANDO RESORT

WALT DISNEY WORLD RESORT

SEA WORLD

Tarpon Springs

Kissimmee

Lake Tohopekaliga

Lakeland

Winter Haven

Tampa

Lake Wales

Lake Kissimmee

St. Petersburg

Tampa Bay

(TOLL)

Wauchula

Bradenton

JOHN AND MABLE RINGLING MUSEUM OF ART

Sarasota

Lake Istokpoga

MARIE SELBY BOTANICAL GARDENS

Arcadia

0   20 mi

0   20 km

© AVALON TRAVEL

EXCURSIONS

in Tampa and St. Petersburg handily). Hotels and restaurants in Sarasota proper are expensive, but more affordable digs are to be found on the barrier islands of Siesta Key and Anna Maria (many accommodations offered only by the week in high season). Another barrier island, Longboat Key, is designed to thrill the high-end golfer.

Orlando

A little like Las Vegas, Orlando draws people with the lure of fantasy, magic, and fun, with fewer vices or ladies in feathered headdresses. But unlike Vegas—where what happens there, stays there, subdued in a fog of excess—what happens in Orlando is the content of scrapbooks, subject of the lion's share of those family holiday photo cards, fodder for countless "what I did on my summer vacation" essays, and, maybe most important of all, the stuff of oft-recounted family memories.

Walt Disney World Resort sets the tone for all the other ancillary and tertiary theme parks and visitor attractions in Orlando. The sprawling Central Florida tourism hub features a brand of magic and fun that is by and large wholesome, but changing all the time as theme parks add, revise, and try to outdo the competition. The thing that holds it all together, that gives it a sense of continuity, is the destination's ongoing flair at appealing to many different kinds of people.

At each attraction, fun has been calibrated to appeal to many different interests and abilities. What started with a shrill-voiced mouse introduced at the Colony Theater in New York on November 18, 1928 has become a whole industry devoted to sussing out the unfulfilled dreams of generations of visitors. Like the sage Cinderella once said, "A dream is a wish your heart makes," which makes all of Orlando something like a psychic cardiologist.

SIGHTS
◖ Walt Disney World Resort
Walt Disney World (WDW) is spread across 27,000 acres, about 43 square miles, half in Orlando and half in Lake Buena Vista. It encompasses four distinct theme parks, two water parks, shopping and entertainment complexes, 22 resort hotels (plus another 10 that aren't Disney owned, but are on the property), six golf courses, a sports complex, and other attractions. For the uninitiated who have a vague notion that WDW is that park with the castle in the middle, thorough investigation cannot be undertaken on a single day. Magic Kingdom, the first of the parks, is divided into seven themed lands, with lots to do for little ones. Epcot, what used to be EPCOT, an acronym for Experimental Prototype Community of Tomorrow, has two "worlds"—Future World, which is mostly about science and technology, and World Showcase, pavilions representing countries around the world. Epcot appeals most to adults, whereas the third park, Disney-MGM Studios lures teens and tweens with its movie-themed rides and attractions. The fourth and newest park, Animal Kingdom, is not a zoo, but rather an animal-themed assemblage of exhibits and thrill rides. All four parks tend to host a festive afternoon parade, an evening celebration (many with fireworks), and special events throughout the year. Costumed Disney characters mill around at all four parks for photo ops and autograph signing.

Typhoon Lagoon and Blizzard Beach are the two themed water parks, each requiring separate entry. Downtown Disney is a shopping and dining complex with an adult nightclub area called Pleasure Island, a huge virtual-reality and video arcade called DisneyQuest, and a theater in which Cirque du Soleil performs La Nouba. The Wide World of Sports complex hosts sporting events like the Atlanta Braves spring training, the Richard Petty Driving Experience enables you to drive a real race car, and 15 miles south the Nature Conservancy

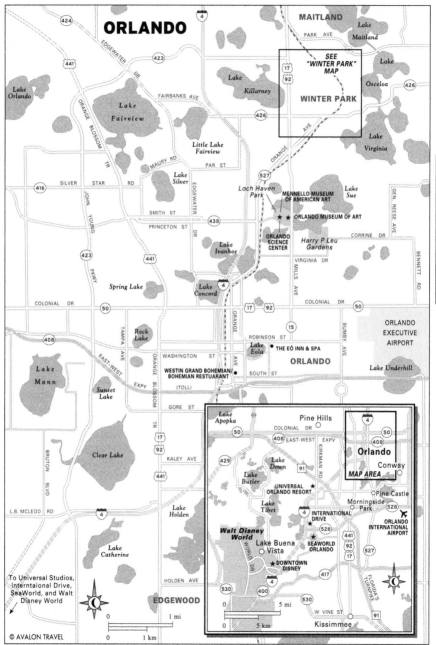

Cinderella's Castle looms over the Magic Kingdom, stunning in its grandeur from far away, but also giving up countless tiny treasures upon close investigation.

oversees Disney Wilderness Preserve. For pricing and information, call 407/939-1289 or visit http://disneyworld.disney.go.com.

Universal Orlando Resort

Universal Orlando Resort began as a direct competitor to Disney-MGM Studios. The idea was the same: build a working film and TV studio that is also a theme park in which guests are immersed in the world of the movies, its dynamic rides, attractions, 3-D movies, and exhibits celebrating the cinema. A massive growth spurt in 1999 yielded a second park, Islands of Adventure as well as three resort hotels, and a dining and nightlife complex called CityWalk. The tagline for Universal Studios Florida is Ride the Movies, whereas the phrase for Islands of Adventure is Live the Adventure. The distinction is a little blurry, but what you need to know is that Islands of Adventure has some of the most hair-raising, sweaty-palmed thrill rides in all of Orlando,

cases in point being Incredible Hulk Coaster and The Amazing Adventures of Spider-Man. And whereas Disney-MGM Studios focuses a little more on nostalgic old films, Universal Studios's efforts are more inspired by popular films, divided into six themed areas within the park. Islands of Adventure draws from classic comics and comic book heroes. For tickets and information, call 407/363-8000 or visit www.universalorlando.com.

SeaWorld Orlando

It's not an amusement park, but it's certainly no aquarium or zoo. SeaWorld Orlando is a celebration of sea life, with a special emphasis on those amazingly smart marine mammals. Shamu and friends are put through their paces in a variety of shows that are constantly being updated and added to. The current killer whale show, *Believe* and the dolphin show, *Blue Horizons,* are offered several times daily along with other live shows that make up the core of the park's attractions. There are a couple thrillish rides, but the park's real strengths are the animal shows and educational walk-throughs of animal environments.

Just across the road from SeaWorld Orlando is its more upscale sibling, Discovery Cove. Limited to 1,000 guests per day by reservation, the lush Caribbean resort allows visitors to swim with a dolphin, snorkel along a saltwater coral reef, frolic amongst stingrays, or just loll in a chaise on a sandy beach. Parent company Anheuser-Busch will open a water park in 2008 to compete with Disney's Lagoon and Blizzard Beach or Universal's Wet 'n Wild. For information and ticket prices, call 800/327-2420 or visit www.seaworld.com.

◖ Downtown Orlando

Downtown? Yes, Orlando has one, located about 20 minutes northeast of all the tourist sprawl. The downtown area and the nearby historic town of Winter Park are home to many of the area's top museums: See Tiffany stained glass at the **Charles Hosmer Morse Museum of American Art**; the work of folk artist Earl Cunningham and others at the **Mennello**

EXCURSIONS

Museum of American Art; a great permanent collection of American art, including works by Georgia O'Keefe and Ansel Adams at the **Orlando Museum of Art**; or a thoughtfully curated show at the **Cornell Fine Arts Museum,** considered one of the country's top college art museums. Kids are entertained at the hands-on **Orlando Science Center** or the 50-acres of botanical gardens at the nearby **Harry P. Leu Gardens,** while sports fans might want to catch an NBA's Orlando Magic game at the arena.

International Drive

Often shortened to I-Drive, this is the most intensive tourist strip of the greater Orlando area, running southwest of downtown roughly parallel to I-4 and linking SeaWorld Orlando and Universal Orlando Resort with the Orange County Convention Center and the two monster outlet malls. For visitors splitting their time between the various theme

SeaWorld's newest show, *Believe*, is billed as the most ambitious project in the park's 41-year history.

COURTESY OF ORLANDO ORANGE COUNTY CVB

parks, I-Drive is an ideal and centralized place to stay, offering midpriced and luxury high-rise hotels along its length. Some of the area's nicer restaurants crowd along I-Drive with many of the half-day tourist attractions (WonderWorks, Ripley's Believe It or Not, SkyVenture, Skull Kingdom). The downside is grueling, bumper-to-bumper traffic during rush hour. It is less crowded in its southern end near the convention center, unless there's a huge convention going on (check the website, www.occc.net, to find out).

Kissimmee

Some say the name was that of a 17th century mission created here to convert the Jororo tribe to Christianity, but everyone agrees that Kissimmee wins Central Florida's Hardest City to Pronounce award. Kissimmee, the Osceola County seat, is 18 miles due south of Orlando and just east of Walt Disney World Resort. Its roots are firmly planted in cattle ranching, with a lingering rough-and-tumble cowboy image. It's where folks go to see the rodeo, do a little bass fishing, ride an airboat through gator-studded waters, or tramp around on the beautiful Florida Trail. Through Kissimmee, the long strip of multi-laned highway called U.S. 192 or Irlo Bronson Memorial Highway is the jackpot for budget-minded Disney visitors. Moderately priced motels, family restaurants and fast food, and a staggering number of mini-golf emporiums dot its length.

Between Kissimmee and Walt Disney World Resort lies the town of Celebration. Clusters of eerily perfect Victorian homes align on neat streets of the Disney Corporation's prototypical community of the future. It's not exactly what Mr. Disney had in mind with EPCOT, but it's close.

FOOD
Walt Disney World Resort

Dining options are so plentiful as to be dizzying—each Disney park has on-site dining ranging from walk-up casual to white-tablecloth fine, then each of the 32 Disney resort properties offer their own eats. A handful of the better options are listed here.

At Disney's Fort Wilderness Resort & Campground, the **Hoop-Dee-Doo Musical Revue** (407/WDW-DINE, three shows nightly, at 5, 7:15, and 9:30 P.M., $51–$59 adults, $26–$30 children) is the big dining kahuna here, and reservations are a must far in advance (up to 180). It's an all-American hoedown with family-style barbecued ribs, corn, baked beans, draft beer, wine, and soft drinks, all enjoyed with a musical comedy review that always gets highest marks from longtime Disney fans. It's one of the longest-running shows at WDW.

Making lists of Orlando's top restaurants nearly every year, **California Grill** (5:30–10P.M. daily, $30–50) at Disney's Contemporary Resort draws locals as well as tourists. It was one of Disney's earliest efforts at luxurious destination dining, with panoramic windows showing off Magic Kingdom (and its fireworks) and a dynamic open kitchen. The food is a very apt facsimile of what made San Francisco such a culinary mecca in the late 1980s—flatbreads, Sonoma goat cheese ravioli, grilled pork tenderloin with polenta and balsamic-sparked cremini mushrooms: simple, bright flavors, with a heavy reliance on seasonal produce. The wine list is a treasure trove for the California Cabophile, even by the glass.

At Disney's Animal Kingdom Lodge, **Jiko–The Cooking Place** (5:30–10P.M. daily, $30–50) is the top offering, with a broad palette of cuisines that range across the Mediterranean, Europe, and the 52 countries on the African continent. It's a lovely dining space, vaguely evocative of *The Lion King*, enlivened by two huge wood-burning ovens. Appetizers tend to be more imaginative than entrées (can't get too whack with the fairly meat-and-potatoes clientele), and the array of wines from South Africa is laudable.

Universal Orlando Resort

Set off to one side of Universal's CityWalk is the biggest **Hard Rock Café** (407/351-7625,

daily 11 A.M.–2 A.M., $11–24) in the world—a veritable "Roman Coliseum of rock," replete with memorabilia from KISS, Elvis, The Beatles, and Bob Dylan, along with an all-American menu of burgers, ribs, and salads. Or kick it up a notch and head to **Emeril's Restaurant Orlando** (407/224-2424, daily 11:30 A.M.–2 P.M. and 5:30 P.M.–10 P.M., an hour later on Fri. and Sat., $25–50) for Emeril Lagasse's upscale spins on Louisiana-style oyster stew, duck, and rib eye. The cocktails are good, but the 12,000-bottle wine list merits some robust consideration. There's also a notable cigar bar and all prime beef—an expense-account paradise.

SeaWorld Orlando

Makahiki Luau Dinner and Show is the big daily dinner event, held at the Seafire Inn as the sun begins its colorful descent over the Waterfront harbor. It is by reservation only (in high season there are two seatings at 5:30 and 8:15 P.M.; the rest of the year dinner is at 6:30 P.M., $6 adults, $30 children 3–9, free for children under 3) and is almost as good as Disney's Spirit of Aloha Show at Disney's Polynesian Resort and better than the Wantilan Luau at the Royal Pacific Resort at Universal. For something more adult-oriented, **Sharks Underwater Grill** is SeaWorld Orlando going fancy-pants (open 11 A.M. to one hour prior to park close, $18–25). It's first come, first served, but you can put your name in for priority seating and come back at a designated time. There's a very commendable à la carte menu of Floribbean dishes—sushi-grade tuna with tropical slaw, Caribbean conch chowder, jumbo lump crab cakes with Key lime mustard mayonnaise—served in an elegant, "underwater" dining room. Not really, but the enormous walls of shark tanks are truly compelling if dinner conversation lapses.

Downtown Orlando

Some of the best dining in this area is to be had in the charming town of **Winter Park,** just northeast of downtown. It's a serious food city, where restaurants engage in fierce

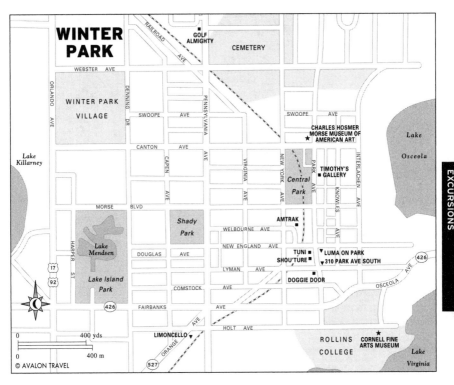

WINTER
PARK

RAILROAD
GOLF ALMIGHTY
CEMETERY

WEBSTER   AVE

ORLANDO   AVE
DENNING   DR
WINTER PARK
VILLAGE
SWOOPE   AVE
PENNSYLVANIA   AVE

CANTON   AVE

Lake
Killarney

CAPEN   AVE
MORSE   BLVD
VIRGINIA   AVE
NEW YORK   AVE

SWOOPE   AVE

CHARLES HOSMER
MORSE MUSEUM OF
★ AMERICAN ART

Lake
Osceola

PARK   AVE
★ TIMOTHY'S
■ GALLERY

INTERLACHEN   AVE

Central
Park

KNOWLES   AVE

Shady
Park

AMTRAK

WELBOURNE   AVE

HARPER   ST
Lake
Mendsen

DOUGLAS   AVE

NEW ENGLAND   AVE

TUNI ■
SHOU'TURE ■
▼ LUMA ON PARK
▼ 310 PARK AVE SOUTH

426

17
92
Lake Island
Park

LYMAN   AVE

COMSTOCK   AVE

DOGGIE DOOR

OSCEOLA   AVE

426

426
FAIRBANKS   AVE

HOLT   AVE

0   400 yds
0   400 m
© AVALON TRAVEL

LIMONCELLO ▼

ORANGE   AVE

527

ROLLINS
COLLEGE

★
CORNELL FINE
ARTS MUSEUM

Lake
Virginia

EXCURSIONS

competition for the approbation of the sophisticated, worldly locals. **Luma on Park** (290 S. Park Ave., 407/599-4111, 5:30–11P.M. daily) may currently get top honors for its incredible array of wines by the glass as well as its contemporary dishes such as Gulf red snapper with corn and local chanterelles or pizzas like the Copper River sockeye salmon with fennel salad, olives, and saffron. At the corner of Park and New England Avenues, it's in a perfect corner spot in the recently remodeled Bank of America building, with a striking two-story illuminated wine vault.

The No. 2 spot is a hard call, as some people favor the comfortable **310 Park Ave. South** (310 S. Park Ave., 407/647-7277, Mon.–Wed. 11 A.M.–10 P.M., Thurs.–Sat. until 11 P.M., Sun. 10 A.M.–10 P.M., $15–30) for an herb-crusted salmon or a simple pork chop. But the family-owned Mediterranean **Limoncello** (702 Orange Ave., 407/539-0900, Tues.–Sun. 5:30–10 P.M., $14–22) also does a brisk business with familiar Italian pastas and such.

SHOPPING

Each of the theme parks boasts its own shopping, mostly of the themed gewgaw variety. For more extensive retail therapy, head to **Prime Outlets Orlando** at the northern tip of International Drive, **Orlando Premium Outlets** at the southern tip of International Drive, or the 120-acre **Downtown Disney,** at the intersection of Buena Vista Drive and Hotel Plaza Boulevard. This last is a shopping and dining complex comprised of the **Marketplace, Pleasure Island,** and the 66-acre **West Side.** The restaurants tend to be outposts of major chains and the shopping is more souvenirs, luxury goods, and zany impulse buys. I have made some excellent purchases here, such as a

Universal's CityWalk keeps retooling and rethinking its concepts, so there is constantly something buzz-worthy along its length.

chili-cheese dog refrigerator magnet (very life-like) and one can of Flarp!, described euphemistically as "noise-making goop." If one were so inclined, one could also buy just-dipped candy apples, a magic trick spinning sphere that appears to hover in space, a battery-operated hamster that runs incessantly inside a clear plastic ball, or a premium cigar.

CityWalk, Universal's 30-acre adult playground of restaurants, nightclubs, and music venues, is chockablock with thousands of pharmaceutical sales reps, orthopedists, certified public accountants, and SYSCO managers who have been cooped up in meetings all day and just want to play. Not that Orlando will adopt the "what happens in Orlando, stays in Orlando" credo anytime soon, but CityWalk may harbor its share of secrets, or at least hazy memories. It sits right at the entrance to both Universal Studios and Islands of Adventure, with a gorgeous 20-screen AMC movie theater. Shopping is nothing particularly upscale or notable, mostly impulse-buy souvenir shops, from the character

apparel and memorabilia at **Cartooniversal** to the obvious incendiary delights of **Cigarz at CityWalk** to the bright cotton clothing for the whole family at **Fresh Produce.**

In downtown Orlando, **Park Avenue** is 10 blocks of shops and galleries interspersed with restaurants, from Swoope Avenue south to Fairbanks Avenue. You'll see Williams-Sonoma, Pottery Barn, Restoration Hardware, Ann Taylor, and some other ubiquitous names, but independent shops abound, from clothing boutiques like the trendy **Tuni** (301 S. Park Ave., 407/628-1609) or **Shou'Ture** (339 S. Park Ave., 407/647-9372) for fashion-forward shoes and a quick pedicure to boot. There are galleries like **Timothy's Gallery** (236 N. Park Ave., 407/629-0707) with ceramics, jewelry, and home accessories; **Golf Almighty** (501 S. Park Ave., 407/273-2362) for your golfing needs; and **Doggie Door** (356 S. Park Ave., 407/644-2969) when you need a treat for the canine back home.

Winter Park Village (500 N. Orlando Ave., 407/571-2502) is a nearby small shopping center with retail shops, about a dozen restaurants, a great chocolate shop, and a 20-screen movie theater.

ACCOMMODATIONS
Walt Disney World Resort

WDW has 32 different resorts, with more than 31,000 guest rooms and 784 campsites—this includes five Disney Vacation Club resort properties, and 10 resorts that are not Disney owned and operated. If the bulk of your time in Orlando will be spent at Walt Disney World Resort theme parks, it makes a lot of sense to stay in one of the Disney Resorts. They are offered at nearly every price point, many of them just adjacent to one of the parks, and there are a host of benefits afforded Disney Resort guests. There are also perks like getting to use your Disney Resort ID like a credit card, or having a package delivery right to your room. Resort identification (your plastic Disney Resort ID) and theme park admission tickets are required to take advantage of these perks. To make a reservation at any Walt Disney World Resort, call 407/934-7639 or visit http://waltdisneyworld.disney.go.com.

Universal Orlando Resort

There are three hotels on property, each with its own flavor and price point, listed here from least expensive to most. Each is within walking distance of Universal Studios, Islands of Adventure, and CityWalk, and guests get Universal Express preferred access to theme park rides and attractions, along with priority seating at most onsite restaurants and shows. There's also courtesy water taxi and bus transportation between the resort and park, complimentary package delivery of in-park purchases to guest rooms, and you can use your resort ID to charge things throughout Universal Orlando.

The Loews's **Royal Pacific Resort** (6300 Hollywood Way, 407/503-3000, rates from $129), has a South Pacific vibe, complete with luscious tropical landscaping and lagoons on a 53-acre property. It's big, with 1,000 rooms and 85,000 square feet of meeting space, so you'll see a preponderance of business and

convention travelers here, swirling around the central fountain of the lobby's Orchid Court or the active lobby bar. If you want to spend a little time up close with one of Elvis's rhinestone jumpsuits or a little footwear from Elton John's closet, head straight for the **Hard Rock Hotel** (5800 Universal Blvd., 407/503-7625, rates from $149), designed in a hip California mission style with 650 rooms. As with other Hard Rocks, the public spaces are chockablock with rock memorabilia, and huge video screens run concert footage. The **Portofino Bay Hotel** (5601 Universal Blvd., 407/503-1000, rates from $159) aims at Mediterranean luxury. Opened in 1999, the hotel features 750 rooms in a kind of Italian seaside village environment. It's won awards like the AAA Four Diamond Award and a place in *Travel + Leisure* magazine's Top 500 Hotels in the World, mostly for its lovely rooms with garden or bay views, and its wide array of amenities.

SeaWorld Orlando

The **Residence Inn Orlando SeaWorld/International Center** (11000 Westwood Blvd., 800/889-9728, www.marriott.com, rates from $109) is six stories in a Floribbean motif, with 350 rooms and one- and two-bedrooms suites with fully equipped kitchens. There's a very nice hot breakfast buffet that is thrown in, with waffles, pancakes, and all the fixings, which you can eat out by the pool. It's a great family hotel, entertaining the kids with a big heated pool, playground, game arcade, and sports courts. **Renaissance Orlando Resort at SeaWorld** (6677 Sea Harbor Dr., 407/351-5555, rates from $179) is located directly across from SeaWorld Orlando, Discovery Cove, and one mile from Orlando's Orange County Convention Center. The hotel boasts 185,000 square feet of meeting and event space with a 10-story atrium (full of waterfalls, exotic birds, and goldfish ponds), 18-hole championship golf course, three lighted tennis courts, and an Olympic-size swimming pool. The 778 rooms have recently been renovated, along with 64 suites. All rooms feature 32-inch flat-panel televisions, king beds with a sleeper sofa or double queen-size beds.

PASCO COUNTY

Naked people. That got your attention. The sleepy, landlocked, mostly residential county to Tampa's north, Pasco County, has at least a day's worth of kooky fun, definitely worth a side trip, a couple of meals, and maybe even an overnight at one of the area's most luscious spa/golf/tennis resorts.

But back to the buff. Lake Como Family Nudist Resort in the town of Land O' Lakes is the area's original nudist community, started in 1947. Since then, Pasco County has become a hotbed of naturist activity, with six all-ages nudist communities and recreational activities (until recently there was naked bowling at the local lanes – the question is, if you're wearing rented bowling shoes, are you really nude?). These days the biggest player is the 120-acre **Caliente Resort and Spa** (21240 Gran Via Blvd., Land O' Lakes, 800/326-7731). Stop in and poke around, unless you're too chicken.

Another Pasco original requiring a little bit of chutzpah is **Skydive City** (4241 Skydive Ln., off Chancey Rd., 813/783-9399, $195, plus $80 if you want the video documenting your whole experience) in Zephyrhills. The town has been a world-famous drop zone since the 1960s, with a world meet (in the trade, it's called a "boogie") in 1972. Why here? According to owner T. K. Hayes, "It's in the middle of nowhere, with not a single picturesque thing about it. It's really about the people – Zephyrhills is the largest skydiving place in the world." Tandem jumping (where a rookie jumps physically harnessed to an instructor) has opened skydiving up to people who never would have had the opportunity – the elderly, the disabled, anyone can do it.

If the bowling flummoxed you, but jumping out of an airplane sounds doable: It takes about an hour to prepare, with a 20-minute briefing. The whole experience is a three- to four-hour adventure, with freefall at 120 mph for about a minute from 13,500 feet, followed by up to six minutes of steering with the parachute open. Hayes says he's never had a student fatality or serious injury (solo students have a higher rate of injury, especially on the landing), very few students lose their lunch, and, he says, "No one comes down and says they wish they'd never done that."

After that, take it down a notch and enjoy a walking tour of downtown **Dade City.** In the rolling hills of eastern Pasco County, the town has more than 50 antiques stores, gift shops, and boutiques. Stop into the historic 1909 Pasco County Courthouse and look at

Downtown Orlando

Hotelier Richard Kessler opened the AAA four-diamond **Westin Grand Bohemian** (325 S. Orange Ave., 407/313-9000, rates from $249) in 2001 and people thought he was a little touched. The laugh's on them, because the hotel has been a hit amongst business travelers, its 250 guest rooms gorgeously kitted out with velvet drapes, plush leather headboards, and crisp white bed linens on pillow-top beds. The hotel's **Boheme Restaurant** consistently wins kudos from food magazines, its luxurious menu featuring dishes like seared foie gras with fig bread pudding and a warm huckleberry sauce, and surprising Asian fillips as in the sushi bento box for two or the Thai spiced duck breast with black bean sauce. A Sunday jazz brunch draws a huge following, and the Bösendorfer Lounge (with one of only two Imperial Grand Bösendorfer pianos in the world) features nightly jazz.

On a much more intimate scale, **The Eō Inn & Spa** (227 N. Eola Drive, 407/481-8485, rates from $139) boasts 17 suites tucked into a 1923-era building overlooking Lake Eola Park and the downtown skyline. A rooftop terrace with whirlpool, a day spa, and an in-house Panera restaurant make it an extremely pleasant stay.

GETTING THERE AND AROUND

From the Tampa Bay area, Orlando is about an hour northeast along I-4. This route is notoriously under construction, and often just the sweet collection of artifacts from the turn of the 20th century. And then have a slice of history with a slice of pie at **Lunch on Limoges** (14139 7th St., 352/567-5685, $12-18). It's a darling throwback to a former era of refined and leisurely lunching, with a daily-changing menu served on Limoges china by nice old waitresses in nurses' uniforms with sensible orthopedic shoes. Excellent chocolate cake, but I don't like that they have a fairly steep minimum order to dine here.

Not far from downtown and worth maybe an hour, **The Pioneer Florida Museum** (15602 Pioneer Museum Rd., 352/567-0262, www.pioneerfloridamuseum.org, Tues.-Sat. 10 A.M.-5 P.M., $5 adults, $4 seniors) consists of nine period buildings dating back to 1878. There's the John Overstreet House, the Lacoochee School, and the Enterprise Methodist Church, all displaying period furniture, clothing, toys, tools. There's also a spooky collection of miniature big-eyed dolls of Florida's first ladies. The museum has good raw material, but it should spend a chunk of volunteer hours redoing some of their signage, which looks a little tired. There often isn't quite enough explanation of what we're looking at — in a historical museum, signs so often tell the story.

If there's time, take a tour around **New Port Richey's Main Street** (www.newportrichey-mainstreet.com, tours 9 A.M.-noon, $10) and then board a boat and ride the **Pithlachascottee River** to see historic homes once owned by Gloria Swanson, Thomas Meighan, and Babe Ruth. Then walk around **Centennial Cultural Park,** which contains the Pasco Fine Arts Council, the Centennial Library, and the 1882 Baker House, one of the oldest structures in Pasco County. If you're hungry, stop in at waterside **Catches** (7811 Bayview St., 727/849-2121).

If you're thinking about bedtime now, **Saddlebrook Resort & Spa** (5700 Saddlebrook Way, 800/729-8383, $300-600) is really Tampa's nicest four-star resort hotel, only it's in the sleepy Pasco town of Wesley Chapel. It has 800 guest rooms, all gorgeous, pools, tennis, the Palmer and the Saddlebrook golf courses (and the Arnold Palmer Golf Academy), and a variety of dining options (if you eat on the Tropics Terrace you can see nesting wood storks). If this is too rich for your blood, **Azalea House** (37719 Meridian Ave., 352/523-1773, $65-79) is a sweet bed-and-breakfast with just a few rooms in Dade City.

For more information about Pasco County, visit www.visitpasco.net.

clogged with tourists, so leave yourself plenty of time in either direction.

Once in the Orlando area, you will find excellent signage that makes it easy to navigate throughout the area and around the various theme parks. **I-4** is the main route to the theme parks and in the greater Orlando area, but it's tricky: It's an east/west highway, but takes a north/south jog from Kissimmee up through Downtown Orlando to the north. Traffic can be fairly miserable in high season. There are several other roads that provide alternate routes: **International Drive** parallels I-4 just to the east and is a long strip of hotels, shopping, restaurants, and other attractions. **Hwy. 192** (known as Irlo Bronson Memorial Highway in parts) runs east/west, from Walt Disney World

Resort in the west through Kissimmee and St. Cloud to the east. Several other local roads—Florida's Turnpike, Central Florida Greeneway (Hwy. 417), and Osceola Parkway—are toll roads, so be sure to have cash in the car.

By Air

Orlando International Airport (1 Airport Blvd., Orlando, general information 407/825-2001, parking information 407/825-7275, www.orlandoairports.net) is located nine miles southeast of downtown Orlando, at the junction of Hwy. 436 (Semoran Boulevard) and Hwy. 528 (Bee Line/Beach Line Expressway). Serving more than 35 million passengers annually, with 898 commercial flights each day, it's a big, orderly, easy-to-use airport serving 51 airlines.

The Nature Coast

The Nature Coast is the rebuttal to Orlando's Disney slickness. Civic-minded boosters have tried to sell this area as "Mother Nature's theme park," but that moniker doesn't quite work. Nothing here is marketed, packaged, or sanitized by crackerjack public relations specialists. It's rural, with the majority of the area set aside as parkland, preserves, reserves, and animal refuges.

In the weathered fishing villages along the coast and the quaint little inland towns, you're likely to see a spiffy fishing boat in every driveway, but you're just as apt to see a dead pickup truck up on blocks in the yard. Residents stay for the affordable living, for the area's easy live-and-let-live tolerance, for the unhurried pace, and—for many, the most important reason— the fish. And that's pretty much why visitors come, too. People drive here to see manatees, black bears, and wading birds; to catch fish; and to dive, to kayak, or to simply contemplate the area's wealth of waterways. There are no white-sand beaches crowded with bikini-clad college kids, no swanky nightclubs with throbbing VIP rooms. From north of Clearwater all the way to the Big Bend (where the Florida peninsula tucks west into the Panhandle), there are precious few multiplexes, museums, or high-fallutin' cultural attractions. All that would get in the way of enjoying one of the least developed stretches of Florida's Gulf Coast.

SIGHTS
Tarpon Springs

There are more than 10,000 species of fresh- and saltwater sponges, simple multicellular animals that sit quietly feeding on plankton and warding off enemies with little toxin-tipped spikes. They are not, as recent cartoons may indicate, loud and obnoxious with a weakness for physical comedy. Still, for some reason, since before the birth of Christ we have been hauling them out of the deep and using their skeletons to clean behind our ears or wipe up a mess.

These days **Tarpon Springs,** a coastal town

15 miles due north of Clearwater, is more about the *idea* of sponges than actual sponges. Since the 1950s and the advent of synthetic sponges, the Greek sponge divers who populated this town have been largely reemployed as fisher-folk, restaurateurs, tour boat captains, etc.

Sponge diving had been a family business in Greece at the end of the 19th century, with naturally adept swimmers assisted by rubber suits and heavy copper helmets to which air was pumped via hose. John Corcoris brought the apparatus to north of Tampa around 1900 and persuaded friends and family, sponge divers all, to relocate from Hydra and Aegena, Greece, to this little Florida backwater. Greeks begot more Greeks and a booming town of Greek restaurants, Greek Orthodox churches, and Greek festivals centered around the sponge industry. Tarpon Springs was the largest U.S. sponge-diving port in the 1930s, but a sponge blight and new synthetic sponge technology caused business to dry up.

The town is still more than one-third Greek, with a sweet, kitschy, Old Florida tourist attraction charm and several fine restaurants. Sponges are everywhere, most of them imported from more sponge-rich far-flung lands (although someone told me there was another flurry of sponge diving here in the 1980s when another bed was found).

It's well worth an afternoon of your time— see the museum and the sponge docks, shop a little, and have dinner.

First stop, **Spongeorama** (510 Dodecanese Blvd., 727/943-2164, Mon.–Sat. 10:30 A.M.–6 P.M., Sun. 11:30 A.M.–6 P.M., free). God I love that name; the building itself is also called the Sponge Factory, but let's stick with Spongeorama. A little down at the heels, the shop/attraction has mannequins dressed as sponge divers and shows an old crackly movie called *Men and the Sea,* which you view before wandering around the little sponge museum with dioramas of sponge-diving history (one gory diorama depicts a diver dying of the

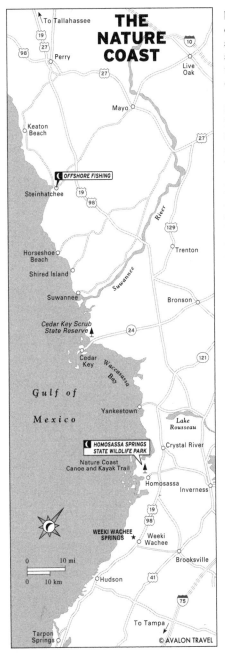

THE
NATURE
COAST

To Tallahassee

Perry

Mayo

Keaton
Beach

Live
Oak

OFFSHORE FISHING

Steinhatchee

River

Trenton

Horseshoe
Beach

Shired Island

Suwannee

Suwannee

Bronson

Cedar Key Scrub
State Reserve

Cedar
Key

Waccasassa
Bay

Gulf of

Mexico

Yankeetown

Lake
Rousseau

HOMOSASSA SPRINGS
STATE WILDLIFE PARK

Crystal River

Nature Coast
Canoe and Kayak Trail

Homosassa

Inverness

WEEKI WACHEE
SPRINGS

Weeki
Wachee

Brooksville

0   10 mi

0   10 km

Hudson

To Tampa

Tarpon
Springs

© AVALON TRAVEL

bends—kids hang out for a long time in front of this one). Afterwards, you buy a couple of specimens (the "wool" ones are highly prized) at the gift shop. Several people have told me that Spongeorama is haunted; maybe it's that diver with the bends.

If you're still angling for more sponge action, **St. Nicholas Boat Line** (693 Dodecanese Blvd., 727/942-6425, $6 adults, $2 children 6–12, free for children under 6) offers a fun, 30-minute narrated boat cruise through the sponge docks, with its own sponge-diving demonstration.

Out on the main drag, Dodecanese Boulevard, there are seven blocks of shops and restaurants. Before you settle on a place to eat, stop into nearby **St. Nicholas Church** (18 Hibiscus St., 727/937-3540), made of 60 tons of Greek marble once on display at the Greek exhibit at the first New York World's Fair. The church is a copy of the Byzantine Revival St. Sophia in Constantinople, with beautiful Czech chandeliers and stained glass. If you happen to be here in January, time a visit for Epiphany on the 6th—this church is the center of the biggest Epiphany celebration in the country. Festivities move from the church to nearby Spring Bayou, where young Greek men dive for a cross that has been blessed and thrown into the water.

Weeki Wachee Springs

The job requirements are tough: a winning smile, powerful athleticism, and a great body. Now add to that the ability to hold one's breath for 2.5 minutes. Florida is home to a variety of rare aquatic creatures, but perhaps none are so singular as the 21 mermaids and mermen who swim through their daily choreographed show at Weeki Wachee Springs.

In 1947, former U.S. Navy frogman Newton Perry thought of a way to bring added draw to one of the United States's most prolific freshwater springs. More than 170 million gallons of 72°F water pour dramatically into the Weeki Wachee River daily. Perry's notion was to gussy up the headwater with a bevy of beautiful mermaids—to this end, he taught a group of powerful swimmers to breathe through submerged air hoses supplied by an air compressor, the

COURTESY OF VISIT FLORIDA

Head to Cedar Key's downtown Dock Street as the sun goes down and your hunger rises.

upshot being a remarkable 30- to 45-minute, entirely underwater extravaganza.

Conceived in the heyday of MGM's trademark aquatic musical spectaculars starring Esther Williams, the show at Weeki Wachee Springs is nonetheless a family affair. There are plenty of ogling opportunities, but these bathing beauties are put through their paces in a show that usually draws from past Disney movies (recent shows have included, unsurprisingly, *The Little Mermaid* and *Pocahontas*).

The audience sits in a small underground amphitheatre in front of a four-inch-thick plate-glass window, behind which the blue waters of the springs teem with fish, turtles, eels, and women in oversized, shimmering tails who twirl, undulate, and lip-synch on cue. Many of the mermaids have been with the show for decades, a fact that can be ascertained with a quick look through photos and memorabilia in the small **Mermaid Museum** (a wall of fame includes early sea nymphs cavorting with Elvis and Don Knotts), opened to commemorate the show's 50th anniversary in 1997.

After getting your picture taken with a mermaid, it's off to the rest of the 200-acre family entertainment park, Florida's only natural spring water park. This includes a flume ride at Buccaneer Bay, a low-key Birds of Prey show, petting zoo, and jungle river cruise.

Weeki Wachee Springs, 6131 Commercial Way, Spring Hill, 352/596-2062, is open daily 10 A.M.–4 P.M. The $19 adults, $15 children 3–10 admission price includes Buccaneer Bay; Weeki Wachee is open year-round but Buccaneer Bay is closed during the winter months and reopens each mid-March.

FOOD
Tarpon Springs
Everyone has a different favorite Greek restaurant here. Mine is **Hellas** (785 Dodecanese Blvd., 727/943-2400, daily 11 A.M.–10 P.M., $10–20), a lively spot with a full bar and a wonderful Greek bakery attached to it. The best entrée is slowly braised tomatoey lamb shanks, served somewhat mysteriously atop spaghetti. There are addictive garlic shrimp, nice gyros in

warm Greek pita, and a delicious Greek salad that comes with a scoop of potato salad hidden in its midst. Others swear by **Mykonos** (628 Dodecanese Blvd., 727/934-4306, daily 11 A.M.–10 P.M., $10–20) for the lamb chops, Greek meatloaf, and slightly more refined atmosphere. Still, **Mama's** (735 Dodecanese Blvd., 727/944-2888, daily 11 A.M.–10 P.M., $7–14) often gets the nod for casual, family-friendly booths and delicious but messy chicken souvlaki sandwiches. If you're visiting on a Saturday night, head over after dinner to the bouzouki club called **Zorba** (508 W. Athens, 727/934-8803), for some zesty belly dancing and an ouzo.

Weeki Wachee Springs Area
For something a little splurgy, **Bare Bones Fish & Steakhouse** (3192 Shoal Line Blvd., Hernando Beach, 352/596-9403, Tues.–Sun. 4–9P.M. $22–35) is presided over by owners Tom and Karen McEachern and features handcut black Angus steaks and an array of Gulf seafood. The low, blue-shuttered building has a warm, wood-paneled dining room and a broad menu. Start with fried asparagus with chipotle ranch, then maybe the onion-crusted wild salmon with basil and brandy cream or the Bare Bones Signature rib eye, chargrilled and topped with mushroom-burgundy sauce.

Cedar Key
Built in 1859, the **Island Hotel and Restaurant** (2nd St. and B St., 352/543-5111, Tues.–Sun. 6–9 P.M., $15–24) is purportedly haunted by 13 ghosts, particularly during grisly weather. Even if you don't believe the story of the restless spirit of a murdered former owner, you'll enjoy the hearts of palm salad (supposedly invented here by the hotel's original owners), the crab bisque, or just a drink in the chummy bar.

For elegant waterside dining, head to the **Island Room Restaurant at Cedar Cove** (10 E. 2nd. St., 352/543-6520, Mon.–Sat 5–10 P.M., Sun. 10 A.M.–9 P.M., $14–28) for Chef Peter Stefani's house-grown veggies and greens or his less pious velvety bread pudding with bourbon sauce. After dinner, if you're not

quite ready to turn in, head over to Dock Street for a game of pool, darts, or some game viewing at **Coconuts of Cedar Key** (330 Dock St., 352/543-6390, 11A.M.–2A.M. daily) or a drink with the locals at **Frog's Landing** (420 Dock St., 352/543-9243, 11A.M.–9P.M. Sun.–Thurs., 11A.M.–10P.M. Fri. and Sat.) or **Seabreeze** (310 Dock St., 352/543-5738, 11A.M.–9P.M. Mon.–Wed., 4:30–9P.M. Thurs., 11A.M.–10P.M. Fri. and Sat., noon–9P.M. Sun.). And when you're feeling fortified and emboldened, order the single weirdest dish the island has to offer—Seabreeze's signature salad is a mélange of lettuce, hearts of palm, peach, pineapple, and dates, "dressed" with a slowly melting scoop of peanut butter ice cream.

Steinhatchee
The dining scene here is dominated by **Fiddler's Restaurant** (1306 Riverside Dr., 352/498-7427, Mon.–Thurs. 4–10 P.M., Fri.–Sun. 11 A.M.–10 P.M., $10–20), a sprawling, lively spot populated by men swapping big fish stories and tucking into fried grouper (you can bring your own cleaned catch and have them cook it up). **Roy's** (100 1st Ave. SW, 352/498-5000, daily 11 A.M.–9 P.M., $13–16), a local favorite for 38 years, doesn't serve any booze but has an exhaustive salad bar, fried seafood, and fat burgers that keep people happy.

RECREATION
Swimming with the Manatees
The West Indian manatee is still listed as an endangered species, but the population has rebounded tremendously in the past few years in this area. Manatee "season" is October 15–March 31, but you'll spot them all year long. Kings Bay in Crystal River has the densest concentration, but the Blue Waters area of the Homosassa River is a little less trafficked by boats, thus a bit quieter. Either way, you can commune with these lumbering mammals from the distance that suits you (up close their size is unsettling—just remember they are herbivores, with blunt teeth so far back in their heads that you could, were it legal, hand feed them with no worries). **Manatee Tour &**

EXCURSIONS

THE SILVER KING

Homosassa is the place. Any fly-fisher will tell you, this little Old Florida town is where the big tarpon congregate, for no reason anyone can fathom. The current world record – 202.8 pounds – was caught right here. But you won't find annual tarpon tournaments broadcast from here on ESPN2. It's a respectful, almost reverent endeavor, with patience often yielding nothing but sunburn. On any given day, you'll see the river dotted with 25 or 30 flats boats navigated with push poles in a hushed silence of profound concentration, everyone waiting to see one roll along the surface in water depths of 5-25 feet. People come from all over the world to the Nature Coast to sight fish, spin casting or fly-fishing for these behemoths before releasing them gently into the warm, clear waters. Tarpon begin to run the last weeks of April and fade out in July. What many consider the "Super Bowl of fishing," tarpon fishing requires a special $50 tag to keep one, and some serious know-how. If you catch one – using live crabs, baitfish, or hand-tied flies – the initial jumps and runs of that angry hooked fish will take your breath away.

If you want to try your hand at chasing giant tarpon on the Gulf or, even better, fly-fishing with light tackle in the backwaters from Homosassa to Cedar Key, try **Capt. Rick LeFiles** (Osprey Guide Services, 6115 Riverside Dr., Yankeetown, 352/447-0829, $350 for a day of reds and trout, $400 for tarpon) or fourth-generation Homosassa **Capt. William Toney** (352/621-9284, www.homosassainshorefish-ing.com, half day $300, full day $400 for 1-2 people, $50 each additional person).

Dive (267 NW 3rd St., Crystal River, 888/732-2692, www.manateetouranddive.com, $29 for tour, $20 for gear) offers two-hour manatee swim and snorkeling trips suitable for the whole family in the waters of Crystal River, and scuba trips in Crystal Springs and Kings Spring, an underwater cavern praised for its excellent visibility, size, and potential for underwater photography (thousands of saltwater fish congregate at the cavern's two exits).

Sunshine River Tours (352/628-3450, www.sunshinerivertours.com, $50) has a similar range of guided ecotourism escapades in Homosassa. If a manatee swim and snorkel tour doesn't sound like a good way to take the waters, you can try your hand at scalloping (July 1–Sept. 10) or just a boat ride to follow the river out to the Gulf of Mexico.

◖ Homosassa Springs State Wildlife Park

How could even the most myopic and woman-starved ancient mariner have mistaken these slow and lugubrious sea cows for mermaids? Manatees, so famous in these parts, can weigh up to 2,000 pounds and look like submerged, limbless elephants, often festooned with algae and barnacles. You'll catch sight of them most often during cooler months, December–March, in the Suwannee River or at Manatee or Fanning Springs State Parks. From boat or shore, look for swirly "footprints" on the water's surface or torpedo-like shapes ambling across the shallow bottom. If you want a guaranteed viewing, stop into Homosassa Springs State Wildlife Park (4150 S. Suncoast Blvd., Homosassa, 352/628-5343, daily 9 A.M.–5:30 P.M.; $9 adults, $5 children), where you can see these marine mammals several ways. Visitors are loaded onto pontoon boats and shuttled through the canopied headwaters of the Homosassa River to a refuge for injured manatees and other animals. Alternately, at 11:30 A.M., 1:30 P.M., and 3:30 P.M., a manatee program allows you to watch docents wade out to feed stubby carrots to a slow-moving swarm of these creatures, many etched with outboard motor scars from run-ins with boats, after which you can walk down to the glass-fronted Fishbowl Underwater Observatory and see eye-to-eye with the gentle giants and the park's other indigenous aquatic creatures. (Mysteriously, the park hosts a hippo named Lucifer—a washed-up animal actor—that former governor Lawton Chiles declared an honorary Florida native.)

Offshore Fishing

Folks visiting this area most often spend their time, and considerable money, on half-day or full-day charters out into the Gulf in search of amberjack, kingfish (the most terrible-tasting of the fiercely beautiful sportfish), redfish, cobia, and grouper. Black grouper limits are five per person, per day, and they must be at least 22 inches long. Big Bend Charters (352/498-3703, www.bigbendcharters.com) takes groups of up to six far out on offshore ($870) nearshore ($600) trips, and on a "thrill" fishing trip that targets a range of species ($990). Keep the grouper you catch, and pawn the rest of it off on someone else. Fresh-caught local grouper is a revelation.

Farther in, spotted sea trout, catfish, and redfish can be coaxed out of the grass flats of Deadman's Bay or the slow-moving Steinhatchee River. Kingfish travel through Steinhatchee spring and fall to stay in the perfect water temperature (72°F or so), and the town is a legendary trout and redfish fishery in the wintertime when the fish move up into the river. Freshwater fishing can be accomplished dockside or from a rented canoe, but it's more fun in a shallow-draft boat with a motor: A 24-foot deck boat with a 200-horsepower Yamaha motor with a bimini will run you $150 per half day, plus fuel at the **River Haven Marina** (1110 Riverside Dr. SE, Steinhatchee, 352/498-0709). First-timers should hire a guide (it's an eminent place to learn saltwater fly-fishing techniques), but if you're striking out on your own, head to one of the local marinas (Sea Hag, River Haven, or Gulf Stream) and listen carefully to suss out the latest hot spots and irresistible baits. (Tip: Wear sunglasses with polarized lenses so you can see into the water more effectively.)

SHOPPING

Inveterate shoppers will be a little flummoxed by the Nature Coast's meager retail options. There is a serviceable **mall** in Crystal River (1801 NW U.S. 19, 352/795-2585) with ubiquitous stores such as Sears, Waldenbooks, and Payless, and Cedar Key's **Dock Street** is host to the kinds of shell-themed giftware and handicrafts stores found in many little seaside towns. For a real local frisson of excitement, sift through the 300 or so booths at **Howard's Flea Market** (6373 S. Suncoast Blvd., Homosassa Springs, 352/628-3532, Fri. 7 A.M.–1 P.M., Sat.–Sun. 7 A.M.–3 P.M.). To safeguard against rain and muggy weather, the market is enclosed, with vendors hawking Nascar merchandise, leather goods, tools, even puppies. A bird aviary and food vendors (good barbecue, excellent old-fashioned root beer) make it fun for the whole family.

ACCOMMODATIONS

People are drawn to the Nature Coast for a raw, unmediated view into the natural world. They come with rods and reels, without hair dryers or sometimes even a decent change of shirt. Thus, this swath of Florida is replete with RV parks, campgrounds, and fish camps that run from rough wooden cabins to no-frills motels. In nearly all the small towns that dot U.S. 19 or the little roads west to the Gulf, you can bet on finding a clean room in a mom-and-pop venture where the decor is uninspired and the amenities limited.

But in addition to these or the more upscale lodgings listed here, the area provides opportunities to indulge a lot of people's moony-eyed fantasy of endless, tranquil mobility: a houseboat stay. You can go "way down upon the Suwannee River" with a 44-foot houseboat rented from **Miller's Marine & Suwannee Houseboats** (County Road 349, Suwannee, 800/458-2628, $640 Fri. afternoon–Sun. afternoon, $132 per day). The crafts rent by the day, weekend, or week, sleep up to eight, and are equipped with showers, bathroom facilities, linens, full kitchens, and cookware. The owners take renters on a warm-up cruise to teach them the basics, then you're on your own with 70 miles of river, countless springs, and an up-close view of the area's wildlife.

We got the anchor stuck, saw a bald eagle,

fished from the comfort of our beds, scratched chigger bites, and generally pretended we were Huckleberry Finn.

Crystal River

The Nature Coast doesn't offer the glut of golfing opportunities of elsewhere in Florida. If you're jonesing to tee off, the **Plantation Inn and Golf Resort** (9301 W. Fort Island Trail, Crystal River, 352/795-4211, www.plantation inn.com) boasts a par-72, 18-hole championship course and a 9-hole executive course for training and practice, in addition to manatee snorkeling tours, guided scuba diving, and 145 guest rooms (with 12 golf villas and 6 condos). Given all the amenities and glitz, room rates are a fairly reasonable $124–350 (which includes greens fees).

Cedar Key

New on the scene, **The Faraway Inn** (3rd and G Sts., 888/543-5330, www.farawayinn.com, $75–160) is set within a quiet, attractive residential area away from traffic and nightlife, but within a short five-minute walk past Victorian and traditional Cracker homes to restaurants, convenience stores, shops, boat launches, the public beach, and the city dock. Faraway Inn was built in the early 1950's on the original site of the 19th-century Eagle Pencil Company Cedar Mill. The inn has little freestanding efficiencies and cottages as well as more motel-like accommodations. It's pet friendly.

Steinhatchee

Steinhatchee Landing Resort (228 NE Hwy. 51, Steinhatchee, 800/584-1709, www .steinhatcheelanding.com, $146–506) is as swanky as it gets along the Nature Coast. The brainchild of patrician Georgian gentleman Dean Fowler, its 35 acres are dotted with dozens of individual one-, two-, and three-bedroom Victorian and Florida Cracker cottages, most equipped with French country furniture, oversize spa tubs, and wildly luxurious appointments for such a down-home fishing village. There's a new swimming pool and patio area, and it accepts pets up to 28 pounds.

If that's too rich for your blood, the same folks own the nearby 17-room budget-friendly **Steinhatchee River Inn** (1111 Riverside Dr., Steinhatchee, 352/498-4049), where the rates range seasonally $72–89.

GETTING THERE AND AROUND

Florida's Nature Coast is west of I-75 and is accessible by the north–south corridor of U.S. 19. Most of the Nature Coast is accessible by car or boat only. There is no public transportation to speak of (okay, there are two southbound and two northbound Greyhound buses that stop daily in Crystal River and Chiefland—but then once you've arrived, you still need a car to see anything). From south to north, Spring Hill (the town in which Weeki Wachee Springs lies), Homosassa, and Crystal River are lined up adjacent to each other right along U.S. 19. To get to Cedar Key, head north on U.S. 19 and then 23 miles southwest on Highway 24, the only road in and out of town (much of which is a quite rural two-lane highway until you cross the causeway into town). Steinhatchee is 33 miles north of Cedar Key on U.S. 19 and then 12 miles west on Highway 51.

Driving in Florida during the summer months can be especially challenging, with periods of heat and humidity punctuated by tremendous thunderstorms. It pays to have your car equipped with the following: first-aid kit, jumper cables, flashlight with new batteries, a jack, and cellular phone (although cell phone service can be sketchy in the more rural communities).

Sarasota

Want a stiff shot of culture? Sarasota's the place to go. Arts vie with more than 35 miles of dazzling Gulf Coast beaches for top draw. An influx of wealthy socialites settled the area starting around 1910, establishing Sarasota as a winter resort for affluent northerners. It was during this time that Sarasota's performing and visual arts institutions were established, to entertain those first hoity-toity tourists. Among the early tourists to be smitten by the town was circus magnate John Ringling. He scooped up property all around Sarasota, moving the circus's winter home here, building himself a winter residence, art museum, circus museum, and college.

All these years later, the city of Sarasota is the undisputed cultural center of the area, with theater, opera, symphony, ballet, art museums, and restaurants to rival those in much bigger cities. Each of the keys maintains its own identity, with glorious beach access being the central unifying theme. Lido and St. Armands are really just extensions of downtown Sarasota, connected by a causeway, and fairly urban. Started as a quiet fishing village, Longboat Key is now strictly the purview of the posh, with tall resort hotels and condominiums and a glut of golf courses. Siesta Key is much more low-rise, with a personality to match. It's relaxed, laid-back, with a high funk-factor. It's the most youthful spot on this part of the Gulf Coast. Casey Key is less of a tourist draw, mostly dotted with single-family homes.

SIGHTS
◖ Marie Selby Botanical Gardens
The word epiphyte comes from the Greek words "epi," meaning "upon," and "phyton," meaning "plant." Beginning their life in the canopy of trees, their seeds carried by birds or wind, epiphytes are air plants, growing stubbornly without the benefit of soil on the branches or trunks of trees. Orchids, cacti, bromeliads, aroids, lichens, mosses, and ferns can even grow on the same tree, a big interspecies

jamboree. And if you want to see some heart-breakingly beautiful and alien epiphytes, spend a long afternoon at Marie Selby Botanical Gardens (811 S. Palm Ave., 941/366-5731, daily 10 A.M.–5 P.M., $12 adults, $6 children 6–11, free for children under 6). The nine-acre gardens on the shores of Sarasota Bay are one of Sarasota's absolute jewels. Marie Selby donated her home and grounds "to provide enjoyment for all who visit the gardens." Meandering along the walking paths through the hibiscus garden, cycad garden, a banyan grove, a tropical fruit garden, and thousands of orchids—there's a lot of enjoyment to be had. The botanical gardens also host lectures and gardening classes, and have a lovely shop (beginners should opt for a training-wheels phalaenopsis—very hard to kill—or an easy-care bromeliad) with an exhaustive collection of gardening books (80 on orchids alone).

◖ John and Mable Ringling Museum of Art
John Ringling's lasting influence on Sarasota is remarkable, but the John and Mable Ringling Museum of Art makes it simply incontrovertible (5401 Bay Shore Rd., 941/351-1660, daily 10 A.M.–5:30 P.M., $19 adults, $16 seniors, $6 students and children 6–17, $6 Florida teachers and students with ID).

In 2007, the museum completed a six-year, $140 million master plan marking the completion of one of the most extraordinary transformations of any museum in North America. It's now one of the 20 largest art museums in North America. Since 2006, the Ringling Museum has opened four new buildings, the Tibbals Learning Center, the John M. McKay Visitors Pavilion, the Ulla R. and Arthur F. Searing Wing, and the Education/Conservation Building, as well as opening the restored Historic Asolo Theater.

The whole museum complex is spectacular, but the art museum is definitely worth its fairly hefty admission price, having been built

COURTESY OF VISIT FLORIDA

The Ringling estate, now known as the John and Mable Ringling Museum of Art, consists of several buildings including Cà d'Zan, the Museum of the Circus, and the original art museum building.

in 1927 to house Ringling's nearly pathological accretion of 600 paintings, sculptures, and decorative arts including more than 25 tapestries. The Mediterranean-style palazzo contains a collection that includes a set of five gargantuan paintings by Peter Paul Rubens, lots of wonderful Spanish work (soulful El Grecos, Velázquez's portrait of King Philip IV of Spain, etc.), and the music room and dining room of Mrs. William B. Astor (Ringling bought all this in 1926 when the Astor mansion in New York was scheduled to be demolished).

The complex also houses the **Museum of the Circus,** a peek into circus history. It achieves a certain level of hyperbole in the interpretive signs when it parallels the ascendance of the circus with the growth of the country more generally. The single most impressive thing about the museum, the thing that caused rampant loitering and inspired commentary like,

"Whoa, cooool," is the Howard Bros. Circus model. It takes up vast space—the world's largest miniature circus, after all—and is a 3/4-inch-to-the-foot scale replica of Ringling Bros. and Barnum & Bailey Circus when the tented circus was at its largest. The model itself takes up 3,800 square feet, with eight main tents, 152 wagons, 1,300 circus performers and workers, more than 800 animals, a 57-car train, and a zillion wonderful details.

Fully restored and reopened in 2002, John Ringling's home on the bay, **Cà d'Zan** (House of John) is also open to the public, an ornate structure evocative of Ringling's two favorite Venetian hotels, the Danieli and the Bauer Grunwald. Completed in 1926, the house is 200 feet long with 32 rooms and 15 baths (a comfort to those of us with small bladders). All kidding aside, there's something about the quality of light much of the year in Sarasota that seems

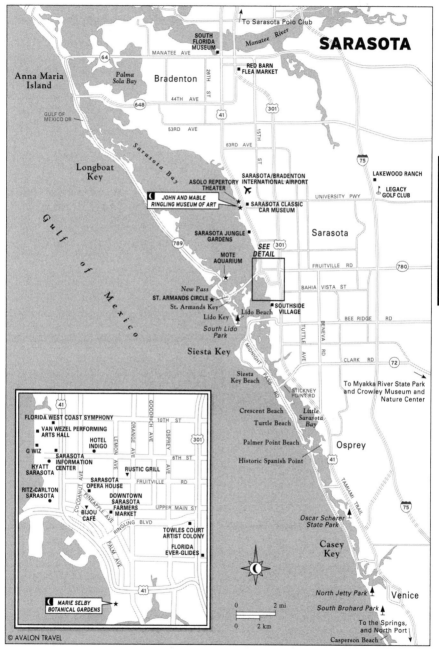

EXCURSIONS

SARASOTA

To Sarasota Polo Club

Manatee River

SOUTH FLORIDA MUSEUM

MANATEE AVE

Anna Maria Island

Palma Sola Bay

Bradenton

RED BARN FLEA MARKET

44TH AVE

GULF OF MEXICO DR

53RD AVE

63RD AVE

Longboat Key

Sarasota Bay

SARASOTA/BRADENTON INTERNATIONAL AIRPORT

LAKEWOOD RANCH

ASOLO REPERTORY THEATER

LEGACY GOLF CLUB

UNIVERSITY PWY

JOHN AND MABLE RINGLING MUSEUM OF ART

SARASOTA CLASSIC CAR MUSEUM

Sarasota

Gulf of Mexico

SARASOTA JUNGLE GARDENS

SEE DETAIL

MOTE AQUARIUM

FRUITVILLE RD

780

BAHIA VISTA ST

New Pass

ST. ARMANDS CIRCLE

St. Armands Key

SOUTHSIDE VILLAGE

BEE RIDGE RD

Lido Beach

Lido Key

South Lido Park

Siesta Key

Siesta Key Beach

CLARK RD

72

To Myakka River State Park and Crowley Museum and Nature Center

Crescent Beach

Little Sarasota Bay

Turtle Beach

Palmer Point Beach

Osprey

Historic Spanish Point

Oscar Scherer State Park

Casey Key

North Jetty Park

Venice

South Brohard Park

To the Springs, and North Port

Casperson Beach

FLORIDA WEST COAST SYMPHONY

10TH ST

VAN WEZEL PERFORMING ARTS HALL

HOTEL INDIGO

G WIZ

SARASOTA INFORMATION CENTER

6TH ST

HYATT SARASOTA

RUSTIC GRILL

FRUITVILLE RD

RITZ-CARLTON SARASOTA

SARASOTA OPERA HOUSE

DOWNTOWN SARASOTA FARMERS MARKET

UPPER MAIN ST

BIJOU CAFÉ

RINGLING BLVD

TOWLES COURT ARTIST COLONY

FLORIDA EVER-GLIDES

MARIE SELBY BOTANICAL GARDENS

0   2 mi

0   2 km

© AVALON TRAVEL

utterly appropriate as host to such a magnificent Venetian Renaissance-style mansion.

FOOD
Downtown

A new addition to the Sarasota culinary landscape, **Derek's Culinary Casual** (514 Central Ave., 941/366-6565, Tues.–Fri. 11:30 A.M.–2:30 P.M., Tues.–Sat. 5–10 P.M., Fri. and Sat. until 10:30 P.M., Sun. until 9 P.M., $19–29) is the brainchild of chef/owner Derek Barnes, former chef at 5-One-6 Burns. In a much larger, high-ceilinged space, he has brought exciting, contemporary American cuisine (complete with a glossary on the back of the menu) to Sarasota's Rosemary District. Tuna gnocchi, pork confit with monkfish medallions, and duck "two ways" (a seared breast paired with crispy pecan-crusted leg confit, German spaetzle, and bitter greens) all aim to bring a new level of sophistication to classic French/Italian/Californian dishes. The wine list is similarly ambitious and fairly priced, but small. While it is still the reservation to nab in Sarasota, service has been known to bobble.

Located in the historic Florida Citrus Exchange, newcomer **Rustic Grill** (400 N. Lemon Ave., 941/906-1111, Sun.–Thurs. 5–10 P.M., Fri. and Sat. until 11 P.M., $24–34) has blown the socks off Sarasota with its stunning Tuscan villa interior and luxurious array of art and antiques. Chef Clinton Combs's open kitchen and wood-burning grill have met the expectations such a gorgeous interior prompt, in an inventive array of small plates and large plates. The waiters need stamina to explain each dish: Grilled local grouper comes with baby fennel confit, haricots vert, calamata tapenade, roasted tomatoes, English pea emulsion, and a blistered red pepper coulis. Whew. Grilled meats are the star of the show, from the bone-in strip loin to a smoky pork tenderloin.

Sarasota's **Bijou Cafe** (1287 1st St., 941/366-8111, Mon.–Fri. 11:30 A.M.–2 P.M., Mon.–Thurs. 5–9:30 P.M., Fri. and Sat. until 10:30 P.M., Sun. until 9 P.M., $19–36) has been a local sparkling jewel since 1986, making everyone's top 10 list and garnering lots

of drippy adjectives from *Zagat, Bon Appetit* and *Gourmet*. It's what you'd call continental-American fare, presided over by chef Jean-Pierre Knaggs and his wife, Shay. Located a couple blocks from Ritz-Carlton Sarasota in a 1920s gas station turned restaurant, the vibe is special-occasion or big-time-business dining. A fairly recent renovation (after a fire) has yielded a new bar, lounge, private room, and outdoor dining courtyards. The wine list is unusual, with a fair number of South African wines (Knaggs is South African), and the menu contains dishes like velvety shrimp and crab bisque, crispy roast duck napped with orange-cognac sauce, or luscious crab cakes with Louisiana rémoulade. All hail the crème brûlée.

It's not exactly downtown, but just slightly south. Still, any list of important downtown restaurants has to include **Michaels On East** (1212 East Ave. S., 941/366-0007, Mon.–Fri. 11:30 A.M.–2 P.M., daily 5:30–10 P.M., $18–31). It's won best-of-Florida accolades from nearly everyone since its opening at the beginning of the 1990s—and it's kept up with all the newcomers, consistently pushing the envelope and wowing diners with its New American take and opulent decor. During the day it's a power-lunching crowd enjoying Wendy's warm chicken salad with dried cranberries, goat cheese, and candied pecans in honey-lemon-basil vinaigrette and a big bottle of bubbly water; at night, romantic dinners à deux include a grilled duck breast paired with Bermuda onion and shiitake fondue, and fig and pecan risotto, all flavors elegantly showcased with a gorgeous big-ticket burgundy or California pinot noir.

St. Armands Circle and Lido Key

Two of the oldest on the stretch are **Café L'Europe** (431 St. Armands Cir., 941/388-4415, daily 11:30 A.M.–3 P.M. and 5–10 P.M., Sun. brunch 11:30 A.M.–3 P.M., $23–40) and the **Columbia Restaurant** (411 St. Armands Cir., 941/388-3987, Mon.–Sat. 11 A.M.–11 P.M., Sun. noon–10 P.M., $8–28). Close together, both feature beautiful dining rooms and wonderful sidewalk dining, but the food's better at

Café L'Europe. The Columbia opened in 1959, making it the oldest restaurant in Sarasota. (Its sister restaurant in Tampa goes one better, being the oldest restaurant in the state of Florida.) The Cuban food is pretty bland and dated, and even its "world-famous" dishes—the 1905 Salad with chopped cheese, olives, and a ho-hum vinaigrette; the sangria; the red snapper Alicante—don't thrill the way they used to. The black bean soup and pompano in parchment seldom disappoint, though. As for Café L'Europe, it's a sophisticated stew of culinary influences that's hard to pin down: The kitchen does an equally adept job with shrimp pad Thai, veal cordon bleu with luxe chanterelle mushroom risotto, and a Mediterranean chicken Kavalla that pairs chicken breast with feta, spinach, and crab.

Southside Village

Pacific Rim (1859 Hillview St., 941/330-8071, Mon.–Fri. 11:30 A.M.–2 P.M., Mon.–Thurs. 5–9 P.M., Fri. and Sat. 5–10 P.M., $7–15) takes you on a very pleasant pan-Asian romp, from Thai curries redolent of basil and galangal to expertly rolled tekka maki sushi and beyond. You can play chef here and select your combinations of meats and veggies to be grilled or wokked.

Nearby **Hillview Grill** (1920 Hillview St., 941/952-0045, Mon.–Sat. 11 A.M.–10 P.M., Sun. 5–9 P.M., $13–29) traffics in another melding of cuisines, this time Cajun and Creole with a dollop of several other ethnic influences. It's more of a neighborhood joint, with easier prices and a relaxed setting. Its more high-flying flights of fancy aren't always successful, but if you stick with dishes like roast chicken with red bliss potatoes or New Zealand lamb chops with apple-mint salsa, you'll be satisfied.

ENTERTAINMENT AND EVENTS
Asolo Repertory Theatre

Celebrating 48 years of professional theater in Sarasota, the Asolo, until 2006 called the Asolo Theatre Company (5555 N. Tamiami Trail, 941/351-8000, www.asolo.org, curtain

The Sarasota skyline has been glamorized in recent years by an influx of cultural venues and visitor attractions.

times generally 2 P.M. and 8 P.M., Nov.–June, prices vary), is a professional company that performs primarily in the 500-seat Harold E. and Esther M. Mertz Theatre at the Florida State University Center for the Performing Arts, a theater originally built as an opera house in 1903 in Dunfermline, Scotland. There's a second, smaller 161-seat black-box Jane B. Cook Theatre on-site for performances of the conservatory season and smaller productions of the Asolo. Students also present a series of original works known as the LateNite series, and the FSU School of Theatre presents a variety of other special events and performances. Recently, the Asolo Rep and the Conservatory perform one show each in the Historic Asolo Theater, located in the Ringling Museum's Visitors Pavilion. All of this means more shows and more variety for Sarasota's theatergoers.

This means that in a single season you might see John Patrick Shanley's riveting *Doubt,* followed by Peter Shaffer's *Equus* (sorry, no Daniel

EXCURSIONS

Radcliffe in this production), Mamet's *Speed the Plow,* and a play adapted by Steve Martin called *The Underpants.*

Festivals

Sarasota supports not one, but two film festivals. By far the more famous of the two is the **Sarasota Film Festival** (www.sarasotafilm festival.com) every April, and every November there's the Sarasota Film Society's 10-day **Cine-World Film Festival** (www.filmsociety.org). February's not a bad month to visit, because you can catch the month-long annual run of the European-style **Circus Sarasota** (www.circus saraasota.org). Sarasota is the self-described "circus capital of the world," after all. Music lovers may want to come in February or March for the repertory season of the **Sarasota Opera** (www.sarasotaopera.org), although in April there's **La Musica International Chamber Music Festival** (www.lamusicafestival.com). Also in April you'll encounter the weeklong **Florida Wine Fest & Auction** (www.florida winefest.com).

RECREATION
Siesta Key Beach

We have a winner of the international whose-beach-is-better competition. In 1987, scientists from the Woods Hole Oceanographic Institution in Woods Hole, Massachusetts, convened to judge the Great International White Sand Beach Challenge, with more than 30 entries from beaches around the world. To this day, Siesta Key Beach remains the reigning world champ, with all other beaches too cowed, or too chicken, to demand a rematch. Its preeminence has long been known—supposedly in the 1950s a visitor from New York, Mr. Edward G. Curtis, sent a pickle jar of Siesta's sand to the Geology Department of Harvard University for analysis. The report came back: "The sand from Siesta Key is 99 percent pure quartz grains, the grains being somewhat angular in shape. The soft floury texture of the sand is due to its very fine grain size. It contains no fragments of coral and no shell. The fineness of the sand, which gives it

its powdery softness, is emphasized by the fact that the quartz is a very hard substance, graded at 7 in the hardness scale of 10."

The real test can't be done with sand in a pickle jar. You need to lie on the sloping strand, run the warmed granules through your fingers, sniff the salt air, and listen to a plaintive gull overhead. That way, too, Siesta Key Beach wins—it's been named America's Best Sand Beach and ranked in Florida's Top Ten Beaches multiple years on the Travel Channel. Dr. Beach named it in his top 10 beaches in America again in 2007 (it's made it into the top 10 numerous times); *National Geographic Traveler* has also named Siesta One of America's Best Beaches. The list goes on.

Siesta Key Beach is on the north side of Siesta Key (it is contiguous with another favorite beach called Crescent Beach—good snorkeling off this one), with white sand so reflective it feels cool on a hot day. Scientists estimate that the sand on this beach is millions of years old, starting in the Appalachians and eventually deposited on these shores. The water is shallow, the beach incline gradual, making it a perfect beach for young swimmers. There are 800 parking spots, which tend to fill up, and the lifeguard stands are painted different colors (as points of reference, so you don't lose your way).

Polo

There are scads of spectator sporting opportunities in Sarasota, but polo trumps a fair number of them. Games are enormous fun, the horses racing around tearing up the lush sod of the polo grounds while their riders focus fiercely on that pesky little ball. For a sport with such an effete pedigree, it's amazingly physical and exciting to watch, whether you're in your fancy polo togs (what's with all the hats?) or your weekend jeans. **Sarasota Polo Club** (Lakewood Ranch, 8201 Polo Club Ln., 941/907-0000, Sun. 1 P.M. mid-December–early April, $10 adults, free for children 12 and under) is in its 17th year, with professional-level players coming from around the world to play on the nine pristine fields. Bring a picnic or buy sandwiches and drinks once you're there. Gates open at 11:30 A.M. and dogs on leashes are welcome. You can also take polo lessons at Lakewood Ranch. Call Scott Lancaster (941/907-1122). Sarasota also boasts high-caliber cricket, lawn bowling, and pétanque.

SHOPPING

The shops of **St. Armands Circle** on Lido Key have been a primary retail draw in Sarasota for a long time, historically known for high-end boutiques. These days the shops cover familiar ground—chains like **Chico's** (443 St. Armands Cir., 941/388-2926), **Tommy Bahama** (300 John Ringling Blvd., 941/388-2888), **Fresh Produce** (1 N. Boulevard of the Presidents, 941/388-1883), and **The White House/Black Market** (317 St. Armands Circle, 941/388-5033)—and a paltry handful of upscale, independently owned boutiques. You'll have better luck noodling in the circle's novelty and giftware shops: **Fantasea Seashells** (345 St. Armands Circle, 941/388-3031), **Wet Noses** (pet stuff, 472 John Ringling Blvd., 941/388-3647), or **Kilwin's** (ice cream and fudge, 312 John Ringling Blvd., 941/388-3200).

Towles Court Artist Colony (Adams Ln. or Morrill St., downtown Sarasota) is a collection of 16 quirky pastel-colored bungalows and cottages that contain artists working furiously and the art they've been working furiously on. You can buy their work and watch them in action most Tuesdays through Saturdays 11 A.M.–4 P.M., or visit Towles Court on the third Friday evening of each month for Art by the Light of the Moon.

Palm Avenue and **Main Street** downtown are lined with galleries, restaurants, and cute shops, and historic **Herald Square** in the SoMa (south of Main St.) part of downtown on Pineapple Avenue has a fairly dense concentration of antiques shops and upscale housewares stores. Also on Pineapple you'll find the **Artisan's World Marketplace** (128 S. Pineapple Ave., 941/365-5994), which promotes self-employment for low-income artisans in developing countries worldwide by selling their baskets, clothing, and handicrafts.

ACCOMMODATIONS

There are scads of condos and beachfront rentals in the greater Sarasota area, but most of these rent only by the week. If that's your time frame, the weeklong rentals often are a more financially prudent choice. Try giving **Argus Property Management** (941/927-6464) a call, or visit **Vacation Rentals by Owner** (www.vrbo.com). There are also golf resort condo communities such as **Heritage Oaks Golf and Country Club** (4800 Chase Oaks Dr., 941/926-7602) and **Timberwoods Vacation Villas & Resort** (7964 Timberwood Cir., 941/923-4966) that rent by the week.

However, if you're only in for a few days, hotels and motels run the gamut from moderately priced and no-frills to truly luxurious. The 12-story **Hyatt Sarasota** (1000 Boulevard of the Arts, 941/953-1234, $229–439) finished the final phases of its $22 million transformation in 2008. The results are a spectacular, and massive, convention hotel right downtown with easy access to Van Wezel Performing Arts Hall, the Municipal Auditorium, and other attractions. It's right in the downtown business district, but waterside, with its own private marina, a floating dock, and a beautiful lagoon-style pool. The 294 guest rooms all have a view of the bay or marina, most with little balconies.

It was controversial when it opened, but the **Ritz-Carlton Sarasota** (1111 Ritz-Carlton Dr., 941/309-2000, reservations 800/241-3333, www.ritzcarlton.com, $410–719), a 266-room, 18-story luxury hotel right downtown, has managed to blend in beautifully, as if it has always been here. Ritz-Carlton's signature service (warm, efficient, but seldom verging on obsequious), spacious rooms with balconies and marble baths, and great amenities make it the top choice among business and high-fallutin' travelers. The downtown location is convenient to restaurants (although there are two laudable ones on-site) and attractions; there's a lovely pool, and the wood-paneled Cà d'Zan Bar & Cigar Lounge is always hopping.

The Ritz has a spa open to guests and members only, and the Members Golf Club located 13 miles from the hotel offers a Tom

Fazio–designed 18-hole championship course. It is a par 72, located on 315 acres of tropical landscape with no real estate development.

One of the most attractive hotels to open in recent years is the **Hotel Indigo** (1223 Boulevard of the Arts, 941/487-3800, $199–233), a sweet boutique job with a canny use of vibrant colors and whimsical design elements. Guest rooms have wall-sized murals and wonderful fabrics in rich blues and greens—altogether it's a fun, contemporary alternative, right in the thick of things. The on-site café is called the Golden Bean, there's a little wine bar called Phi, and a fitness studio called, well, Phitness Studio. Still, I'd spend my time in one of the cushioned Adirondack chairs or out on the lovely patio.

GETTING THERE AND AROUND

Sarasota is along I-75, the major transportation corridor for the southeastern United States. Sarasota County is approximately one hour south of Tampa. U.S. 301 and U.S. 41 (Tamiami Trail) are the major north–south arteries on the mainland; the Gulf Drive (County Road 789) is the main island road. The largest east–west thoroughfares in Sarasota are Highway 72 (Stickney Point Road); County Road 780 (University Parkway); and (to the islands) Ringling Causeway, which takes you right to Lido Beach.

Downtown streets and roads run east–west; avenues and boulevards run north–south. The main street downtown is called, um, Main Street. From downtown, go east across the John Ringling Causeway to access St. Armands Circle and Lido Key. Continue north to Longboat Key, where there's not a lot of draw beyond swanky hotels, golf courses, a few restaurants, and slightly inconvenient beach access and parking. To reach Siesta Key, head south on U.S. 41 (also called the Tamiami Trail), then take a right onto either Siesta Drive or Stickney Point Road—the former takes you to the northern, residential section of the key; Stickney takes you closer to the funky Siesta Village. The public beaches on Siesta Key are among the finest in the state.

By Air
Sarasota-Bradenton International Airport (SRQ) (6000 Airport Cir., at the intersection of U.S. 41 and University Pkwy., 941/359-2770) is certainly the closest airport, served by commuter flights and a half dozen major airlines or their partners, including Continental, Delta, Northwest, AirTran, and US Airways. Still, many people fly into **Tampa International Airport** (813/870-8700), which offers more arrival and departure choices, and often better fares on flights and even rental cars.

BACKGROUND
The Land

Florida is bounded on the north by Alabama and Georgia, to the east by the Atlantic, to the south by the Straits of Florida, and to the west by the Gulf of Mexico. The east coast of the state is comparatively straight, extending in a rough line 470 miles long. The Gulf side, on the other hand, has a more sinuous and convoluted coastline, measuring roughly 675 miles. In all, Florida's 2,276-mile coastline is longer than that of any other state in the continental U.S. It's nearly pancake flat, without notable change in elevation, and young by geological standards, having risen out of the ocean a scant 300–400 million years ago.

TAMPA

Busch Gardens, Ybor City, the Florida Aquarium, Tampa Bay Buccaneers, Tampa Bay Rays, and Tampa Bay Lightning. But notice I didn't mention the beach. Tampa fronts Tampa Bay, not the Gulf of Mexico. A huge port city—the largest pleasure and industrial port in the southeast—it doesn't have any beaches to speak of. Before you despair, though, it's an excellent vacation destination, especially for families. There's a magical confluence of warm weather, affordable accommodations, professional sports, children's attractions, and strangely posh shopping that seems to suit every taste.

Containing the biggest and best airport on

COURTESY OF VISIT FLORIDA

Florida's west coast, Tampa is a natural embarkation point for a Gulf Coast vacation. It's located adjacent to Pinellas County and, when combined with St. Petersburg, is the largest metropolitan area in the state. There is huge suburban sprawl in the north, where Busch Gardens and University of South Florida are, but farther to the south it's cheek by jowl: There's the elegant historic residential and commercial neighborhood of Hyde Park, the Cuban center of town in Ybor City (once famous for cigars, now more famous for bars), and MacDill Air Force Base, which takes up the entire southern third of the Tampa peninsula and is home to the U.S. Central Command. The Hillsborough River runs through the city, providing a peaceful natural counterpoint to all the more frantic, citified pleasures.

ST. PETERSBURG AND PINELLAS COUNTY

St. Petersburg, the last you heard, was a retirement community. It's different now--an influx of high-tech firms, mostly employing youngish people, has prompted a shift in the demographics. Pinellas County as a whole has seen enormous growth and fiscal health recently, a notable destination for family vacations. St. Petersburg itself faces Tampa to the east, with seven miles of inviting parkland touching placid Old Tampa Bay. On the west side of the peninsula, Clearwater Beach, protected by Honeymoon Island to the north, is a wide, welcoming swath of Gulf water lapping at white sand, backed by restaurants, souvenir shops, boogie-board-and-bikini boutiques, etc.

The city of St. Petersburg exerts its pull with a vibrant downtown of pastel art deco buildings and cultural attractions like the Salvador Dalí Museum, Florida International Museum, orchestral music at the Mahaffey Theater, or theater at American Stage. St. Petersburg is also home to some of the most sophisticated restaurants in the greater Tampa Bay area.

Along the Gulf side of Pinellas County, Clearwater is not necessarily the most famous community. St. Pete Beach to the south, which is a distinct community from the larger, more urban St. Petersburg to its east, draws beach lovers from around the world. It's a classic Florida beach town, with late-night waterside clubs, deepwater fishing, and low-slung motels with views of the beach. And there's a lot of beach, many local strands ranking high in international beach polls. Caladesi Island, Honeymoon Island, and Fort De Soto Park are all noteworthy Pinellas beaches.

CLIMATE
Heat and Humidity

Florida is closer to the equator than any other continental American state, located on the southeastern tip of North America with a humid subtropical climate and heavy rainfall April–November. Its humidity is attributed to the fact that no point in the state is more than 60 miles from salt water and no more than 345 feet above sea level. If this thick steamy breath on the back of your neck is new to you, humidity is a measure of the amount of water vapor in the air. Most often you'll hear the percentage described in relative humidity, which is the amount of water vapor actually in the air divided by the amount of water vapor the air can hold. The warmer the air becomes, the more moisture it can hold.

When heat and humidity combine to slow evaporation of sweat from the body, outdoor activity becomes dangerous even for those in good physical shape. Drink plenty of water to avoid dehydration and slow down if you feel fatigued or notice a headache, a high pulse rate, or shallow breathing. Overheating can cause serious and even life-threatening conditions such as heatstroke. The elderly, small children, the overweight, and those on some medications are particularly vulnerable to heat stress.

During the summer months, expect temperatures to hover around 90°F and humidity to be somewhere near 100 percent. The most pleasant times of the year along the length of the Florida peninsula fall between December and April—not surprisingly, the busiest time for tourism. The best approach for packing in preparation for a visit to Florida is layering—with a sweater for over-air-conditioned interiors or chilly winds, and lots of loose, wicking material for the heat.

Rain

It rains nearly every day in the summer in the Tampa Bay area. And not just a sprinkle. Due to the abundance of warm, moist air from the Gulf of Mexico and the hot tropical sun, conditions are perfect for the formation of thunderstorms. There are 80–90 thunderstorms each summer, generally less than 15 miles in diameter—but vertically they can grow up to 10 miles high in the atmosphere. These are huge, localized thunderstorms that can drop four or more inches of rain in an hour, while just a few miles away it stays dry. The bulk of these tropical afternoon thunderstorms each summer are electrical storms.

Lightning

With sudden thunderstorms comes lightning, a serious threat here. About 50 people are struck by lightning each year in the state. Most of them are hospitalized and recover, but there are about 10 fatalities annually. Tampa is the Lightning Capital of the U.S., with around 25 cloud-to-ground lightning bolt blasts on each square mile annually. The temperature of a single bolt can reach 50,000 degrees Fahrenheit, about three times as hot as the sun's surface. There's not much you can do to ward off lightning except to avoid being in the wrong place at the wrong time. The summer months of June, July, August, and September have the highest number of lightning-related injuries and deaths. Usually lightning occurs during daylight hours, with the highest concentration between 3 P.M. and 4 P.M., when the afternoon storms peak. Lightning strikes usually occur either at the beginning or end of a storm, and can strike up to 10 miles away from the center of the storm. Keep your eye on approaching storms and seek shelter when you see lightning.

Locals use the 30-30 rule: Count the seconds after a lightning flash until you hear thunder. If that number is under 30, the storm is within six miles of you. Seek shelter. Then, at storm's end, wait 30 minutes after the last thunder clap before resuming outdoor activity.

Hurricanes

At the time of this writing, Tampa Bay has repeatedly dodged a bullet. The last time the area took a direct hurricane hit was 1921, but the law of averages says that won't last. Hurricanes are violent tropical storms with sustained winds of at least 74 mph. Massive low-pressure systems, they blow counterclockwise around a relatively calm central area called the eye. They form over warm ocean waters, often starting as storms in the Caribbean or off the west coast of Africa. As they move westward, they are fueled by the warm waters of the tropics. Warm, moist air moves toward the center of the storm and spirals upward, releasing driving rains. Updrafts suck up more water vapor, which further strengthens the storm until it can be stopped only when contact is made with land or cooler water. In the average hurricane just one percent of the energy released could meet the energy needs of the U.S. for a full year.

In Florida, the hurricane season is July–November. These storms have been named since 1953. It used to be just female names ("Hell hath no fury like a woman scorned," or some such nonsense), but now there's gender parity in the naming. Really powerful hurricanes' names are retired, kind of like sports greats' jerseys.

The 2004 hurricane season was the last really destructive year in Florida, with Charley, Frances, Ivan, and Jeanne wreaking quite a bit of havoc on the Gulf Coast in rapid succession. Despite dire predictions, recent years have been meteorologically uneventful on Florida's Gulf Coast.

Hurricane Safety

Monitor radio and TV broadcasts closely for directions. Gas up the car, and make sure you have batteries, water supply, candles, and food that can be eaten without the use of electricity. Get cash, have your prescriptions filled, and put all essential documents in a large resealable bag. In the event of an evacuation, find the closest shelter by listening to the radio or TV broadcasts. Pets are not allowed in most shelters. There are designated pet shelters, but all animals must be up to date on shots. Alternatively, an increasing number of hotels and motels accept animals for a nominal daily fee.

History

The southernmost state in the U.S., Florida was named by **Ponce de León** upon his visit in 1513, clearly taken with the lush tropical wilderness. This expedition, the first documented presence of Europeans on the mainland of the U.S., was ostensibly "to discover and people the island of Bimini." On the return voyage he rounded the Dry Tortugas to explore the Gulf of Mexico, entering Charlotte Harbor (about an hour south of Tampa and St. Petersburg). He soon realized that Florida was more than a large island. Near Mound Key he encountered the fierce Calusa people, and while on Estero Island repairing his ship he narrowly escaped Calusa capture. Eight years later he returned and headed to the Calusa territory with 500 of his men, aiming to establish a permanent colony in Florida. In an ensuing battle with the Calusa, Ponce de León was pierced in the thigh by an arrow and carried back to his ship. He never returned again.

Many of the subsequent explorers' missions were less high profile. In 1516 **Diego Miruelo** mapped Pensacola Bay. In 1517, **Alonso Alvarez de Pineda** went the length of the Florida shore to the Mississippi River, confirming Ponce de León's assertion that Florida was not an island. In 1520, **Vasquez de Ayollon** mapped the Carolina coast (which at the time Spain claimed in the vast region they called "Florida").

Panfilo de Narvaez was a veteran Caribbean soldier, hired by Spanish authorities in 1520 to overthrow Hernán Cortés's tyrannical rule. After a lengthy imprisonment by Cortés, Narvaez went back to Spain and obtained a grant to colonize the Gulf Coast from northern Mexico to Florida. Together with **Cabeza de Vaca,** an armada of five ships, and 400 soldiers, Narvaez landed north of the mouth of Tampa Bay in 1527. Spanish–Native American relations deteriorated quickly during this period; the Spaniards' ruthless hunt for gold and riches met with violence on the part of the Indians.

Then came **Hernando de Soto.** In the spring of 1539 he sailed for Tampa Bay with seven vessels, 600 soldiers, three Jesuit friars, and several dozen civilians with the intent of starting a settlement. Where he went exactly is a topic of much debate: Some say he landed in Manatee County, others believe it was in Charlotte Harbor. Like many of the conquistadores before him, de Soto was attracted to the stories of Indian riches to the north, so he sent his fleet back to Cuba, left only a rudimentary base camp on the Manatee River, and set off inland from the coast. He and his men never found what they sought, moving ever northward into Georgia, South Carolina, Tennessee, Alabama, Mississippi, and Arkansas, where he died of fever.

There were religious missions to the state during the same time—Dominican priest **Father Luis Cancer,** three additional missionaries, and a Christianized Indian maiden named Magdalene arrived on the beaches outside Tampa Bay in 1549. Given the Native Americans' experience with white men, it's probably no wonder that Father Cancer was quickly surrounded and clubbed to death. The survivors in his party hightailed it back to Mexico to put the skids on future missionary proposals for Florida.

Long after Hernando de Soto sailed into the bay, the area went largely untouched by whites for another couple of hundred years. Dutch cartographer Bernard Romans named the Hillsborough River and the upper arm

COURTESY OF ST. PETERSBURG/CLEARWATER AREA CVB

Fort De Soto's guns were never fired in a war. They were test-fired in the early 1900s on targets pulled by ships in the Gulf of Mexico.

of Tampa Bay in 1772, in honor of Lord Hillsborough, British secretary of state for the colonies. The U.S. purchased Florida from Spain in 1821, with traders setting up shop along what is now downtown Tampa in 1855.

On the other side of Tampa Bay, intrepid Frenchman Odet Philippe, established a large orange grove near Safety Harbor in 1842. In what was to become Pinellas County, Scottish merchants settled Dunedin and the Russian immigrants who worked the Orange Belt Railroad and named St. Petersburg after their Russian hometown.

It wasn't until Henry B. Plant extended his railroad into Tampa in 1884 and started a steamship line from Tampa to Key West to Havana, Cuba, that the area really began to grow. In 1891, Plant built the Tampa Bay Hotel, which launched the city as a winter resort for the northern elite. Around the same time, O. H. Platt purchased 20 acres of land across the Hillsborough River creating Tampa's first residential suburb, Hyde Park (named after Platt's hometown in Illinois). Hyde Park was,

and still is, the residential area of choice for many prominent citizens. Many of the 19th-century bungalows and Princess Anne–style cottages are still occupied today, and the Old Hyde Park Village collection of boutiques and restaurants is one of the city's biggest draws.

Around the same time, Don Vicente Martinez Ybor, an influential cigar manufacturer and Cuban exile, moved his cigar business from Key West to a scruffy stretch of land east of Tampa in 1885. His first cigar factory drew others, and the Spanish, Italian, German, and Cuban workers who settled here to work in the area's more than 200 cigar factories created a vivacious Latin community known as Ybor City.

When the U.S. declared war on Spain in 1898, Tampa was the port of embarkation for troops headed to Cuba. A vital colonel named Theodore Roosevelt organized his Rough Riders at the Tampa encampment. Not long after that, another Tampa neighborhood, Davis Islands, developed during the Florida land boom. Two little islands off downtown Tampa, where the Hillsborough River empties into Hillsborough Bay, became booming real estate developments.

In some ways, Henry Ford's affordable $400 Model T foreshadowed the real estate boom in the area in the early 1920s. It was the beginning of road-tripping, folks hopping in the car in search of sun, sand, and a little fun. They found what is now Pinellas County, the peninsula that hangs down Florida's west side like a thumb, with its beaches and Intracoastal waterway, and they found the growing city of Tampa to the east. People liked what they saw.

They bought up land, building big resort hotels, affordable motels, and homes.

Growth continued apace through the Roaring Twenties, slowing, as it did everywhere, during the Great Depression. Since then, the Tampa Bay area hasn't been buoyed by the tourist dollar to the degree other Gulf Coast cities have, and thus has been less susceptible to the ups and downs of Florida travel (first 9/11, then the walloping hurricane season of 2004, counterbalanced by Europeans' enthusiasm about the weakness of the dollar).

Government and Economy

STATE GOVERNMENT

In 1968, Florida adopted a new state constitution. The governor is elected for a term of four years, and the legislature has a senate of 40 members and a house of representatives of 120 members. The state also elects 23 representatives and 2 senators to the U.S. Congress and has 27 electoral votes.

It's easy enough to say that the state is fairly solidly Republican. But it's more complicated than that. In a state that was historically Democrat, recent explosive population growth has brought with it many Republicans, leaving the state approximately evenly split between the two parties. It's because of that, combined with its large number of electoral votes, that Florida is considered by political analysts to be a key swing state in presidential elections. Tampa, once a hotbed of Democratic union support, is now much more heavily influenced by pro-business Republicans. As a whole, Florida went for Nixon in 1968 and 1972, but Carter in 1976, Reagan in 1980 and 1984, Bush in 1988, Bush, just barely, in 1992, Clinton in 1996, then depending on your take on the 2000 election, either Bush by a hair or Gore by a bigger hair, and Bush again by a little in 2004.

As for state government, Democrat Lawton Chiles, elected governor in 1990 and reelected in 1994, was succeeded by Republican John Ellis "Jeb" Bush, elected in 1998 and reelected in 2002. Republican Charlie Crist (attorney general under Bush) was elected in 2006, with Jeff Kottkamp as lieutenant governor, Bill McCollum as attorney general, and Alex Sink as CFO. The next state constitutional officer elections occur in 2010.

INDUSTRY

Florida has historically been a poor state. It spent its early years luring any kind of industry here with big tax breaks and incentives, sometimes even free land. And there have been many waves of takers. The deepwater ports along the Gulf prompted ship-building booms as far back as the 1830s, with industries like cotton-shipping utilizing the gentle open water and connecting rivers and Intracoastal Waterway.

Cheap labor, lax laws, rich natural resources, a general anti-union sentiment, and no state income tax—it's a recipe for get-rich-quick, environmentally damaging industries. And Florida has had them, from timber and turpentining to paper mills and chemical plants. It wasn't until the Clean Water Act in 1972—which regulates the discharge of pollutants into U.S. waters and makes it illegal for industry to discharge pollutants without a permit—that people in Florida started scratching their heads about all the dead fish washing up on the shores. It's gotten better, but the Gulf states (Florida, Texas, and Louisiana in particular) are still among the top offenders for allowing permit violations for high-hazard chemicals. The industries in question are varied, linked mainly by their propensity for toxic discharge and their political clout. State and federal agencies charged with monitoring are perennially hamstrung by Florida politicians.

Agriculture also plays a mighty role in the commercial well-being of the state. In 2005 (the last available statistics), Florida ranked 2nd in the value of vegetables and melon production with receipts of $1.4 billion, 3rd in fruit and nuts with receipts of $1.5 billion, 5th in all crops with receipts of $5.4 billion, and 10th in total cash receipts. Horticultural products (meaning plants and floriculture) are big business, too, hiking up total state agricultural revenues past $6.8 billion.

Cattle ranches and dairy farms are dense in the middle of the state, and from Gulf waters commercial fishers haul millions of pounds of fish and shellfish, and sport fishers haul millions more. The lumber industry is still going strong in some parts of the state, while high-tech companies have flocked to the St. Petersburg/Tampa area recently, drawn by good weather and low housing costs.

All this is still beside the point in some ways. Tourism is the state's number one industry, plain and simple. From January 1 through December 31, 2006, more than 83.9 million people visited Florida, according to data released by Visit Florida, the state's marketing arm. It's an approximately $65 billion business, with 50,000 restaurants, 4,000 hotels and accommodations, and some of the world's top tourist attractions (Walt Disney World, Kennedy Space Center, did I mention Walt Disney World?).

FLORIDA'S MILITARY

There are currently 11 active military installations in Florida. This follows a 2005 shakeup at the hands of the U.S. Department of Defense when they announced their preliminary 2005 Base Realignment and Closure list (it recommended closing 33 major bases and realigning, either enlarging or shrinking, 29 others).

Though shrinking, the military has in recent years been the state's third top economic sector behind tourism and agriculture, with 64,500 people employed in the armed forces directly.

Many of the bases and two of the unified commands are along the Gulf Coast. **U.S. Central Command** (CENTCOM) is at MacDill Air Force Base in Tampa and is responsible for U.S. security interests in 25 nations that stretch from the Horn of Africa, through the Gulf region, into Central Asia. The command was activated in January 1983 as the successor to the Rapid Deployment Joint Task Force. A few years after that, in 1987, **U.S. Special Operations Command** (USSOCOM) was established as a unified combatant command also at MacDill, composed of army, navy, and air force special operations forces. Its mission is to support the geographic commanders-in-chief, ambassadors, and their country teams and other government agencies by preparing special operations forces. Its annual budget is nearly $5 billion, 1.3 percent of the overall defense budget.

EDUCATION

Centrist Governor Crist may be good news for education in the state. In his first year in office, he managed to shield public schools from budget cuts, but an impending property tax amendment may undo all that. First vetoing a public college tuition increase, he changed his mind and okayed a 5 percent increase--good news for a beleaguered system with too many students and too few resources.

Still more good news, Crist intends to overhaul the Florida standardized testing system. Governor Jeb Bush's A+ Plan woefully misused the FCAT standardized tests. Like his brother's No Child Left Behind program, it used standardized tests as a means of teacher accountability, withholding funds from schools whose students fail to meet the established standards. It ranked schools with a letter grade, the highest ranked schools getting the greatest funding, and then handed out state vouchers to students in the failing schools. The problem is, this ostensible "choice" is no choice at all when the best schools are often already at maximum capacity.

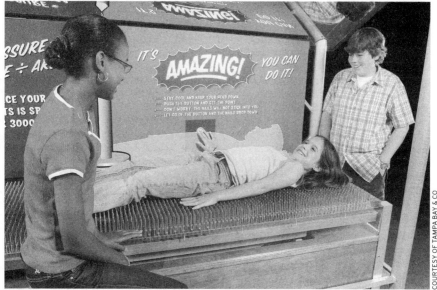

COURTESY OF TAMPA BAY & CO

One of the largest educational science centers in the Southeast, Tampa's Museum of Science and Industry has more than 450 interactive exhibits.

The bottom line: Florida's public education does not compete on a national level. After eight years of Jeb Bush's governance, a state report came out evaluating Florida schools in 14 categories, finding the state above the national average in only three categories (third-grade reading is going okay, and the number of students returning for a second year at community colleges is commendable). In areas such as scores on the ACT and SAT college-entrance exams, student-teacher ratios, high-school graduation rates, and reading and math scores on the National Assessment of Educational Progress exams administered to students across the country, Florida was deemed subpar.

Money is part of the problem. The amount spent per student ranks 43rd among 50 states (as an example, in 2004 New Jersey spent $13,338 per pupil, Florida spent $6,793). The state also lags in average teacher salary and funding of colleges (adjusted for cost of living, though, beginning teachers' salaries are slightly above average). Crowding is another problem. Class-size reductions have not kept up with those of other states, and the schools have seen a significant demographic bubble in elementary-age kids in the past few years.

But the problems are clearly just as much about ideology. The state has failed to prioritize the education of its students, as much at the elementary school levels as at the college level. With some of the lowest tuitions and teacher salaries in the country, Florida universities prove one thing: Cheap tuition means inferior education, with poor services, crowded classrooms, delayed graduation (because classes aren't available), and disgruntled faculty.

ENVIRONMENTAL ISSUES

In 1827, Ralph Waldo Emerson visited the Florida territory's new capital city and wrote in his diary that the place had been "rapidly settled by public officers, land speculators, and desperadoes." That seems to be still the case.

In reading the *New Yorker*'s review of the biopic *Monster,* the story of Aileen Wuornos, I was struck by David Denby's assessment of the state in which the real-life Wuornos was executed in 2002:

> The scuzzy central-Florida setting gives [Charlize] Theron some acting ground to stand on. In such recent American movies as the Matt Dillon thriller *Wild Things*, Larry Clark's *Bully*, John Sayles's *Sunshine State*, the Charlie Kaufman–Spike Jonze fantasia *Adaptation*, and Frederick Wiseman's documentary *Domestic Violence*, as well as Carl Hiaasen's novels, Florida has appeared as a kind of bedraggled kingdom of chaos. The swamps, the threadbare woods, the sagging, loose-hinged bungalows, the roadhouses with their grizzled and beer-bellied bikers, the long, droning freeways, cars tooling along to somewhere or other. . . . Florida is the place where life doesn't shape up . . . [where] there's no structure, nothing hard or dense enough to mold people into coherent human beings."

Sounds pretty grim, huh? But still, I know what he means. There's a Wild West making-up-the-rules-as-they-suit-me frontier spirit in this state, a state in which environmentalism has been slow to catch on. For nearly two centuries land speculators have ridden roughshod over the wilderness, buying and selling it in ever-smaller parcels. Mismanaged growth has been the norm, with government officials routinely called to the carpet for cozying up to land developers.

Millions of acres have been bulldozed to make way for strip malls and condo developments—nothing new, really, it happens all over. It's the same story of insufficient infrastructure, deficient water supply, and oversubscribed highways that is told of most recently plundered natural settings. And with something like 1,000 new residents moving to Florida every day, something's gotta give.

Still, the state's commitment to the environment is not hopeless. There's been an enormous grassroots effort in the past decade in Florida, regular people who have balked at the shady characters and get-rich-quick schemes that have so wantonly reduced the state's resources and diminished natural habitats. If their efforts gain purchase, the state's natural treasures—which are truly so vast and so breathtaking—might be preserved and, in some cases, restored.

People and Culture

DEMOGRAPHICS

Florida ranks fourth in the U.S. in population, behind California, Texas, and New York. In 2006, the population was estimated to be 18,089,888 (up from 9,746,961 in 1980). If you count Tampa/St. Petersburg/Clearwater as a single metropolitan area, it beats Miami for sheer numbers—2,396,000 versus 2,253,000 at the last census. On the Gulf Coast, the other most populous areas are Sarasota/Bradenton (590,000), Fort Myers/Cape Coral (441,000), Pensacola (412,000), Tallahassee (285,000), and Naples (251,000). Nearly 1,000 new people move to Florida each day, and despite a slight slowdown in the 1990s, Florida remains one of the fastest-growing states in the nation.

Age

Florida's age distribution is in a state of flux: In 1990, there were 2,355,938 Floridians aged 65 and older (18.2 percent of the total population), whereas in 2000 the census counted 2,807,598 in this group (17.6 percent of the total). So the percentage of those over 65 has shrunk some, but the number of people over 85 has grown tremendously (maybe people just live longer in this climate). Growth in the over-85 population is forecast to expand around 60 percent between 2000 (the last census) and 2010. The area around Tampa has gotten younger in recent years. For instance, the youth population (those age 0–19) has shown increasing growth rates over the last 30 years, from 15.5 percent 1970–1980 to 25.2 percent 1990–2000.

Race

The population of the Gulf Coast is still primarily white (17.8 percent nonwhite at the last census, but projected to be 20 percent by 2010), with the greatest ethnic diversity in the Tampa Bay area. The state's Hispanic population is expected to reach 22 percent of the population by 2010.

Religion

In modern times, the Gulf Coast is primarily Christian. Jewish retirees don't, for whatever reason, settle along the Gulf Coast, with the exception of Sarasota (3–6 percent Jewish, as compared to the east coast of the state from Coral Gables up through Palm Beach, which is roughly 13–15 percent Jewish). The southernmost part of the state is dominantly Catholic, as is the area just north of Tampa up through what is known as the Nature Coast. By and large, though, Floridians are Protestant, especially as you get closer to the Georgia and Alabama borders.

Snowbirds

First, what's a snowbird? It's a temporary resident in Florida, someone who comes from a colder, less hospitable winter climate to bask in the Sunshine State all winter. Snowbirds are usually of retirement age, or nearing it. But it gets more specific. New Yorkers account for 13.1 percent of Florida's temporary residents, followed by Michiganders at 7.4 percent, Ohioans at 6.7 percent, Pennsylvanians at 5.8 percent, and Canadians at 5.5 percent. The average length of stay is five months. If Florida has roughly seven million households, there are an estimated 920,000 temporary residents during the peak winter months and another 170,000 during the late summer.

RESOURCES
Suggested Reading

TAMPA
Travel Guides

Murphy, Bill. *Fox 13 Tampa Bay One Tank Trips With Bill Murphy.* St. Petersburg: Seaside Publishing, 2004. An offshoot of a television segment Murphy does, the books showcase 52 Florida-based adventures that are all within a full tank of Tampa. It's lots of off-the-beaten path attractions, all worthy of your time, from Pioneer Florida Museum in Dade City to the excellent camping at Fort De Soto Park.

Fiction

Hiaasen, Carl. He's everywhere in Florida, bigger than a novelist, bigger than a *Miami Herald* columnist. He's like a rock star around here (good because he owns a Fender Strat that Dave Barry helped him pick out), with so many titles it's hard to really put forth a favorite with any kind of stalwart conviction. The most recent is his nonfiction golf book called *The Downhill Lie* (New York: Knopf, 2008), before that *Nature Girl, Skinny Dip, Basket Case, Sick Puppy, Lucky You, Stormy Weather, Strip Tease, Native Tongue, Skin Tight, Double Whammy,* and *Tourist Season.* What you, the reader, need to know, beyond the fact that he has a penchant for two-word titles, is that he loves the rich and iconoclastic zaniness that is south Florida, has a real fondness for smart hookers with a heart of gold, finds tough-guy baldies especially amusing, and is a bulldoggish environmentalist. In addition to his novels, Hiaasen has also published two collections of his newspaper columns, *Kick Ass* and *Paradise Screwed,* and an eviscerating anti-Disney book called *Team Rodent.* (Caveat emptor: Hiaasen keeps snakes as pets. They feature heavily in his books.)

Wayne White, Randy. *Sanibel Flats.* New York: St. Martin's Press, 1991. Randy Wayne White was a fishing guide at Tarpon Bay down on Sanibel for 13 years. A prolific mystery novelist, he writes mostly about areas just slightly to the south of Tampa and St. Petersburg, with numerous novels featuring super tough-guy Doc Ford solving various mysteries *(Black Widow, Hunter's Moon, The Deadlier Sex, Cuban Death-Lift, The Deep Six, The Heat Islands, The Man Who Invented Florida, Captiva, North of Havana, The Mangrove Coast, Ten Thousand Islands, Shark River, Twelve Mile Limit, Everglades, Tampa Burn,* and *Dead of Night).* In all his books, Florida is one of the main characters, lovingly and lavishly described in all its loony glory. Wayne White is a columnist for *Outside* magazine and *Men's Health* and he's written lots of other books of essays and such, including *Batfishing in the Rain Forest* and a fish cookbook.

Drama

Cruz, Nilo. *Anna in the Tropics.* Theatre Communications Group, 2003. This play won Cruz the Pulitzer Prize for drama in 2003. It is a romantic drama, loosely a retelling of Tolstoy's *Anna Karenina,* that depicts a Cuban-American family of cigar makers in Ybor City (Tampa) in 1930. It tells the story of the factory's new "lector," a person hired to read aloud great works of literature and the day's news to the cigar workers. A beautiful stage play—keep your eyes open for any performances of it during your visit.

ST. PETERSBURG
Nonfiction

Klinkenberg, Jeff. *Pilgrim in the Land of Alligators: More Stories about Real Florida.* Gainesville: University Press of Florida, 2008. *St. Petersburg Times* writer Klinkenberg may have invented the term Real Florida, which means the Old Florida, without Disney, fancy golf courses, or really anything glamorous. This book is an assemblage of largely humorous essays he's written for the paper that tell great stories about the people, flora, and fauna in west-central Florida. Klinkenberg wrote two other compelling books of essays entitled *Seasons of Real Florida* and *Dispatches from the Land of Flowers: A Snake Man, a Sad Poet, a Lightning Stalker and Other Stories About Real Florida.* Gainesville: Down Home Press, 2004 and 1996, respectively.

Fiction

MacDonald, John. *Condominium.* New York: Fawcett, reissue edition, 1985. For most of his life MacDonald was considered a pulp fiction writer, and prolific, who spent more than half his life in west-central Florida, first in Clearwater, then in Sarasota and Siesta Key. This book still seems fresh, especially in light of 2004's hurricane season. The setting is Golden Sands, a Sunbelt condo in the path of Hurricane Ella. It's a multicharacter disaster book, think *The Towering Inferno* or something like that. (*Cape Fear,* by the way, was based on a MacDonald book.)

Wildlife

Adams, Alto. *A Florida Cattle Ranch.* Sarasota, FL: Pineapple Press, 1998. You'll learn about Cracker cows, scrub, and the hardscrabble world of Florida ranching.

Arnov, Boris. *Fish Florida: Saltwater/Better than Luck-The Foolproof Guide to Florida Saltwater Fishing.* Gulf Publishing, 2002. This is a fairly good beginner book: it describes a kind of fish, let's say amberjack, then tells you how it fights (fiercely); appropriate tackle, whether you're spinning or plug casting or fly fishing; and technique for live bait or light tackle casting. It also gives catch and size limits and other regulations.

Maehr, David. *Florida's Birds: A Field Guide And Reference.* Sarasota, FL: Pineapple Press, 2005. For birders and rookies alike, birds can be quickly identified in this book via picture (pretty ones with birds grouped by similar species), text, or index. Maps indicate when migratory birds are present or breeding, and where.

Maehr, David. *The Florida Panther: Life and Death of a Vanishing Carnivore.* Washington, D.C.: Island Press, 1997. The author makes these endangered cougars spring to life in their last frontier in the Big Cypress National Preserve and around the Okaloacoochee Slough.

Sobczak, Charles. *Alligators, Sharks & Panthers: Deadly Encounters with Florida's Top Predator—Man.* Sanibel, FL: Indigo Press, 2006. It chronicles gristly attacks, but with an underlying environmentalist's message about humans mucking about in creatures' natural habitats.

Tekiela, Stan. *Birds of Florida Field Guide.* Minnesota: Adventure Publications, 2005. It's a great small-sized book organized by bird color. This makes it easy to narrow things down when you've just spotted a flash of wing color in your binoculars.

Even better than these books, though, is a sand- and waterproof *Florida's Gulf Coast Birds* flip map illustrated by Ernest C. Simmons (visit www.floridabooks.com if you can't find it in area bookstores). It puts birds into rough groups—wading birds, shore birds, wetland birds, birds of prey, and others.

Shells

Williams, Winston. *Florida's Fabulous Seashells: And Other Seashore Life.* Tampa: World Publications, 1988. It's light enough to pack in your beach bag, with good color photos and interesting text about the marine animals.

Witherington, Blair and Dawn. *Florida's Seashells.* Sarasota, FL: Pineapple Press, 2007. This one is a little heavier.

CHILDREN'S LITERATURE

DiCamillo, Kate. *Because of Winn Dixie.* Cambridge, MA: Candlewick Press, 2001. A major motion picture a few years back, this book about 10-year-old India Opal Buloni and her ugly dog Winn-Dixie (named for where she found him) has captured the attention of lots of families. It's a great story, set in a fictional town of Naomi, Florida (I like to think it's modeled on someplace down toward Port Charlotte). Opal's had kind of a hard life, so it might be too much for a really sensitive kid.

Rawlings, Marjorie Kinnan. *The Yearling.* New York: Simon Pulse, 50th edition, 1988. Rawlings wrote 10 books while a resident in Cross Creek, Florida, the most popular of which was *The Yearling,* which won a Pulitzer Prize in fiction in 1939. It tells the story of scrappy young Jody Baxter and his pet fawn Flag, who together roam the Florida scrublands wrestling big swamp gators and cavorting with bear cubs. Rawlings second-best book is called simply, *Cross Creek,* also with the same earthy Florida Cracker dialect.

Smith, Patrick D. *A Land Remembered.* Sarasota, FL: Pineapple Press, 1998. Beginning with Tobias MacIvey's arrival in Florida in 1858, this young-adult historical novel tells the story of three generations of Floridians carving out a hardscrabble life for themselves in the wilds of central Florida. This sweeping story is rich in Florida history.

Internet Resources

TAMPA

Tampa Bay Convention and Visitors Bureau
www.visittampabay.com

This is a good site for background on the Bay Area as well as travel strategies and accommodations.

Creative Loafing
http://tampa.creativeloafing.com

The local alternative weekly newspaper has a site that beats the *Tampa Tribune's,* hands down. The writing is provocative and witty, and the paper's arts critics have impeccable taste.

ST. PETERSBURG

St. Petersburg/Clearwater Area Convention & Visitors Bureau
www.floridasbeach.com

Very similar to the Tampa Convention & Visitors Bureau site, this one focuses, not surprisingly, on the beaches. It's easy to book a room from this site, and it features excellent downloadable maps.

St. Petersburg Times
www.tampabay.com

The Gulf Coast's best daily metro paper has an equally superlative website, the place to go if you want to be versed in local politics or find out the day's most exciting events. The paper's movie, book, and pop music reviews are notably good, and a team is working on making the site more usable with the introduction of sortable databases.

GENERAL
Visit Florida
www.flausa.com

For a good introduction to the Gulf Coast, contact the state's official tourist information organization, Visit Florida (or call 888/7FLA-USA) for a copy of their excellent annual *Visit Florida* guide, the *Florida Events Calendar,* or *Florida Trails.* Online resources include a number of electronic travel guides (for which you can order printed versions if you prefer). Visit Florida also has a 24-hour multilingual tourist assistance hotline at 800/656-8777.

Florida Secrets, The Insider's Guide to Unique Destinations
www.florida-secrets.com

The graphics have a cheese factor and it's heavy on the advertising, but the site is a treasure trove of little-known destinations in Florida, divided up on the Gulf Coast by southwest, west-central, eastern, and western Panhandle.

FISHING
Fish We Catch in Florida
www.redfishhunter.com/fish

If you're looking for a no-nonsense description of what you're likely to catch, what they look like, how to nab them, and then whether they're worth eating, this is the site for you.

Florida Fishing
www.floridafishing.com

It's a clearinghouse of fishing guides, fishing charters, and fishing captains in the state, divided by region.

CAMPING
Florida Association of RV Parks & Campgrounds
www.floridacamping.com

It's an easy-to-use comprehensive database of Florida campgrounds, including amenities information for each site. You can also go on their website and order a print version of the guide. To make reservations at a Florida state campground (or in any state), however, you must utilize www.reserveamerica.com.

PARKS AND FORESTS
Florida State Parks Department
www.floridastateparks.org

Find a park, its affiliated camping and lodging, or get a bead on what events are coming up along the Gulf Coast. The site also has maps and directions to Florida's state parks, and it runs an amateur photo contest of state park photography.

Florida Trail Association
www.florida-trail.org

The Florida Trail Association is a nonprofit that builds, maintains, promotes, and protects hiking trails across the state of Florida, especially the 1,400-mile Florida Trail. From this site you can download all kinds of trail maps and park brochures.

Index

A

accommodations: see hotels; Hotels Index
Adventure Island: 20
age distribution: 165-166
AirFest at MacDill Air Force Base: 92
airforce base tours: 24
air travel: Orlando 141; Sarasota 156; trip
   planning 7
alligators: 106-107
Alvarez de Pineda, Alonso: 160
AMC Veterans 24: 88
American Stage Theatre: 85
American Stage Theatre Company at the
   Raymond James Theatre: 86
American Victory Mariner's Memorial &
   Museum Ship: 15
amusement parks: Adventure Island 20; Busch
   Gardens 20; Universal Orlando Resort 134;
   Walt Disney World Resort 132, 134; Weeki
   Wachee Springs 144
Anclote Key Preserve State Park: 102
animal attractions: Big Cat Rescue 23; Busch
   Gardens 21; Lowry Park Zoo 22; SeaWorld
   Orlando 134; Walt Disney World Resort
   132; see also aquariums; wildlife/wildlife-
   watching
antiques: 96
aquariums: Clearwater Marine Aquarium 26;
   Florida Aquarium 16; The Pier (Downtown St.
   Petersburg) 25; Sawgrass Lake Park 105
arts: 78-90; highlights 77; Mainsail Arts
   Festival 92; Sarasota 149-150, 153-154, 155
Arts Center, The: 83
Asolo Repertory Theatre: 153
Ayollon, Vasquez de: 160

B

background: 157-166
Baisden Gallery: 84
bakeries: Tampa 30
ballooning: 24
bars: 65-71
baseball: 115-117
Bay Area Renaissance Festival: 92
Bayshore Boulevard: 15
Baywalk: 93
BayWalk 20 and IMAX: 89
Beach Art Center: 78
Beach Drive Northeast: 93

beaches: 99-103; itinerary suggestions 11-12;
   Sarasota 154
Beach Theatre: 89
Belleair beaches: 103
Big Cat Rescue: 23
bike rentals: 25, 101, 102, 111
biking: 110-112
bird-watching/attractions: Anclote Key
   Preserve State Park 103; Boyd Hill Nature
   Preserve 103; Busch Gardens 22; Canoe
   Escape 112; Florida Aquarium 17; Fort De
   Soto State Park 101; Honeymoon Island State
   Recreation Area 101; Sawgrass Lake Park
   105; Shell Key 104; suggested reading 168
Bleu Acier: 84
boat rides/tours: Clearwater Marine Aquarium
   26; dolphin tours 16, 104; Homosassa
   Springs State Wildlife Park 146; houseboat
   rentals 147; Lowry Park Zoo 22; manatee
   tours 145; Pasco County 141; The Pier
   (Downtown St. Petersburg) 25; pirate ships
   104; sailboat rentals 99; sailing classes 104;
   Tarpon Springs 143; yacht dinner cruise 31;
   yachting 19; see also canoeing and kayaking;
   fishing
bookstores: 96-97
Boyd Hill Nature Preserve: 103
Brooker Creek Preserve: 103
Busch Gardens: 20
Busch Gardens and North Tampa: hotels 122;
   map ; restaurants 40-41; sights 20-23;
   where to go 5

C

Cabeza de Vaca: 160
Cà d'Zan: 150
Caladesi Island: 98
camping: Anclote Key Preserve State Park 103;
   Fort De Soto State Park 101; Hillsborough
   River State Park 103; Internet resources 170
Cancer, Luis: 160
Canoe Escape: 111
canoeing and kayaking: Caladesi Island 99;
   Canoe Escape 112; Fort De Soto State Park
   101; Hillsborough River State Park 103; kayak
   tours 104; Lettuce Lake Park 105; Weedon
   Island Preserve Cultural and Natural History
   Center 108
car travel: Nature Coast 148; Orlando 140-141;
   Sarasota 156; trip planning 7

INDEX **177**

YZ
yacht dinner cruise: 31
yachting/yacht races: 19
Ybor City: hotels 121; map ; restaurants 38-40; shops 96; sights 19-20; where to go 5
Ybor City State Museum: 83
ZbookZ New & Used Books: 97
zoos: 22

Hotels Index

Nightlife Index

Restaurants Index

MOON TAMPA & ST. PETERSBURG

Avalon Travel
a member of the Perseus Books Group
1700 Fourth Street
Berkeley, CA 94710, USA
www.moon.com

Editor: Shaharazade Husain
Series Manager: Erin Raber
Copy Editor: Emily Lunceford
Graphics Coordinators: Stefano Boni,
  Domini Dragoone
Production Coordinators: Darren Alessi,
  Amber Pirker
Cover Designer: Stefano Boni
Map Editor: Albert Angulo
Cartographers: Kat Bennett, Chris Markiewicz
Cartography Director: Mike Morgenfeld
Indexer: Jean Mooney

ISBN-10: 1-59880-141-4
ISBN-13: 978-1-59880-141-5
ISSN: 1944-916X

Printing History
1st Edition – March 2009
5 4 3 2 1

Front cover photo: Tampa's Sunshine Skyway Bridge,
  © Joseph Sohm/Digital Railroad
Title page photo: Ybor City at dusk,
  Courtesy of Visit Florida
Interior frontmatter photos: pages 2, 3, 4, 6, 7, 11, and
12, Courtesy of Visit Florida. pages 5, 8, 9, and 10
© Laura Reily

Printed in the United States by RR Donnelly

KEEPING CURRENT

If you have a favorite gem you'd like to see included in the next edition, or see anything
that needs updating, clarification, or correction, please drop us a line. Send your
comments via email to feedback@moon.com, or use the address above.

MAP SYMBOLS

▦▦▦	Expressway	**◖**	Highlight	✗	Airfield	⚲	Golf Course
▦▦▦	Primary Road	○	City/Town	✈	Airport	◻	Parking Area
▦▦▦	Secondary Road	◉	State Capital	▲	Mountain	⛬	Archaeological Site
▪▪▪▪	Unpaved Road	✪	National Capital	✛	Unique Natural Feature	⛪	Church
▪▪▪	Trail	★	Point of Interest			⛽	Gas Station
⋯⋯	Ferry	•	Accommodation	☙	Waterfall	Λ	Campground
▬▬	Railroad	▾	Restaurant/Bar	⚑	Park		Mangrove
▦▦▦	Pedestrian Walkway	▪	Other Location	⬕	Trailhead		Reef
⫿⫿⫿	Stairs	**Ⓢ**	Toll Booth	⛷	Skiing Area		Swamp

CONVERSION TABLES

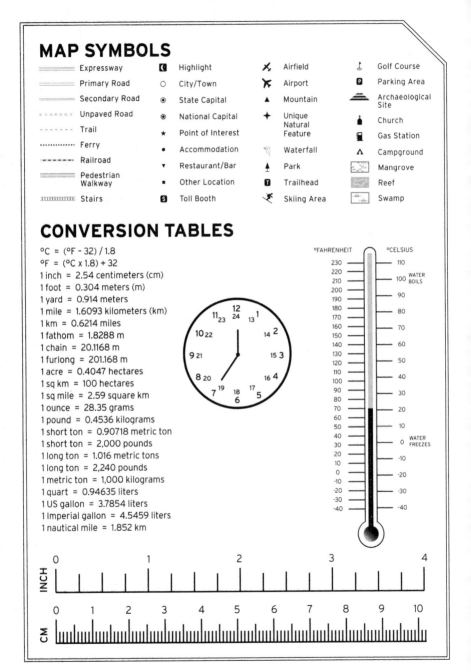

°C = (°F - 32) / 1.8
°F = (°C x 1.8) + 32
1 inch = 2.54 centimeters (cm)
1 foot = 0.304 meters (m)
1 yard = 0.914 meters
1 mile = 1.6093 kilometers (km)
1 km = 0.6214 miles
1 fathom = 1.8288 m
1 chain = 20.1168 m
1 furlong = 201.168 m
1 acre = 0.4047 hectares
1 sq km = 100 hectares
1 sq mile = 2.59 square km
1 ounce = 28.35 grams
1 pound = 0.4536 kilograms
1 short ton = 0.90718 metric ton
1 short ton = 2,000 pounds
1 long ton = 1.016 metric tons
1 long ton = 2,240 pounds
1 metric ton = 1,000 kilograms
1 quart = 0.94635 liters
1 US gallon = 3.7854 liters
1 Imperial gallon = 4.5459 liters
1 nautical mile = 1.852 km

Maps

Odessa

582

9

Tarpon Springs

Lake Tarpon

Keystone Lake

611
77

19

Honeymoon Island

ALDERMAN RD

Palm Harbor

5

RACE TRACK RD

GUNN HWY

Clearwater Harbor

586

Oldsmar

TAMPA RD W

Caladesi Island

MAIN ST

580

58

8

Dunedin

COURTNEY CAMPBELL

60

Clearwater Beach Island

SUNSET POINT RD

N HERCULES AVE

CAUSEWAY

GULF TO BAY BLVD

Clearwater

LAKEVIEW RD

Clearwater Beach

BELLEAIR RD

Old Tampa Bay

Sand Key

BAY DR

HOWARD FRANKLAND

Largo

ULMERTON

S BELCHER RD

RD

GANDY

113TH ST N

SEMINOLE

KEENE

RD

687

WALSINGHAM RD

68TH ST N

19

102ND AVE

BLVD

RD

Pinellas Park

PARK BLVD

68TH ST

Seminole

PARK BLVD

(DR MLK ST)

9TH ST N

16TH ST N

4TH ST N

62ND AVE N

ST. PETERSBURG

TYRONE BLVD N

5TH AVE N

275

Treasure Island

CENTRAL AVE

6

Downtown St. Petersburg

G u l f

7

Gulfport

54TH AVE S

St. Pete Beach

Long Key

Isla Del Sol

o f

M e x i c o

SUNSHINE SKYWAY BRIDGE (TOLL)

Cabbage Key

© AVALON TRAVEL

Mullet Key

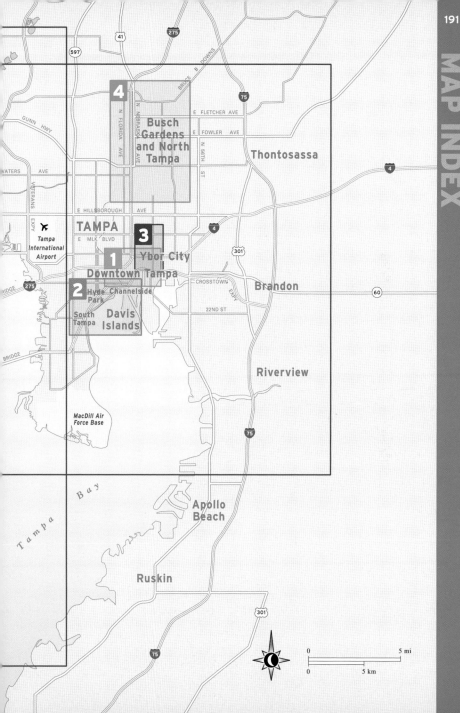

41
275
597

4

75

BRUCE B DOWNS

N FLORIDA AVE

N NEBRASKA AVE

E FLETCHER AVE

E FOWLER AVE

N 56TH ST

Busch Gardens and North Tampa

Thontosassa

GUNN HWY

WATERS AVE

VETERANS EXPY

E HILLSBOROUGH AVE

4

TAMPA

E MLK BLVD

✈
Tampa International Airport

3

4

301

Ybor City

1

Downtown Tampa

275

2

Hyde Channelside
Park

CROSSTOWN EXPY

Brandon

60

South Tampa

Davis Islands

22ND ST

BRIDGE

BRIDGE

Riverview

MacDill Air Force Base

B a y

Apollo Beach

T a m p a   B a y

Ruskin

301

75

0   5 mi

0   5 km

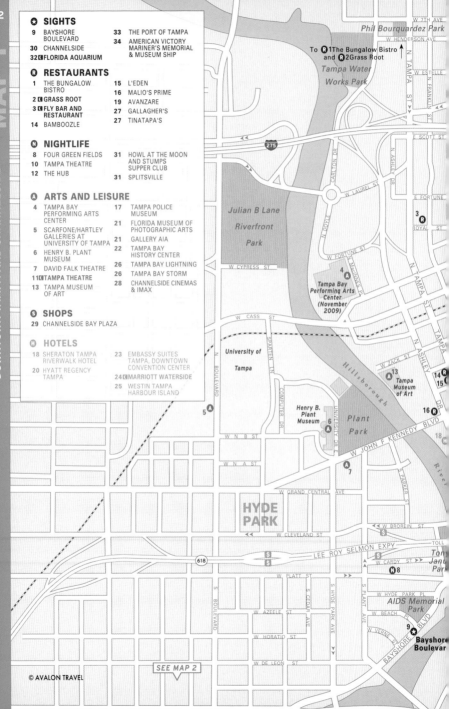

⊙ SIGHTS

9 BAYSHORE BOULEVARD
30 CHANNELSIDE
32 ⓒ FLORIDA AQUARIUM
33 THE PORT OF TAMPA
34 AMERICAN VICTORY MARINER'S MEMORIAL & MUSEUM SHIP

ⓡ RESTAURANTS

1 THE BUNGALOW BISTRO
2 ⓒ GRASS ROOT
3 ⓒ FLY BAR AND RESTAURANT
14 BAMBOOZLE
15 L'EDEN
16 MALIO'S PRIME
19 AVANZARE
27 GALLAGHER'S
27 TINATAPA'S

ⓝ NIGHTLIFE

8 FOUR GREEN FIELDS
10 TAMPA THEATRE
12 THE HUB
31 HOWL AT THE MOON AND STUMPS SUPPER CLUB
31 SPLITSVILLE

ⓐ ARTS AND LEISURE

4 TAMPA BAY PERFORMING ARTS CENTER
5 SCARFONE/HARTLEY GALLERIES AT UNIVERSITY OF TAMPA
6 HENRY B. PLANT MUSEUM
7 DAVID FALK THEATRE
11 ⓒ TAMPA THEATRE
13 TAMPA MUSEUM OF ART
17 TAMPA POLICE MUSEUM
21 FLORIDA MUSEUM OF PHOTOGRAPHIC ARTS
21 GALLERY AIA
22 TAMPA BAY HISTORY CENTER
26 TAMPA BAY LIGHTNING
26 TAMPA BAY STORM
28 CHANNELSIDE CINEMAS & IMAX

ⓢ SHOPS

29 CHANNELSIDE BAY PLAZA

ⓗ HOTELS

18 SHERATON TAMPA RIVERWALK HOTEL
20 HYATT REGENCY TAMPA
23 EMBASSY SUITES TAMPA, DOWNTOWN CONVENTION CENTER
24 ⓒ MARRIOTT WATERSIDE
25 WESTIN TAMPA HARBOUR ISLAND

Phil Bourquardez Park

To ⓡ1 The Bungalow Bistro and ⓡ2 Grass Root

Tampa Water Works Park

Julian B Lane Riverfront Park

Tampa Bay Performing Arts Center (November 2009)

University of Tampa

Henry B. Plant Museum

Plant Park

Tampa Museum of Art

HYDE PARK

LEE ROY SELMON EXPY

AIDS Memorial Park

Bayshore Boulevard

SEE MAP 2

© AVALON TRAVEL

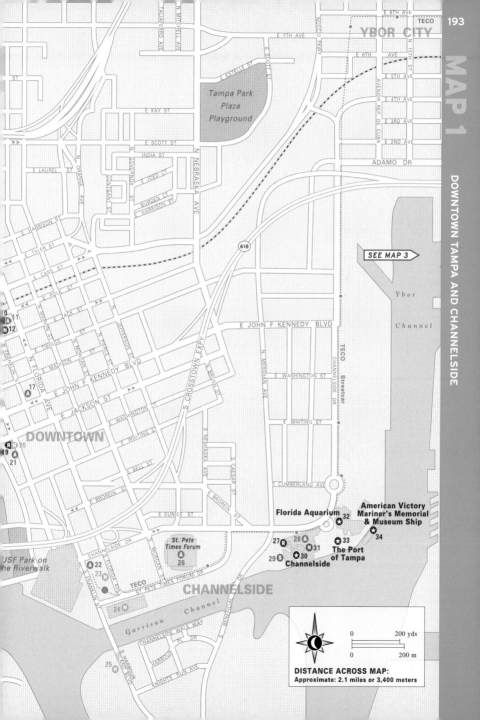

MAP 1

DOWNTOWN TAMPA AND CHANNELSIDE

TECO

YBOR CITY

E 8TH AVE

E 7TH AVE

E 6TH AVE

E 5TH AVE

E 4TH AVE

E 3RD AVE

E 2ND AVE

NUCCIO PKWY

AVENIDA REP. DE CUBA

N 15TH ST

ADAMO DR

Tampa Park
Plaza
Playground

E KAY ST

E SCOTT ST

INDIA ST

E LAUREL ST

E JOED CT

BURDEN CT.

HARRISON ST.

N ORANGE AVE

N CONSTANT AVE

GOVERNOR ST

N NEBRASKA AVE

E ESTELLE ST

E SCOTT ST

N MITCHELL AVE

N TALIAFERRO AVE

ST

E HARRISON ST

E TYLER ST

E CASS ST

E POLK ST

E ZACK ST

N HARMON ST

E TWIGGS ST

E MADISON ST

N MORGAN ST

N PIERCE ST

JEFFERSON ST

N FLORIDA AVE

N FRANKLIN ST

E JOHN F KENNEDY BLVD

E JACKSON ST

WASHINGTON ST

E WHITING ST

DOWNTOWN

E BELL ST

E BROREIN ST

S NEBRASKA AVE

S CAESAR ST

BROREIN ST

E EUNICE ST

A 17

R 20
9 19
A 21

618

E JOHN F KENNEDY BLVD

N MERIDIAN AVE

E WASHINGTON ST

E WHITING ST

E CUMBERLAND AVE

SEE MAP 3

Ybor

Channel

TECO
CHANNELSIDE DR

Streetcar

Florida Aquarium **32**

American Victory
Mariner's Memorial
& Museum Ship

34

27 **R**   **28** **A**
          N **31**   **33**
29 **S**   **30**

The Port
of Tampa

Channelside

St. Pete
Times Forum
A
26

CHANNELSIDE DR

N MORGAN ST

N FLORIDA AVE

N FRANKLIN ST

ST. PETE TIMES FORUM DR

USF Park on
the Riverwalk

A 22
23

TECO

CHANNELSIDE

Channel

BENEFICIAL DR

24 **Ⓠ**

Garrison   Channel

CHANNELSIDE WALK WAY

PL DR

HARBOUR

S HARBOUR ISLAND BLVD

KNIGHTS RUN AVE

25 **Ⓠ**

0   200 yds

0   200 m

DISTANCE ACROSS MAP:
Approximate: 2.1 miles or 3,400 meters

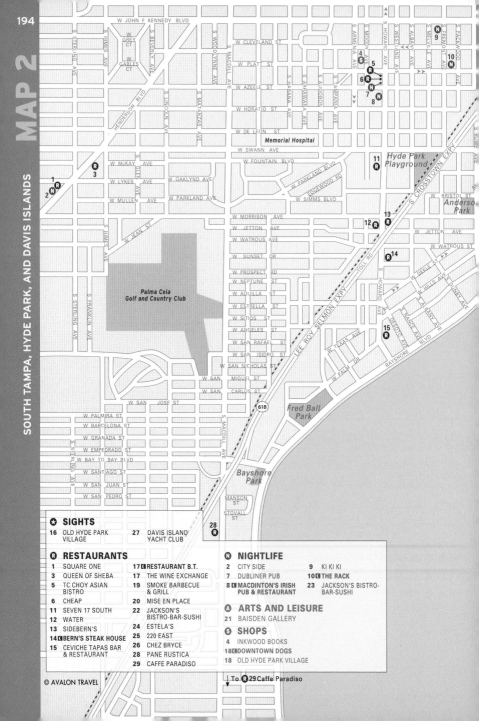

⊙ SIGHTS

16	OLD HYDE PARK VILLAGE	27	DAVIS ISLAND YACHT CLUB

® RESTAURANTS

1	SQUARE ONE	17	RESTAURANT B.T.
3	QUEEN OF SHEBA	17	THE WINE EXCHANGE
5	TC CHOY ASIAN BISTRO	19	SMOKE BARBECUE & GRILL
6	CHEAP	20	MISE EN PLACE
11	SEVEN 17 SOUTH	22	JACKSON'S BISTRO-BAR-SUSHI
12	WATER	24	ESTELA'S
13	SIDEBERN'S	25	220 EAST
14	BERN'S STEAK HOUSE	26	CHEZ BRYCE
15	CEVICHE TAPAS BAR & RESTAURANT	28	PANE RUSTICA
		29	CAFFE PARADISO

Ⓝ NIGHTLIFE

2	CITY SIDE	9	KI KI KI
7	DUBLINER PUB	10	THE RACK
8	MACDINTON'S IRISH PUB & RESTAURANT	23	JACKSON'S BISTRO-BAR-SUSHI

Ⓐ ARTS AND LEISURE

21	BAISDEN GALLERY

Ⓢ SHOPS

4	INKWOOD BOOKS
18	DOWNTOWN DOGS
18	OLD HYDE PARK VILLAGE

© AVALON TRAVEL

To ® 29 Caffe Paradiso

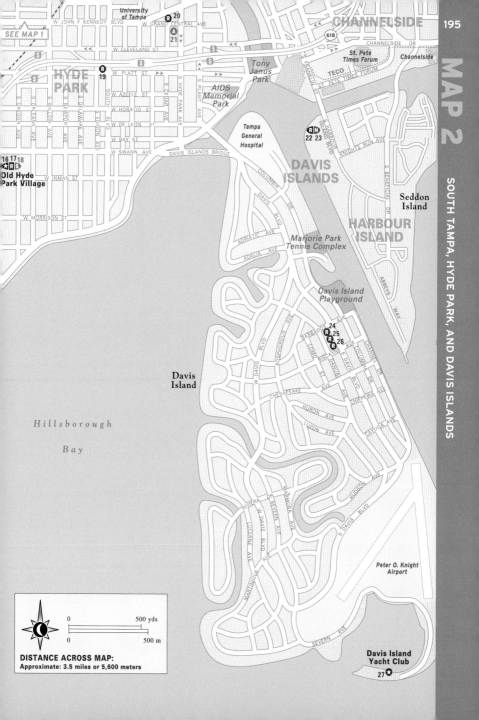

SEE MAP 1

University of Tampa

W JOHN F KENNEDY BLVD
W GRAND CENTRAL AVE

R 20
A 21

CHANNELSIDE

W CLEVELAND ST

618

CHANNELSIDE DR

Channelside

St. Pete Times Forum

Tony Jands Park

TECO
Pete Times Forum

HYDE PARK

R 19

W PLATT ST

W AZEELE ST

W HORATIO ST

W DE LEON ST

W BAY ST

W SWANN AVE

DAVIS ISLANDS BRIDGE

AIDS Memorial Park

Tampa General Hospital

R N 22 23

KNIGHT'S RUN AVE

DAVIS ISLANDS

Seddon Island

16 17 18
Old Hyde Park Village

W INMAN ST

W MORRISON ST

COLUMBIA DR

DAVIS BLVD

ADRIATIC AVE

ADALIA AVE

Marjorie Park Tennis Complex

HARBOUR ISLAND

ABBEYS WAY

S BENEFICIAL DR

Davis Island Playground

Hillsborough

Bay

Davis Island

BOSPHOROUS BLVD

DAVIS BLVD

W DAVIS BLVD

CHESAPEAKE AVE

BARBADOS AVE
COMO ST

24
R 25
R 26
BISCAYNE AVE

E DAVIS BLVD

COLUMBIA DR

CHANNEL DR

CHIPPEWA AVE

CAYUGA AVE

HUDSON AVE

HURON AVE

LUZON AVE

RIVIERA DR

W DAVIS BLVD

W SEVERN AVE

MARMORA AVE

LUCERNE AVE

MARTINIQUE AVE

S DAVIS BLVD

Peter O. Knight Airport

SEVERN AVE

0   500 yds
0   500 m

DISTANCE ACROSS MAP:
Approximate: 3.5 miles or 5,600 meters

Davis Island Yacht Club
27

MAP 2

SOUTH TAMPA, HYDE PARK, AND DAVIS ISLANDS

Cuscaden Park

E 17TH AVE

E 17TH AVE
E COLUMBUS DR

E 15TH AVE

E 15TH AVE
E 14TH AVE

NUCCIO PKWY
NUCCIO PKWY

E 12TH AVE

E 11TH AVE

E PALM AVE
E PALM AVE

Hillsborough Community College-Ybor Campus

Centro Ybor

12  A

E 9TH AVE

YBOR CITY

Ybor Square
1 N **2** N

H **3**

6 7 R N **9** A **10**

13 R

Centennial Park

17 S

E 8TH AVE

TECO Streetcar

R **8**

4 N **5**

R **14**

E 7TH AVE (E BRAODWAY AVE)

7th Avenue

N **11**

N **15**

R **16**

R **18**

E 6TH AVE

E 5TH AVE

E 4TH AVE

E 3RD ST

E 2ND ST

ADAMO DR

PENNY ST

SEE MAP 1

● SIGHTS

5 ◖ 7TH AVENUE
9 CENTRO YBOR

® RESTAURANTS

6 ADOBE GILA'S
6 SAMURAI BLUE SUSHI AND SAKE BAR
6 TAMPA BAY BREWING COMPANY
13 MEMA'S ALASKAN TACOS
14 BERNINI OF YBOR
16 ACROPOLIS GREEK TAVERN
18 COLUMBIA RESTAURANT

Ⓝ NIGHTLIFE

1	NEW WORLD BREWERY	8	CLUB SKYE
2	ORPHEUM	11	CLUB PRANA
4	CZAR VODKA BAR	15	COYOTE UGLY
7	ADOBE GILAS		

Ⓐ ARTS AND LEISURE

10 MUVICO THEATERS
12 YBOR CITY STATE MUSEUM

Ⓢ SHOPS

17 YBOR CITY

Ⓗ HOTELS

3 DON VICENTE DE YBOR HISTORIC INN

0   200 yds
0   200 m

DISTANCE ACROSS MAP:
Approximate: .7 miles or 1,145 meters

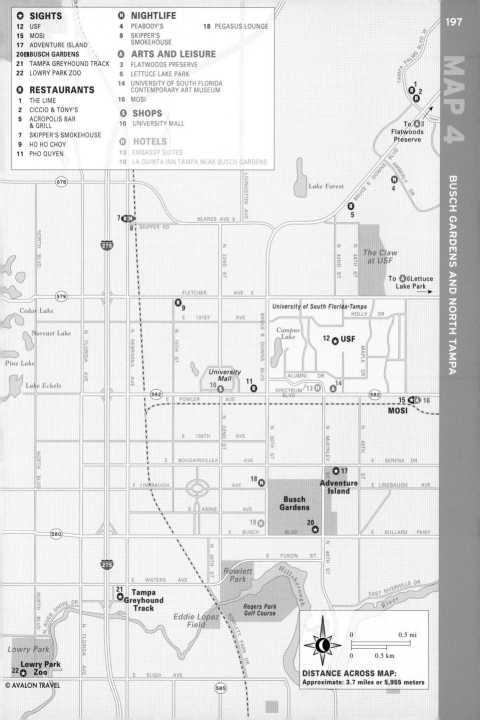

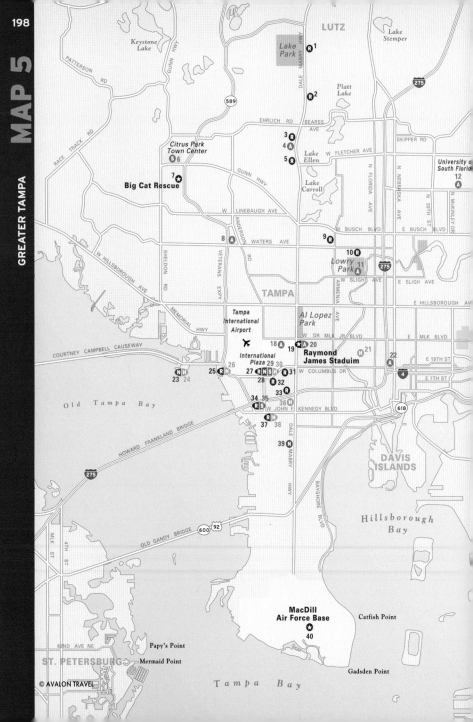

LUTZ

Keystone Lake

Lake Stemper

Lake Park

Platt Lake

Citrus Park Town Center

University of South Florida

Big Cat Rescue

Lake Ellen

Lake Carroll

TAMPA

Lowry Park

Tampa International Airport

Al Lopez Park

Raymond James Staduim

International Plaza

Old Tampa Bay

DAVIS ISLANDS

Hillsborough Bay

MacDill Air Force Base

Catfish Point

ST. PETERSBURG

Papy's Point

Mermaid Point

Gadsden Point

Tampa Bay

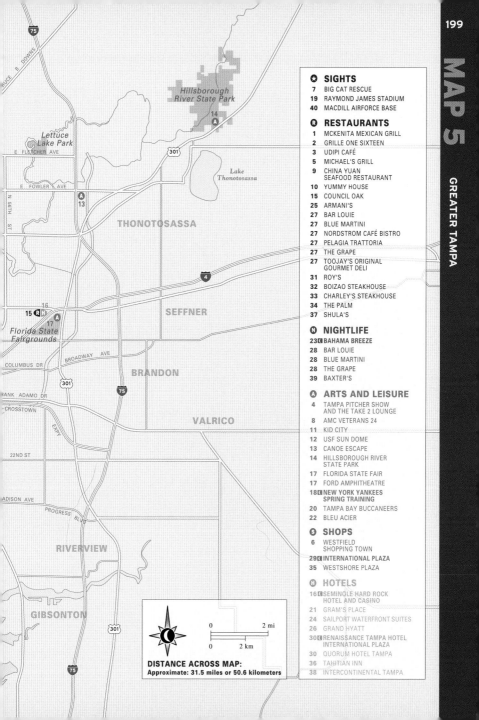

DISTANCE ACROSS MAP:
Approximate: 31.5 miles or 50.6 kilometers

✪ SIGHTS
- **7** BIG CAT RESCUE
- **19** RAYMOND JAMES STADIUM
- **40** MACDILL AIRFORCE BASE

℞ RESTAURANTS
- **1** MCKENITA MEXICAN GRILL
- **2** GRILLE ONE SIXTEEN
- **3** UDIPI CAFÉ
- **5** MICHAEL'S GRILL
- **9** CHINA YUAN SEAFOOD RESTAURANT
- **10** YUMMY HOUSE
- **15** COUNCIL OAK
- **25** ARMANI'S
- **27** BAR LOUIE
- **27** BLUE MARTINI
- **27** NORDSTROM CAFÉ BISTRO
- **27** PELAGIA TRATTORIA
- **27** THE GRAPE
- **27** TOOJAY'S ORIGINAL GOURMET DELI
- **31** ROY'S
- **32** BOIZAO STEAKHOUSE
- **33** CHARLEY'S STEAKHOUSE
- **34** THE PALM
- **37** SHULA'S

🌙 NIGHTLIFE
- **23C** BAHAMA BREEZE
- **28** BAR LOUIE
- **28** BLUE MARTINI
- **28** THE GRAPE
- **39** BAXTER'S

🎭 ARTS AND LEISURE
- **4** TAMPA PITCHER SHOW AND THE TAKE 2 LOUNGE
- **8** AMC VETERANS 24
- **11** KID CITY
- **12** USF SUN DOME
- **13** CANOE ESCAPE
- **14** HILLSBOROUGH RIVER STATE PARK
- **17** FLORIDA STATE FAIR
- **17** FORD AMPHITHEATRE
- **18C** NEW YORK YANKEES SPRING TRAINING
- **20** TAMPA BAY BUCCANEERS
- **22** BLEU ACIER

🛍 SHOPS
- **6** WESTFIELD SHOPPING TOWN
- **29C** INTERNATIONAL PLAZA
- **35** WESTSHORE PLAZA

🏨 HOTELS
- **16C** SEMINOLE HARD ROCK HOTEL AND CASINO
- **21** GRAM'S PLACE
- **24** SAILPORT WATERFRONT SUITES
- **26** GRAND HYATT
- **30C** RENAISSANCE TAMPA HOTEL INTERNATIONAL PLAZA
- **30** QUORUM HOTEL TAMPA
- **36** TAHITIAN INN
- **38** INTERCONTINENTAL TAMPA

MAP 6

DOWNTOWN ST. PETERSBURG

200

Tropicana Field

DOWNTOWN
ST. PETERSBURG

✪ SIGHTS

- 18 THE PIER
- 39 DOWNTOWN AREA

❶ RESTAURANTS

- 7 MARCHAND'S GRILL
- 9 MOON UNDER WATER
- 10 PARKSHORE GRILL
- 12 ❻ MFA CAFÉ
- 16 L'OLIVIER
- 29 THE TABLE
- 30 ❻ BELLA BRAVA
- 31 GLOBE COFFEE LOUNGE
- 37 CEVICHE
- 43 CAFE ALMA
- 46 ❻ PACIFIC WAVE

❶ NIGHTLIFE

- 3 THE PALLADIUM
- 19 CHA CHA COCONUTS
- 28 STATE THEATRE
- 33 ❻ JANNUS LANDING
- 34 THE GARDEN
- 35 VINTAGE ULTRA LOUNGE
- 44 PUSH ULTRA LOUNGE

⒜ ARTS AND LEISURE

- 2 COLISEUM
- 4 THE PALLADIUM
- 13 MUSEUM OF FINE ARTS
- 14 FLORIDA INTERNATIONAL MUSEUM
- 17 ST. PETERSBURG MUSEUM OF HISTORY
- 21 FINN GALLERY
- 22 GLASS CANVAS GALLERY AND CROATIAN NATIVE ART GALLERY
- 27 THE ARTS CENTER
- 32 FLORIDA CRAFTSMEN GALLERY
- 36 NESTOR HAVERLY GALLERY
- 41 THE STUDIO@620
- 42 FLORIDA HOLOCAUST MUSEUM
- 45 AMERICAN STAGE THEATRE
- 47 ❻ TAMPA BAY RAYS
- 48 MAHAFFEY THEATER AT THE PROGRESS ENERGY CENTER
- 49 ❻ SALVADOR DALÍ MUSEUM

🏨 HOTELS

- 5 LA VERANDA BED AND BREAKFAST
- 6 MANSION HOUSE BED AND BREAKFAST
- 8 ❻ RENAISSANCE VINOY RESORT & GOLF CLUB

ⓢ SHOPS

- 1 PATTY & FRIENDS ANTIQUE MALL
- 11 KABLOOM OF ST. PETERSBURG
- 11 ❻ MAISON ROUGE
- 15 BAYWALK
- 20 THE PIER
- 23 ❻ HASLAM'S BOOK STORE
- 24 CENTRAL AVENUE ANTIQUE MARKETPLACE
- 25 GAS PLANT ANTIQUE ARCADE
- 27 MILAGROS
- 40 BEACH DRIVE NORTHEAST
- 38 ❻ PONCE DE LEON HOTEL

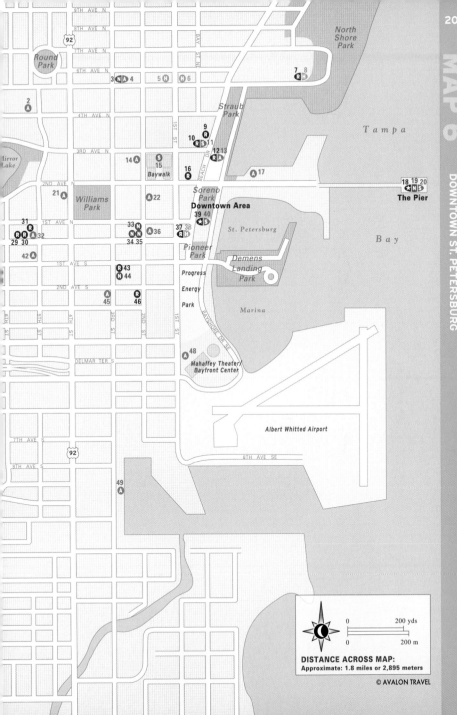

DISTANCE ACROSS MAP:
Approximate: 1.8 miles or 2,895 meters

© AVALON TRAVEL

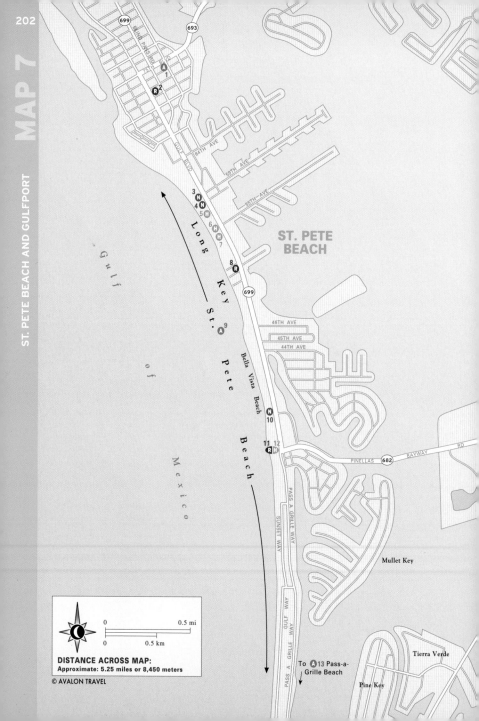

ST. PETE
BEACH

Long Key St. Pete Beach

Gulf of Mexico

Bella Vista Beach

Mullet Key

Tierra Verde

Pine Key

Pass-a-Grille Beach

Gulf Way

Sunset Way

Pass-a-Grille Way

To 13 Pass-a-Grille Beach

PINELLAS BAYWAY RD

64TH AVE
59TH AVE
55TH AVE
46TH AVE
45TH AVE
44TH AVE

GULF BLVD

ISLAND PARKWAY

699
693
699
682

DISTANCE ACROSS MAP:
Approximate: 5.25 miles or 8,450 meters

0   0.5 mi
0   0.5 km

© AVALON TRAVEL

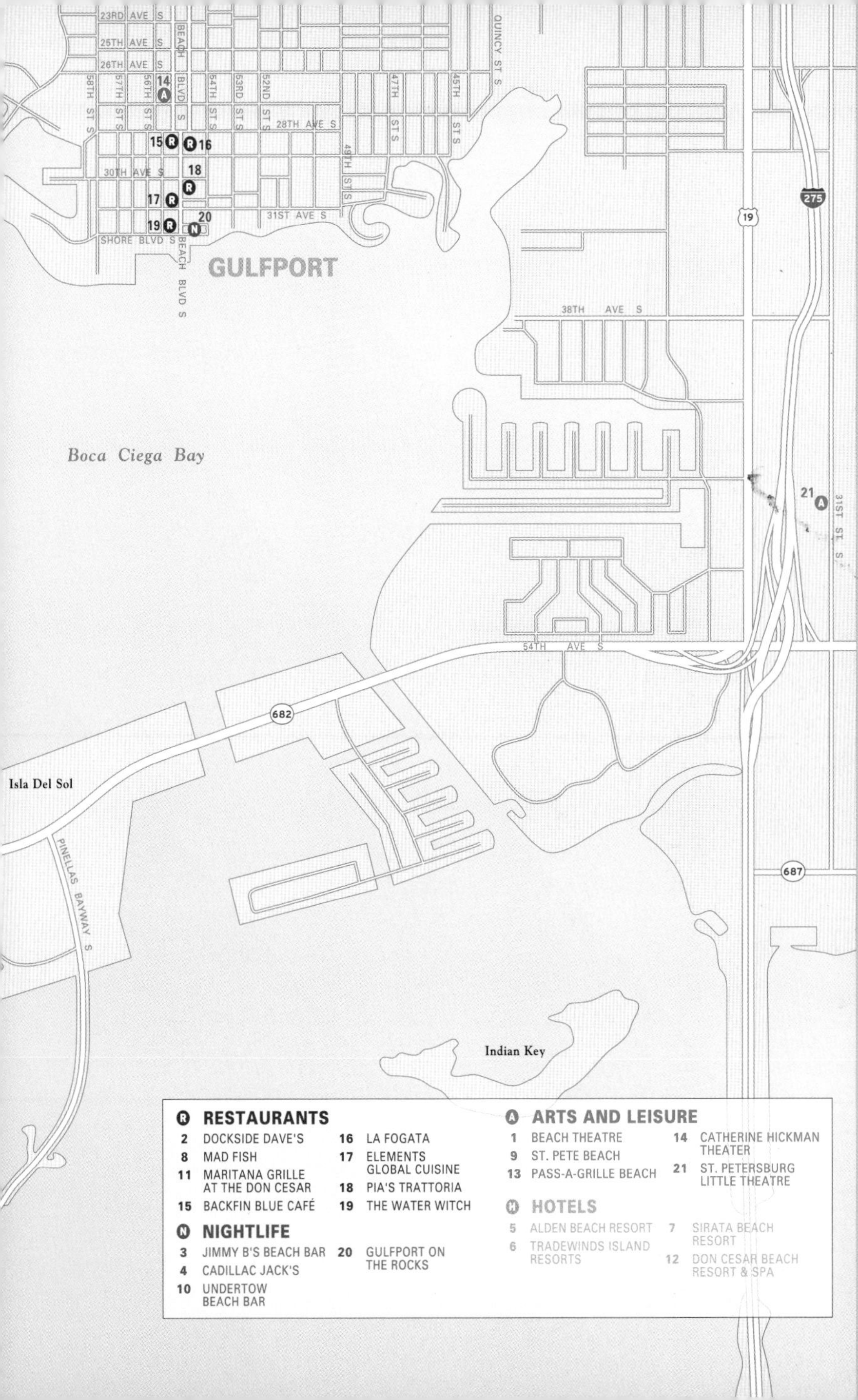

MAP 7

ST. PETE BEACH AND GULFPORT

QUINCY ST S

23RD AVE S
25TH AVE S
26TH AVE S

58TH ST S
57TH ST S
56TH ST S
54TH ST S
53RD ST S
52ND ST S

BEACH BLVD S

14
A

28TH AVE S

47TH ST S

45TH ST S

15 R R 16

30TH AVE S

18

17 R

19 R

20
N

31ST AVE S

31ST ST S

49TH ST S

SHORE BLVD S

BEACH BLVD S

GULFPORT

Boca Ciega Bay

38TH   AVE   S

21
A

31ST ST S

275

19

682

54TH   AVE   S

Isla Del Sol

PINELLAS BAYWAY S

687

Indian Key

R RESTAURANTS

2	DOCKSIDE DAVE'S	16	LA FOGATA
8	MAD FISH	17	ELEMENTS GLOBAL CUISINE
11	MARITANA GRILLE AT THE DON CESAR	18	PIA'S TRATTORIA
15	BACKFIN BLUE CAFÉ	19	THE WATER WITCH

N NIGHTLIFE

3	JIMMY B'S BEACH BAR	20	GULFPORT ON THE ROCKS
4	CADILLAC JACK'S		
10	UNDERTOW BEACH BAR		

A ARTS AND LEISURE

1	BEACH THEATRE	14	CATHERINE HICKMAN THEATER
9	ST. PETE BEACH	21	ST. PETERSBURG LITTLE THEATRE
13	PASS-A-GRILLE BEACH		

M HOTELS

5	ALDEN BEACH RESORT	7	SIRATA BEACH RESORT
6	TRADEWINDS ISLAND RESORTS	12	DON CESAR BEACH RESORT & SPA

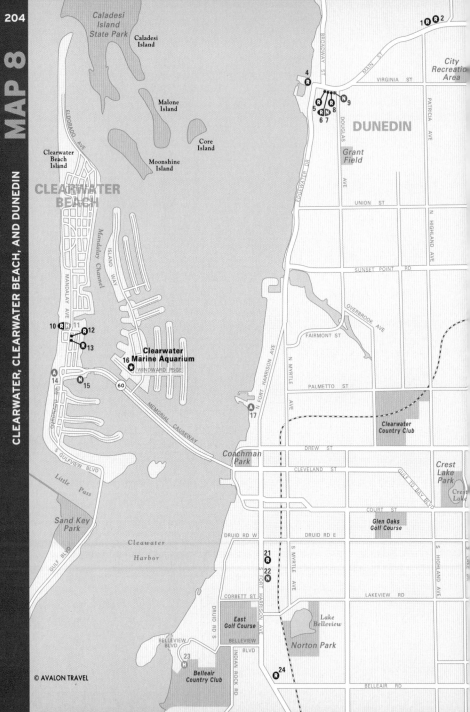

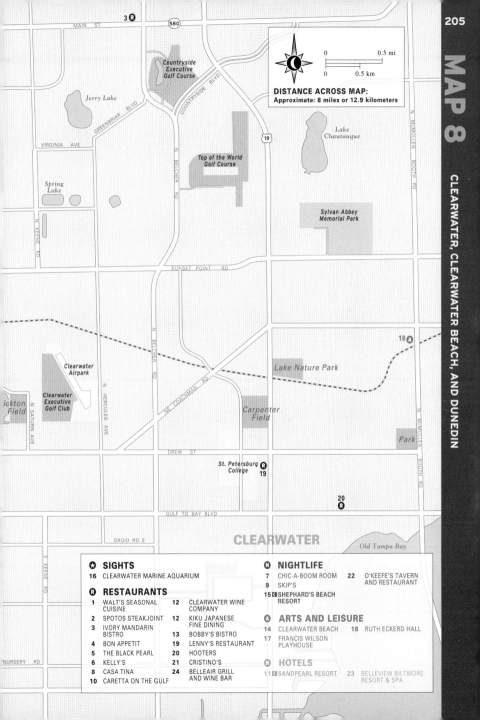

MAIN ST 3 ℞ 580

Countryside Executive Golf Course

Jerry Lake

GREENBRIAR BLVD

COUNTRYSIDE BLVD

19

Lake Chautauque

VIRGINIA AVE

N BELCHER RD

Top of the World Golf Course

Spring Lake

Sylvan Abbey Memorial Park

N KEENE RD

SUNSET POINT RD

N MCMULLEN BOOTH RD

DISTANCE ACROSS MAP:
Approximate: 8 miles or 12.9 kilometers

0   0.5 mi
0   0.5 km

Clearwater Airpark

Clearwater Executive Golf Club

ickton Field

N SATURN AVE

N HERCULES AVE

N BELCHER RD

NE COACHMAN RD

Lake Nature Park

18 Ⓐ

Carpenter Field

Park

N MCMULLEN BOOTH RD

DREW ST

St. Petersburg College 19 ℞

20 ℞

GULF TO BAY BLVD

DRUID RD E

S KEENE RD

NURSERY RD

CLEARWATER

Old Tampa Bay

○ SIGHTS
16 CLEARWATER MARINE AQUARIUM

℞ RESTAURANTS
1	WALT'S SEASONAL CUISINE	12	CLEARWATER WINE COMPANY
2	SPOTOS STEAKJOINT	12	KIKU JAPANESE FINE DINING
3	IVORY MANDARIN BISTRO	13	BOBBY'S BISTRO
4	BON APPETIT	19	LENNY'S RESTAURANT
5	THE BLACK PEARL	20	HOOTERS
6	KELLY'S	21	CRISTINO'S
8	CASA TINA	24	BELLEAIR GRILL AND WINE BAR
10	CARETTA ON THE GULF		

Ⓝ NIGHTLIFE
7	CHIC-A-BOOM ROOM	22	O'KEEFE'S TAVERN AND RESTAURANT
9	SKIP'S		
15	SHEPHARD'S BEACH RESORT		

Ⓐ ARTS AND LEISURE
14	CLEARWATER BEACH	18	RUTH ECKERD HALL
17	FRANCIS WILSON PLAYHOUSE		

Ⓗ HOTELS
11	SANDPEARL RESORT	23	BELLEVIEW BILTMORE RESORT & SPA

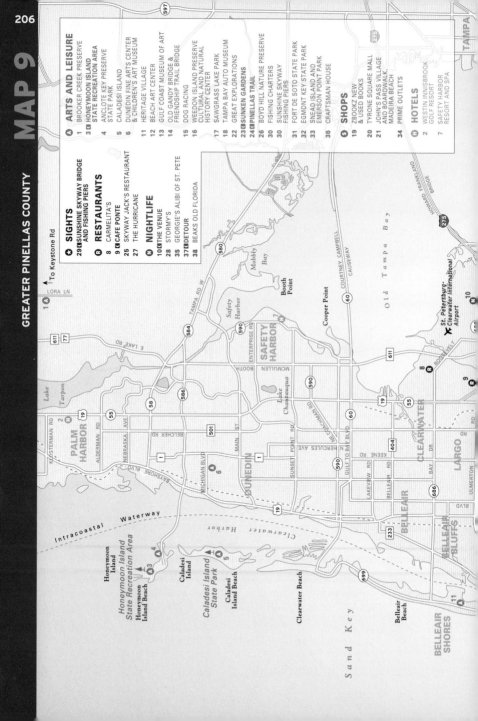

SIGHTS

29 🅢 SUNSHINE SKYWAY BRIDGE AND FISHING PIERS

RESTAURANTS

8 CARMELITA'S
9 🅔 CAFE PONTE
25 SKYWAY JACK'S RESTAURANT
27 THE HURRICANE

NIGHTLIFE

10 🅣 THE VENUE
28 STORMYS
35 GEORGIE'S ALIBI OF ST. PETE
37 🅓 DETOUR
38 BEAKS OLD FLORIDA

ARTS AND LEISURE

1 BROOKER CREEK PRESERVE
3 🅗 HONEYMOON ISLAND STATE RECREATION AREA
4 ANCLOTE KEY PRESERVE STATE PARK
5 CALADESI ISLAND
6 DUNEDIN FINE ARTS CENTER & CHILDREN'S ART MUSEUM
11 HERITAGE VILLAGE
12 BEACH ART CENTER
13 GULF COAST MUSEUM OF ART
14 OLD GANDY BRIDGE & FRIENDSHIP TRAIL BRIDGE
15 DOG RACING
16 WEEDON ISLAND PRESERVE CULTURAL AND NATURAL HISTORY CENTER
17 SAWGRASS LAKE PARK
18 TAMPA BAY AUTO MUSEUM
22 GREAT EXPLORATIONS
23 🅢 SUNKEN GARDENS
24 🅟 PINELLAS TRAIL
26 BOYD HILL NATURE PRESERVE
30 FISHING CHARTERS
30 SUNSHINE SKYWAY FISHING PIERS
31 FORT DE SOTO STATE PARK
32 EGMONT KEY STATE PARK
33 SNEAD ISLAND AND EMERSON POINT PARK
36 CRAFTSMAN HOUSE

SHOPS

19 ZBOOKZ NEW & USED BOOKS
20 TYRONE SQUARE MALL
21 JOHN'S PASS VILLAGE AND BOARDWALK, MADEIRA BEACH
34 PRIME OUTLETS

HOTELS

2 WESTIN INNISBROOK GOLF RESORT
7 SAFETY HARBOR RESORT AND SPA

MAP 9

GREATER PINELLAS COUNTY

MacDill Air Force Base

Friendship Trail Bridge

OLD GANDY BLVD

14

92

600

602

Weedon Island Preserve

Papy's Point

Mermaid Point

Weedon Island 16

Tampa Bay

GANDY BLVD

15

687

Coquina Key

Point Pinellas

Sunshine Skyway Bridge and Fishing Piers

To 32 Egmont Key State Park, 33 Snead Island and Emerson Point Park, and 34 Prime Outlets

DR MARTIN LUTHER KING ST

4TH ST N

22

23

SEE DETAIL

Sawgrass Lake Park

17

ST. PETERSBURG

9TH ST N

16TH ST N

9TH ST S

687

16TH ST S

Lake Maggiore

26

54TH AVE S

62ND AVE S

275

SUNSHINE SKYWAY BRIDGE (TOLL)

29 30

118TH AVE N

118TH AVE N

18

Pinellas Park

102ND AVE N

102ND AVE N

19

62ND AVE N

54TH AVE N

AVE N

AVE N

22ND AVE N

5TH AVE N

CENTRAL AVE

AVE

19

GULFPORT

15TH AVE S

22ND AVE S

25

R

Boca Ciega Bay

Isle del Sol

SEMINOLE

693

694

68TH ST

60TH ST

PARK BLVD

62ND

54TH

AVE N

46TH AVE N

38TH

TYRONE BLVD

690

49TH ST N

58TH ST S

54TH ST S

24

4

SUNSHINE

Lake Seminole

595

19

DAIRY RD

S BELCHER RD

St. Pete Beach

To 31 Fort DeSoto State Park

PASS-A-GRILLE BEACH

Treasure Island

19

SEMINOLE

113TH ST N

Pinellas Trail

21

Madeira Beach

Redington Beach

NORTH REDINGTON SHORES

REDINGTON SHORES

INDIAN SHORES

Suncoast Seabird Sanctuary

Beach

71

233

WALSINGHAM RD

102ND AVE

PARK BLVD

112TH ST N

Gulf of Mexico

GULF BLVD

27 28

19 S

20

DISTANCE ACROSS MAP:
Approximate: 24 miles or 38,625 meters

N

0   2 mi
0   2 km

SEE DETAIL (inset)

24TH ST N

25TH ST N

38

26TH ST N

37

3RD AVE N

BURLINGTON AVE N

2ND AVE N

1ST AVE N

CENTRAL AVE

36

1ST AVE S

Seminole Park

3RD ST N

2ND ST N

1ST ST N

35

www.moon.com

MOON.COM is all new, and ready to help plan your next trip! Filled with fresh trip ideas and strategies, author interviews, informative blogs, a detailed map library, and descriptions of all the Moon guidebooks, Moon.com is all you need to get out and explore the world—or even places in your own backyard. As always, when you travel with Moon, expect an experience that is uncommon and truly unique.